Instructor's Resource Manual

to accompany

Carson • Butcher • Mineka
ABNORMAL PSYCHOLOGY AND MODERN LIFE
Tenth Edition

Prepared by

Frank J. Prerost
Western Illinois University

HarperCollins*CollegePublishers*

Instructor's Resource Manual to accompany Carson/Butcher/Mineka ABNORMAL PSYCHOLOGY AND MODERN LIFE, Tenth Edition

CONTENTS

PREFACE

TO THE INSTRUCTOR

Every course in abnormal psychology can be a unique experience because each instructor and each group of students bring a unique combination of interests, skills, and experience. However, most instructors who teach the course face similar problems. Perhaps the most pressing is the limited time available to prepare for lecture and recitation. This **Instructor's Resource Manual** is designed to help lighten your busy schedule by providing a variety of supportive aids to make each chapter of **ABNORMAL PSYCHOLOGY AND MODERN LIFE Tenth Edition** more accessible and engaging for your students.

To this end, various chapter-related resources that will assist you in preparing for specific class sessions have been developed. Although a great many of the ideas presented here will appeal primarily to first-time instructors, the intention is to offer "something for everyone" so that even the most skillful and experienced instructor using this text will find lecture topics, discussion ideas, and reading assignments to fit into his or her scheme of teaching the course.

USING THE CHAPTER RESOURCES WITH THE TEXT

Beginning on page one of this **Instructor's Resource Manual**, an assemblage of chapter outlines, learning objectives, key terms, Focus on Research material, readings, lecture ideas, and activities and projects have been supplied for each chapter of the text. These components are described as follows:

Chapter Outlines: Text material for each chapter is described through a detailed outline of the text sections.

Learning Objectives: A number of specific learning objectives are listed for each chapter which direct attention toward its major points.

Key Terms: The significant terms introduced in each chapter are listed for your convenience.

Focus on Research: Each chapter suggests two or more articles, extracted from the professional literature, that expand or provide a different perspective on selected text topics. Articles are first cited, then synopsized. They can be used to form the basis of part of a class lecture or recitation or they may be assigned to students for outside reading. Questions designed to stimulate classroom discussion about these topics are provided after the synopsis.

Readings: These books and articles supplement other resources given in the chapter and in the text and can be used as background for lecture or, in some cases, assigned to students. Recent research and review articles are included which address topics of interest to many students.

Discussion and Lecture Ideas: This section offers several topics which would be useful in preparing lectures and/or generating class discussion in small groups. Many of these ideas are based on a single book or article. The majority are accompanied by one or more specific follow-up questions to provoke discussion of related items. Complete references are given within the topic.

Activities and Projects: Suggestions are provided for research projects, in-class activities, and other "hands-on" ideas that you might want to try in a small discussion or recitation group. Some projects require preparation on your part in order to make full use of the activity. The purpose of these various activities is to stimulate student interest and involvement in the study of abnormal psychology, as well as to illustrate first-hand some of the important concepts introduced in the text. Some of he activities are designed for in-class participation; other projects require out-of-class   ities on the part of the student.

It goes without saying that there is more information contained in this **Instructor's Resource Manual** than any instructor could reasonably expect to use in a single term. As stated at the outset, the objective of this manual is to anticipate a multitude of different teaching approaches, levels of teaching experience, types of students, lengths of course terms, and attitudes toward the use of instructor's resource manuals, and to produce a "cafeteria" of potentially useful suggestions wherein most instructors will find something of value. If u would like to see more (or less!) of any specific type of information presented in this manual, please let us know. After all, the Eleventh Edition of **ABNORMAL PSYCHOLOGY AND MODERN LIFE** may only be a few years away!

Frank J. Prerost
Western Illinois University
Macomb, Illinois

ANCILLARY PACKAGE

Test Bank
by Gerald I. Metalsky and Rebecca Laird, Lawrence University

Expertly authored, completely revised, and reviewed by the parent text authors, this Test Bank includes more than 2,500 multiple-choice, short answer, and essay items. Each question is page-referenced; keyed according to chapter, type, learning objective, and skill level (factual, applied, or conceptual); and cross-referenced to the Study Guide. Thorough and authoritative.

TestMaster DOS
TestMaster Mac

The complete Test Bank is also available on TestMaster for IBM and Macintosh computers. The TestMaster software lets you choose test questions randomly by selecting a chapter, question type, and quantity, or manually by choosing specific item numbers. Questions can also be selected by viewing them on screen or by doing computer searches for groups of questions that meet specific criteria. The TestMaster software enables you to edit existing questions or add your own questions to the chapter disks. Tests can be printed in several different formats and can include figures such as graphs, charts, and tables.

THE WORLD OF ABNORMAL PSYCHOLOGY Telecourse
produced by The Annenberg/CPB Collection and Toby Levine Communications

Developed in conjunction with **ABNORMAL PSYCHOLOGY AND MODERN LIFE**, this highly-acclaimed 13-part video series provides interviews and commentaries from researchers, clinicians, and teachers, as well as with patients and members of their families. **THE WORLD OF ABNORMAL PSYCHOLOGY** is available on VHS, BETA, and Laserdisc. Individual tapes, as well as the complete series, are available to text adopters through the HarperCollins Media Program. Contact your local representative regarding cost and availability.

Telecourse print materials to accompany **THE WORLD OF ABNORMAL PSYCHOLOGY** include:

- paperback version of **ABNORMAL PSYCHOLOGY AND MODERN LIFE, Tenth Edition**
- Telecourse Study Guide
- Telecourse Faculty Guide, including Test Bank
- Computerized Test Bank
- Video Guide

For more information on the cost of **THE WORLD OF ABNORMAL PSYCHOLOGY** program or on specific hardware requirements, please contact your local HarperCollins representative.

FOR THE STUDENT

Study Guide
by Don Fowles, University of Iowa

Respected scholar and former **Journal of Abnormal Psychology** editor Don Fowles authors this complete Study Guide. In addition to providing essential learning tools such as the chapter overview and objectives, key terms, and a full range of study questions, Dr. Fowles offers two new innovative features designed for the serious student of psychology. The first -- "Names You Should Know" -- identifies individuals who have contributed significantly to the field, many of whom will become increasingly familiar to students as they pursue their studies. The second new feature, entitled "Critical Thinking about Difficult Topics," departs from strictly text-based inquiry and asks students to consider challenging and often unresolved issues. Indispensable, comprehensive, this Study Guide accommodates students at all levels of learning.

SuperShell II
for IBM and Macintosh
by Suzanne de Beaumont, University of Buffalo

This interactive, text-specific computer program offers students additional learning opportunity. For each text chapter, SuperShell II includes a comprehensive outline, key terms and concepts, plus more than sixty multiple-choice, true/false, and short answer questions. Available for both IBM and Macintosh computers.

ORGANIZING THE COURSE

ABNORMAL PSYCHOLOGY AND MODERN LIFE is probably the most comprehensive abnormal psychology text available, with ample coverage for the fullest and most demanding upper-division semester course. For shorter courses, lower-division courses, or courses in which a special emphasis is desired or in which supplementary reading is to be assigned, instructors may want to use only certain chapters of the text. Several different selections of chapters can still provide an adequate introduction to the field as well as flexibility in meeting the needs of specific classes. Instructors are probably well aware that many students will read unassigned chapters or sections because of the high intrinsic interest.

Probably most instructors will assign the following chapters:

Chapter 1	(definitions, myths, scope, and sequence overview)
Chapter 3	(general causes of abnormal behavior)
Chapters 5-14	(major syndromes)
Chapters 16, 17	(therapy)

Alternative #1
Use of entire text for comprehensive coverage

The advantages of this approach are that students are provided with a comprehensive perspective on abnormal behavior, and the instructor is largely relieved of the burden of content coverage and is provided with a degree of flexibility in terms of focus and methods of instruction.

PART 1		PERSPECTIVES ON ABNORMAL BEHAVIOR
	1	Abnormal Behavior in Our Times
	2	Historical Views of Abnormal Behavior
	3	Causal Factors and Viewpoints in Abnormal Psychology
PART 2		PATTERNS OF ABNORMAL BEHAVIOR
	4	Stress and Adjustment Disorders
	5	Panic, Anxiety, and Their Disorders
	6	Mood Disorders and Suicide
	7	Somatoform and Dissociative Disorders
	8	Psychological Factors and Physical Illness
	9	Personality Disorders
	10	Substance-Related and Other Addictive Disorders
	11	Sexual Variants, Abuse, and Dysfunctions

Alternative #2
Use of selective chapters for specific focus

This approach is often used for shorter courses and for those with special needs and instructional objectives. Four differing areas of focus follow.

Focus on major syndromes with brief coverage of therapy

Focus on psychosocial and sociocultural aspects of abnormal psychology

Focus on therapy

<u>Focus on behavior modification</u>

Alternative #3
Use of selective chapters for limited survey

This approach has proven particularly suitable for lower-division and shorter courses in which the students have a limited background in psychology.

FILMS ABOUT ABNORMAL PSYCHOLOGY

Abnormal Behavior (CRM, 26 min). Covers a wide spectrum of psychopathology including a discussion of the stress situations that confront individuals, the theories of Freud, Maslow, Rogers, and Fromm, and interviews with patients in psychiatric hospitals.

Abnormal Behavior: A Mental Hospital (McG, 28 min). A documentary of life in a modern psychiatric hospital. Includes a tour of the hospital, therapy sessions, and diagnostic sessions.

Access (RSC, 20 min.). Co-winner at the International Rehabilitation Film Festival. Shows the adjustment of two middle-aged adults confined to wheelchairs.

Aging (CRM, 22 min). A survey of the styles of aging in America, focusing on patterns associated with successful adjustment. The film rebuts the common stereotypical idea that the elderly constitute one homogenous group.

Albert Ellis: A Demonstration with a Young Divorced Woman (IRL, 30 min). Ellis describes his technique after he has interviewed a 29-year-old divorced woman experiencing guilt feelings about her sexual relationships.

Alcoholism (DA, 26 min). This film discusses the difference between the use and the abuse of alcohol. Interviews with young people accentuate the growing problem of alcoholism with this age-group.

Alcoholism: A Model of Drug Dependency (CRM, 20 min). Examines the problem of alcohol in our society. Illustrates how insecure people turn to alcohol to relieve tension and soon become addicted.

An Approach to Growth: Awareness Training (CRM, 26 min). Filmed at the Lomi School in Kauai, Hawaii, this film shows a variety of exercises and therapies such as Hatha Yoga, bioenergetics, breathing, kinesthetics, dreams, and Gestalt therapy. Subjects are seen talking and acting out their problems in a group.

An Ounce of Prevention (HR, 20 min). Examines the causes of alcoholism, the damage it inflicts upon the individuals and their families, and the newest treatment and prevention programs.

Anxiety: The Endless Crisis (IU, 59 min). Two mental health authorities discuss the causes of anxiety and the difference between state anxiety and trait anxiety.

Anything They Want to Be (EMC, 12 min). Explores sex-role stereotypes in intellectual and career-oriented activities during the elementary and secondary school years.

Autism's Lonely Children (PCR, 20 min). An excellent film, best in its class. Shows many of the psychological disorders of childhood.

Behavior Modification: Teaching Language to Psychotic Children (EMC, 43 min). Shows Lavaas using operant techniques to teach speech to psychotic children aged 4 to 8. Shows that self-destructive acts must first be suppressed, using punishment and shock.

Behavior Theory in Practice (PCR, 20 min). A series of four films that describe findings of Skinnerian research and applied implications. Part I: Discussion and demonstration of operant behavior. Part II: Schedules of reinforcement, shaping, and programmed instruction. Part III: Discrimination and motivation--reinforcement, punishment, avoidance, and intracranial self-stimulation. Part IV: Sequences of behavior, chains of response, alternative responses, and multiple-stimulus control.

Behavior Therapy Demonstration (PCR, 32 min). Demonstrates the use of behavior therapy on a young woman suffering from extreme nervousness and anxiety. Situations that cause anxiety are first identified, then the subject is given exercises to use in combating these feelings. An excellent film for presenting the basic technique of behavior therapy.

Behavior Therapy with an Autistic Child (USPHS, 40 min). Demonstrates the treatment of an autistic child by operant conditioning techniques.

B. F. Skinner and Behavior Change (UCEMC, 42 min). Shows Skinner in a variety of situations--working in his lab, addressing students, talking with colleagues--and reviews his most important contributions to psychology. More of a homage than a critical presentation, but a good introduction to the man and his work.

Biofeedback: Listening to Your Head (IDEAL, 22 min). Explores the use of brain-wave conditioning to control diseases and emotional problems and to open up new avenues of communication.

The Brain: Creating a Mental Elite (ECEMC, 22 min). Examines three major areas of brain research: chemical stimulation, electrical stimulation, and environmental conditioning. Includes discussions with noted scientists Wilder Penfield in Montreal, Roy John in New York, and Mariam Diamond and David Krech in Berkeley. Writer C. Clarke also comments on some imaginative possibilities.

Bulimia (CRM, 12 min). This film explores the motivations of bulimia victims and discusses methods used to combat the disorder.

Carl Rogers Conducts an Encounter Group (APGA, 70 min). Dr. Rogers outlines the factors he thinks most important in facilitating a group, the levels on which it should operate, the importance of honest expression of feelings by facilitators as well as group members, and physical contact in the group. The film also offers a glimpse of Rogers as he relates to a group and the quality of his personal action with people.

Depression: The Shadowed Valley (IU, 59 min). Examines the many forms of depression through discussions with patients describing the origin of their problems and how they feel. Also presents the treatments of depression.

Depression: A Study in Abnormal Behavior (CRM, 27 min). Follows a 29-year-old teacher through severe depression and her treatment with a variety of methods, including chemotherapy, electro-convulsive therapy, and group therapy. The value of the film is that it serves as a model of abnormal behavior, enabling the narrator to explain the variety of approaches to the understanding and treatment of abnormal behavior.

Dialogues, Dr. Carl Rogers, Parts I and II (UCEMC, 100 min). Follows a young girl through her schizophrenic episode and the therapy sessions which eventually lead to her recovery.

Emotional Development: Aggression (CRM, 30 min). Describes the way in which aggression develops, what keeps it going, and how it can be changed. The film uses actors to portray the general psychological principles involved.

Emotional Illness (IU, 30 min). Acts as a good introductory film for discussions of abnormal behavior. Defines neurotic, psychotic, and psychosomatic.

Essie (FMK, 55 min). The many psychological stages through which the terminally ill patient passes are depicted with a focus on the counseling of patient, family, and friends.

Face to Face (UCEMC, 39 min). Informative interview with Carl Jung when he was eighty-four. Captures a considerable amount of his personality while exploring important aspects of his life and work.

Facing Reality (McG, 12 min.). Another brief film, this one illustrates a number of defense mechanisms.

Fighting Fear with Fear (McG, 26 min). CBS News 21st Century series showing Thomas Stampfl's controversial "implosion" technique -- to break down her neurosis, a 23-year-old secretary is bombarded with the terrifying situations she fears most.

Freud: The Hidden Nature of Man (IU, 29 min). Analyzes Freud's revolutionary theories of the power of the unconscious. Uses the technique of dramatic reenactment, with actors playing Freud, his ideas, and his patients.

Frustration/Aggression: It's Not Fair (CRM, 14 min). Presents the frustrations encountered by Tom and Terry in one day and the results of those frustrations when they get together that night for a date.

Handling Marital Conflicts (McG, 14 min). A reasonable summary of some of the more common marital conflicts and some negative and positive ways of handling them.

Harry: Behavioral Treatment of Self-Abuse (RP, 38 min). A mentally retarded person's bizarre symptomology is controlled through behavioral means.

Home Sweet Homes: Kids Talk About Joint Custody (FMK, 20 min). Five children are interviewed concerning the problems they have had adjusting to divorce, separation, and joint custody.

Hey! What About Us? (EMC, 10 min). Discusses sex-role stereotyping in physical activities in schools, including physical education classes and playground games.

How Are You? (RSC, 15 min.) An animated film which portrays mental health and mental illness at an introductory level.

Human Aggression (HR, 22 min). Human aggression is portrayed vividly by following an adolescent gang -- the "Skulls" -- through part of their day. Film focuses on the causes of aggression and presents the experimental findings and theories of Bandura, Walers, and Milgram.

I Don't Have to Hide (FNL, 28 min). Covers a wide range of themes associated with bulimia and anorexia nervosa.

I'm Dependent, You're Addicted (TL, 47 min.). This film gets just a little hysterical, but does a good job of discussing medical evidence on marijuana, LSD, uppers, and downers. A good summary, particularly if you feel a little weak in this area.

In Cold Blood (SW, 134 min). Chilling film version of Truman Capote's book. Chronicles the brutal murder of an entire family by two psychopathic young men.

Individual Differences (CRM, 16 min). Examines the broad range of human characteristics constituting normality and contrasts tests that attempt to discriminate between personality differences and developmental traits.

Journey into Self (EMC, 47 min). Academy Award-winning documentary of an intensive sixteen-hour encounter group of eight adults, all strangers to one another. Group is led by Carl Rogers and Richard Farson.

Jung Speaks of Freud (UCEMC, 29 min). Unrehearsed interview with Carl Jung at his home in Zurich in 1957. He explains the strong influence of Sigmund Freud's work on his own early studies. Dr. Jung's strong accent sometimes obscures the audio portion of the film.

King of Hearts (UA, 105 min). Examines the question of what abnormal behavior *is*. A very touching film which is sure to raise issues, make people laugh and cry. Excellent film to be used as an introduction to this course.

Madness and Medicine (CRM, 49 min). An excellent documentary narrated by Howard K. Smith, which investigates mental institutions and the patients living in these hospitals. Discusses the use of electroconvulsive therapy and psychosurgery.

Mental Health: New Frontiers of Sanity (EMC, 22 min). Documents the extent of mental health problems in North America and traces the history of therapy.

Mental Retardation: The Long Childhood of Timmy (McG, 53 min). Warm portrayal of a victim of Down syndrome who must make the transition from his family to a school for the retarded.

Mind of Man (IU, 119 min). Explores recent discoveries about the powers and workings of the mind. Documents experiments in which people have consciously controlled their oxygen needs and blood pressure, functions previously thought to be involuntary. Also covers latest findings on development of the mind in fetus and infant; how drugs affect the mind; mysteries of sleeping and dreaming; and brain structure, including chemical changes occurring within it and electrical energy it generates. Thorough and comprehensive.

Mind Over Body (TL, 49 min). Shows how routine illnesses and body injuries are influenced by the patient's psychological state. Includes discussion of autonomic conditioning of heartbeat, blood flow, and brain waves.

Miracle of the Mind (McG, 26 min). Reviews research into the nature of the brain and chemical and electronic means of improving its functioning. Considers the notion that drugs can increase motivation, competitiveness, and intelligence.

Mother Love (NYU, 26 min.). Probably the best of all the films showing Harlow's study of monkeys raised with different types of surrogate mothers.

Mysteries of the Mind (NGS, 60 min). The film delves into the workings of the human brain during sleep, work, and leisure and considers how control of pain can be accomplished.

Nature vs. Nurture (IU, 30 min). Discusses the relative roles of heredity and environment in determining behavior and personality. Explains how the genes in the chromosomes act as carriers of inherited characteristics. Considers the statistics of heredity as discovered by Mendel. Explains the facts of family resemblances and the role of cultural, economic, and psychological factors in social inheritance. Features Dr. Edwin G. Boring of Harvard University.

Obsessive-Compulsive Neurosis (McG, 30 min). Examines several instances of obsessive-compulsive behavior and interprets the meaning of these behaviors.

Old Age (TL, 45 min). From the *Family of Man* series. Studies aging as it occurs in five cultures.

One Flew Over the Cuckoo's Nest (UA, 129 min). The film adaptation of Ken Kesey's award-winning novel, which won an unprecedented number of Academy Awards. An excellent film depicting life in a mental hospital.

One Man's Madness (TL, 31 min). The first-hand account of a writer who becomes a manic depressive. Footage of the subject's hospital treatment is included, and, with a hidden camera, some unnerving scenes unfold. Guaranteed to stimulate discussion among your students.

One Step at a Time: An Introduction to Behavior Modification (CRM, 30 min). BM is explained and shown in use in a variety of settings: a normal classroom, an MR classroom, and a mental hospital.

Pavlov's Experiment--The Conditioned Reflex (COR, 19 min). Gives a realistic recreation of Pavlov's famous experiment on classical conditioning of a reflex in a dog. What better way to begin a discussion of learning?

A Perfectly Normal Day (CCF, 28 min). Helps develop methods of coping with the stresses of daily living.

People: Roots of Prejudice (IU, 30 min). A very well-done television show about stereotypes and the formation of attitudes. Avoids the problem of preaching to the audience.

Personality (CRM, 30 min). In-depth analysis of the personality of a college senior. Through interviews with the subject, his parents, girl friend, and roommate, viewers gain understanding of the complexity of personality development. The role of the psychologist and his techniques, such as the Draw-a-Person Test and the Thematic Apperception Test, are effectively demonstrated.

Pink Triangles (CDF, 35 min). Prejudices against lesbians and gay men are explored and discussed.

Professor Erik Erikson (AIM, 50 min.). A summary of Erikson's stages of personality development by Erikson himself. Very insightful film.

Psychoanalysis (IU, 30 min). Psychoanalysts enact episodes from several analytic sessions. Patient in question is convinced he is becoming a failure and the viewer observes the psychoanalyst getting to the root of the problem.

The Psychology of Eating (HBJ, 25 min). Another of Harcourt's new series of films in psychology. This one, narrated by Eliot Valenstein, promises to be a welcome addition to the few films dealing with aspects of motivation.

Repulsion (SW, 105 min). Catherine Deneuve stars in this Polanski film depicting a young woman experiencing a schizophrenic episode. Polanski's filming of visual hallucinations is excellent.

Rock-a-Bye Baby (TL, 28 min). A very good summary film about the effects of early experience on development.

Scenes from a Marriage (C5, 143 min). Directed by Ingmar Bergman and starring Liv Ullman, this film attempts to depict the problems encountered by a couple who are no longer able to communicate with each other.

Schizophrenia: The Shattered Mirror (IU, 60 min). One of the three or four best films you could show. Follows a real schizophrenic patient. Shows institutional care and current research on schizophrenia. Often hard to believe that the folks in the film are not actors.

Sex-Role Development (CRM, 23 min). Discusses the biological and social influences that interact in forming sex-role stereotypes and perpetuating sex-role discrimination. Shows how stereotypes are transmitted to children and suggests alternative approaches.

Spellbound (SW, 104 min). Gregory Peck stars in this Hitchcock thriller which is filled with scenes about hypnosis, amnesia, and dream interpretation.

Stress (PCR, 11 min). Demonstrates Hans Selye's general-adaptation syndrome.

The Suicide Clinic: A Cry for Help (IU, 28 min). Indicates that the suicide attempt is a cry for help, sympathy, and understanding. Links most suicides with long-term depression involving love, work, or physical illness.

Suicide: But Jack Was a Good Driver (CRM, 14 min). Two friends of a boy who was killed in a car accident reflect upon his activities and conversations during the month before his death. Their reflections provide insight into the causes of suicide and the subtle communication of intentions to commit suicide.

Suicide: It Doesn't Have to Happen (UCEMC, 20 min). The story of a teacher who prevents a student's suicide by referring the student to a suicide prevention center. Discusses the symptoms of suicide and ways to deal with them.

Teaching and Demonstrating Gestalt Therapy (FI). Fritz Perls discusses and demonstrates the use of Gestalt therapy.

Techniques of Nonverbal Psychological Testing (IFB, 20 min). Introduces techniques employed by those intimately involved with the diagnostic aspects of evaluating "difficult" children who cannot be assessed by ordinary means.

The Autistic Child: A Behavioral Approach (ERI, 28 min). This film demonstrates the acquisition of language skills among autistic children.

The Boys in the Band (SW, 120 min). The film adaptation of the Broadway production about a "gay" birthday party. A very witty, yet poignant, film about homosexuality.

The Boy Who Turned Off (NCF, 28 min). The relationship between an autistic child and his family is explored.

The Obsessive-Compulsive Neurosis (McG, 28 min). A middle-aged man has been unable to keep a job for five years because of his obsessive-compulsive condition. This film describes the patient's feelings about his symptoms and his progress in therapy.

The Thin Edge (IU, 59 min, for each segment). Five separate films, first aired on public television, dealing with five psychological traits: depression, aggression, guilt, anxiety, and sexuality. Because of their length, you may want to consider choosing one of these films as a class project, then ask students to supplement the film's and the text's discussion with outside reading.

The Three Faces of Eve (FI, 95 min). The classic film depicting the course of Eve's struggles with multiple personalities.

Three Approaches to Psychotherapy (PFI, 50 min). Demonstrations of client-centered, Gestalt, and rational-emotive therapies. Shows Carl Rogers, Fritz Perls, and Albert Ellis.

Titicut Follies (Z, 89 min). An excellent documentary about the treatment of patients in a mental hospital in Bridgewater, Massachusetts.

Unconscious Motivation (IU, 40 min). Shows how psychological tests and interview techniques are able to uncover a situation implanted in the "unconscious" of two subjects through hypnosis.

The Violent Mind (IBIS). This is a three-part program investigating the psychology of violent human behavior. It provides both a cultural and a biological framework for understanding violence and draws heavily upon the works of Freud, Lorenz, and Fromm.

Violent Youth: The Unmet Challenge (HR, 23 min). Features a discussion with three incarcerated juveniles, in which they describe their feelings about themselves, society, and their crimes.

Warriors' Women (DTF, 27 min). This is a portrait of Vietnam veterans' wives who struggle with the emotional problems of their husbands.

What Happens in Emotions? (IU, 30 min). Discusses bodily functions that operate during emotional states. Uses charts and diagrams to explain the sympathetic and parasympathetic nervous systems. Stresses the way in which facial expressions provide clues in determining different emotions.

Women and Sexuality: A Century of Change (ALT, 36 min). Views about women and sex held in the past are contrasted to those of today.

Word is Out (NYF, 124 min). This film interviews 26 homosexual men and women and examines their feelings, thoughts, and reactions to their sexual orientation.

Film Distributors

AIM	Associated Instructional Materials, 600 Madison Avenue, New York, NY 10022
ALT	Atlanta Films, 15 West 68th Street, New York, NY 10023
APGA	American Personnel and Guidance Association Film Distribution Center, 1607 New Hampshire Ave., N.W., Washington, DC 10009
C5	Cinema 5, 595 Madison Avenue, New York, NY 10022
CCF	Cally Curtis Films, 111 North Las Palmas Avenue, Hollywood, CA 90038
CDF	Cambridge Documentary Films, Inc., P.O. Box 385, Cambridge, MA 02139
COR	Coronet Instructional Films, 65 East South Water Street, Chicago, IL 60601
CRM	CRM McGraw-Hill Films, Del Mar, CA 92014
CW	Chuck Whitner Enterprises, 2307 Santa Monica Boulevard, Suite 189, Santa Monica, CA 90404
DA	Document Associates, Inc., 211 East 43rd Street, New York, NY 10017
DTF	Dorothy Tod Films, 20 Bailey Avenue, Montpelier, VT 05602
EB	Encyclopedia Britannica Films, Inc., 1822 Pickwick Avenue, Glenview, IL 60025
ERI	Efficacy Research Institute, 569 Salem End Road, Framingham, MA 01701
FI	Films Incorporated, 38 West 32nd Street, New York, NY 10001
FIF	Faces International Films Inc., 8444 Wilshire Boulevard, Beverly Hills, CA 90211
FL	Film Library, Division of Safety and Hygiene, 246 North High Street, 4th Floor, Columbia, OH 43215
FMK	Filmmakers Library, 133 East 58th Street, New York, NY 10022
FNL	Fanlight Productions, 47 Halifax Street, Jamaica Plains, NY 02130
HBJ	Harcourt Brace Jovanovich, 757 Third Avenue, New York, NY 10017
HCW	Hurlock Cine-World, Inc., 13 Arcadia Road, Old Greenwich, CT 06870
HR	HarperCollins Publishers, Inc. 10 East 53rd Street, New York, NY 10022
IBIS	IBIS Media, Box 308, Pleasantville, NY 10570
IDEAL	Ideal School Supply Company, 1100 South Lavergne Avenue, Oak Lawn, IL 60453
IFB	International Film Bureau, 332 South Michigan Avenue, Chicago, IL 60604
IRL	The Institute for Rational Living, 45 East 65th Street, New York, NY 10021
IU	Audio-Visual Center, Division of University Extension, Indiana University, Bloomington, IN 47405
LCA	Learning Corporation of America, 711 Fifth Avenue, New York, NY 10022
McG	Contemporary/McGraw-Hill Films, 1221 Avenue of the Americas, New York, NY 10020
NCF	National Carousel Films, Inc., 241 East 34th Street, Room 24, New York, NY 10016

NET	National Educational Television, Audio-Visual Center, Indiana University, Bloomington, IN 47401
NDF	New Day Films Co-op Inc., P.O. Box 315, Franklin Lakes, NY 07417
NGS	National Geographic Society, Educational Services, Department 80, Washington, DC 20036
NYF	New Yorker Films, 16 West 61st Street, New York, NY 10023
NYU	New York University Film Library, 26 Washington Place, New York, NY 10003
PCR	Pennsylvania State University Psychology Cinema Register, University Park, PA 16802
PFI	Psychological Films, Inc, 189 North Wheeler Street, Orange, CA 92669
RP	Research Press, Box 3177Y, Champaign, IL 61821
RSC	Rehabilitation Services Commission, 4656 Heaton Road, Columbus, OH 43229
SB	Stephen Bosostou Productions, P.O. Box 2127, Santa Monica, CA 90404
SW	Swank, P. O. Box 231, South Jefferson Avenue, St. Louis, MO 63166
TL	Time-Life Films, Inc., 43 West 16th Street, New York, NY 10011
UA	United Artists/16, 729 Seventh Avenue, New York, NY 10019
UCEMC	University of California Extension Media Center, Film Distributor, 2223 Fulton Street, Berkeley, CA 94720
UFC	United Films of Canada, 7 Hayden Street, Suite 305, Toronto, Ontario, Canada M4Y 2P2
Z	Zipporah Films, 54 Lewis Wharf, Boston, MA 02110

CHAPTER 1

Abnormal Behavior in Our Times

CHAPTER OUTLINE

I. Popular Views of Abnormal Psychology
    A. The study of problems of coping exhibited by people
        1. Albert, the popular professor who commits suicide
        2. Sue, the lawyer who has an alcohol problem
        3. Manuel, who showed poor impulse control
    B. The limits of psychological resourcefulness are examined
    C. Mental disorders have often been portrayed by writers
        1. Shakespeare's characters such as Macbeth and Iago
        2. Autobiographical explorations of abnormality
            a. Vonnegut's The Eden Express
            b. Green's I Never Promised You a Rose Garden
            c. Sutherland's Breakdown
            d. Ward's The Snake Pit
            e. Kesey's One Flew Over the Cuckoo's Nest
        3. We all have a fascination with bizarre behavior
            a. Attempts at "armchair" diagnoses
            b. The popular misconceptions about abnormal behavior
II. What Do We Mean by Abnormal Psychology?
    A. Dilemmas of Definition
        1. The DSM-IV definition
        2. Cultural relativists reject the notion of sick societies
            a. Nazi obedience is viewed as adaptive
            b. One group may select normality for others in society
        3. Problems in validity for defining abnormality through cultural relativism
            a. Are one set of values as good as another?
            b. Therapists must seek conformity to social norms
    B. Mental Disorder as maladaptive
        1. Does behavior foster well-being?
        2. Abnormal behavior prevents growth and fulfillment
            a. Actualization is seen as worth striving to attain
            b. Behavior is evaluated in terms of its consequences on well-being and growth
        3. The several distinct fields of practices are reviewed

          a.   Psychiatry and clinical psychology are compared
          b.   Psychiatric social work focuses on the social enviroment

III.   Classifying Abnormal Behavior
    A.   DSM classification of mental disorders
        1.   Describing the nature or clinical picture of abnormal behaviors
            a.   Classification systems permit clear communication
            b.   Classification is a step toward treatment
        2.   The DSM-IV was published in 1994 by the American Psychiatric Association
        3.   The International Classification of Diseases, 9th Edition governs worldwide classification
        4.   The DSM classification has distinct clinical usefulness
            a.   Only operational criteria are used for definition
            b.   Subjectivity in diagnosis is diminished
        5.   The DSM has a diagnosis made according to five axes or dimensions
            a.   Axes I, II, and III deal with the patient's current condition
                1)   Axes I and II list the categories of mental disorder
                2)   Axis III requires a medical exam and assesses physical state
            b.   Axes IV and V assess life situation and success in coping, respectively
    B.   The problem of labeling
        1.   Labels often appear to criticize the person
        2.   The person may act out the label
        3.   Society may stigmatize the "labeled" person
            a.   People may act negatively toward the patient
            b.   Patients are seen as "dangerous" because of their labels
        4.   Professionals must be cautious in assigning a label to a patient
            a.   Some professionals prefer the term client
            b.   The need for confidentiality is very important
IV.   The Extent of Abnormal Behavior
    A.   Frequencies of particular disorders are of great interest to professionals
        1.   Research efforts are guided by frequencies
        2.   Allocation of treatment resources depends upon the extent of the disorder
    B.   Epidemiology studies the distribution of mental disorders
        1.   Prevalence identifies the active cases
        2.   Incidence is the rate of occurrence
    C.   The NIMH Catchment Area studies provide information about mental disorder in our society
        1.   Thirty-three percent of the sample were likely to have some psychological disorder
        2.   Most are treated in outpatient facilities
V.   Research in Abnormal Psychology

A. Observation of behavior
   1. Overt behavior forms the basis of classification
   2. Self-reports of inner thoughts has a limit as a data base
   3. The observational method is a systematic technique to record behavior
      a. Hypotheses help to make sense of the observed behavior
      b. Hypotheses guide empirical research
   4. Hypotheses about causation guide treatment strategies
      a. Various perspectives explain the same behavior differently
      b. Treatments vary depending upon a therapist's theoretical perspective

B. Sampling and generalization
   1. Studies that examine groups of people are valued over single cases
      a. May identify multiple causes for disorders
      b. Can generalize results to other cases
   2. Sampling is a technique to find representatives of the disorder being researched
      a. Erroneous conclusions can emerge from faulty sampling
      b. Control groups are used for comparisons

C. Correlation and causation
   1. Correlation or association of variables is not evidence of causation
      a. Many conditions or symptoms occur together, but their relationship can take many forms
      b. Complexity is the rule in abnormal behavior
   2. Path analysis can be used to disentangle complexities
   3. Correlations can provide useful information for inference
      a. Epidemiological studies use correlations extensively
      b. Assists in developing hypotheses for future research

D. Experimental strategies
   1. The experimental method strives to control extraneous variables
   2. There are limitations to using the experimental method
      a. Ethical restraints limit possible conditions
      b. It is impossible to control all variables influencing behavior
   3. Analogue studies simulate conditions that cannot be manipulated
      a. Learned helplessness studies are analogue investigations
      b. But limitations in generalization exist for analogue research

E. The clinical case study
   1. Case studies examine causation of problems and treatment methods
      a. $N=1$ experiments use the patient as his/her own control
      b. A single observer can bias results
   2. Case studies allow for in-depth examination of a patient

F. Retrospective versus prospective strategies
   1. Prospective research is supplementing traditional retrospective form
      a. Looking forward strengthens causal hypotheses when correct
      b. Populations with risk factors are followed
   2. Prospective studies have produced equivocal results
      a. The methodology is still evolving

                b.   Excessive confidence was initially placed in them

VI.   The Orientation of the Book
      A.   A scientific approach to abnormal behavior is based on data from various fields
      B.   An awareness of our common human concerns using sources outside of science
      C.   Respect for the dignity, integrity, and growth potential of the person
      D.   Focuses on the psychosocial factors involved in abnormal behavior
      E.   Methods of asessment and treatment are reviewed following discussion of problems

VII.   Unresolved Issues on Classification
      A.   The DSM-IV uses a disease metaphor for mental disorder
      B.   Some professionals differ on the value of DSM-III-R classification
            1.   Complex human behavior is overly simplified
            2.   Is it possible to divide behavior into normal and abnormal?
            3.   Symptoms are the foundation for categorization
      C.   Alternatives have been proposed
            1.   The dimensional approach views behavior as a level of intensity
            2.   The prototypal approach objects to clear categories and "pigeon holes"

LEARNING OBJECTIVES

1.   List some popular plays, movies, and books that describe abnormal behavior and explain why such sources are often inaccurate.

2.   Desribe two broad perspectives on abnormal behavior and explain how each views the goals of therapy.

3.   List three aspects of abnormal behavior that must be considered by those who wish to understand it.

4.   List several reasons why a classification system is needed in abnormal psychology and explain the meaning of validity and reliability in reference to such a system.

5.   Differentiate between the DSM and ICD classification systems and describe the five axes of DSM-IV.

6.   Compare DSM-IV and DSM-III-R and describe two limitations of DSM classifications and labeling in general.

7.   Explain why the observation of behavior is basic to psychology and its importance to the development of hypotheses.

8.   Explain why research on groups of people is usually preferred to single case studies and why those groups must be representative of larger populations.

9.   Explain why correlational research cannot establish cause and effect but has been extremely useful in epidemiologic research.

10.   Explain why experimental studies are often inappropriate for abnormal psychology, and indicate how analogue studies have been used in their place.

11.   Describe the clinical case study, and explain why it is easy to draw erroneous conclusions from this method of research.

12.   Compare the advantages and disadvantages of retrospective and prospective research in

abnormal psychology.

13. List and explain three concepts about the study of abnormal psychology on which this text is based.
14. List and describe three broad approaches to the classification of abnormal behavior and some of the assumptions underlying each.
15. Explain why the authors prefer a prototypal model of classification to the categorical one that is in place.

KEY TERMS

abnormal behavior	abnormal psychology
psychopathology	clinical psychology
psychiatry	psychiatric social work
clinical picture	functional psychoses
reliability	validity
DSM-IV	acute
chronic	mild
moderate	severe
episodic	epidemiology
prevalence	incidence
observational method	hypotheses
sampling	control group
criterion group	correlation
causation	experimental method
analogue studies	case study
retrospective research	prospective research
categorical classification	dimensional classification
propotypal classification	syndrome
lifetime prevalence	

FOCUS ON RESEARCH 1

Nathan, P. (1994). "DSM-IV: Empirical, Accessible, Not Yet Ideal." Journal of Clinical Psychology, 50, 110.

This author gives a summation to the revision process of the the DSM-IV. The process took five years until the final draft of the DSM-IV was completed. The author was one of the several hundred task force members who completed the process. In this article he discusses the major achievements and continuing shortcomings in the DSM.

He considers this revision to have greater breadth of coverage than in previous editions because of the number of diagnosticians and researchers who were involved in the task force. Thirteen work groups had the responsibility for a major diagnostic category. The membership requirements were sensitive to disciplinary bases, gender, racial and ethnic diversity and primary work settings. The result was the inclusion of more women, nonpsychiatrists, and clinicians than in previous revisions.

A three stage empirical process was begun in 1988 by the work groups. The initial step was to complete a systematic literature review. This was followed by an analysis of existing clinical data. The process concluded with field trials. With this process, any unresolved diagnostic issues diminished in number. The field trials completed by the task force were more extensive than in previous efforts. Thus, the diagnostic categories in this revision were influenced by both extensive literature review and field trials. The DSM-IV pays substantial attention to the significance of gender and, ethnicity-related diagnoses, and provides a guideline for cultural formulation.

After describing the important improvements in this revision, the author suggests a number of continuing problems in the DSM-IV. The revision is criticized for promoting a medical or disease model which many claim cannot be supported and may be of limited usefulness. Even though the empirical base of the revision was substantial, some decisions were still made using a "best estimate" strategy. Another criticism centers on the perceived undue responsiveness of the task force to politically popular issues. Finally, defying efforts to make the DSM-IV compatible with the ICD-10, the completed revision retains important differences in some categories.

Questions for Discusssion

1. How important is the DSM revision process? Who is affected by the outcome?

2. The DSM-IV is substantially larger than previous editions. What factors contributed to the increase in absolute size of the DSM? Have new disorders been identified?

FOCUS ON RESEARCH 2

Lukoff, D., Lu, F. and Turner, R. (1992). "Toward a More Culturally Sensitive DSM-IV." Journal of Nervous and Mental Disease, 180, 673-682.

This article provides an interesting insight into one effort to expand the way the DSM-IV would categorize abnormal behavior. One of the criticisms directed at the DSM-III-R classification system was the lack of concern for religious and spiritual dimensions of life. These authors suggest that this reflects a cultural insensitivity toward individuals who have religious and spiritual experiences in both Western and non-Western cultures. They term this insensitivity the "religious gap" between clinciians and clients.

The authors show that the DSM typically refers to religious matters as illustrations of psychopathology. They discuss the relationship of associating religion with psychopathology by reviewing the long history of this tendency in psychiatry beginning with Freudian perspectives.

Since psychiatry assigns a primacy to biology over culture, a continuing lack of sensitivity to the cultural forces of religion has been seen. The research literature since Freud has largely ignored religion. Further, the authors state that neither psychiatrists nor psychologists are given adequate training to prepare them to deal with issues related to religion.

The authors presented their proposal to the Task Force which prepared the DSM-IV. The proposal called for the inclusion of a new "z" code category reflecting psychoreligious or psychospiritual problems. This category would involve problems emerging from beliefs and practices associated with organized religious institutions, and problems a person may be experiencing in relations to his/her perception of a transcendent being or force.

The authors' presentation of their proposal provides an excellent illustration of how the professional community attempts to correct perceived shortcomings in the current practice of mental health issues. Since the DSM-IV has a wde ranging impact on the mental health community, insight into this process can be useful for students.

Questions for Discussion

1.   What are the possible reasons for the perceived shortcomings in the DSM?
2.   What is the importance of updating the DSM?
3.   What problems, if any, could this proposal create?
4.   What are the positives of having this categorization?

FOCUS ON RESEARCH 3

Fances, A., Pincus, H., Widiger, T., Davis, W., and First, M. (1990). "DSM-IV: Work in Progress." American Journal of Psychiatry, 147, 1439-1448.

This article provides a thorough discussion of the development of DSM-IV. A historical review initiates the article and discusses the paradigm shift toward descriptive mental diagnosis that was meant to be neutral with regard to etiology and theoretical orientation which began in DSM-III. That edition contained the two methodological innovations of using a multiaxial system and explicit diagnostic criteria. Some limitations of DSM-III included the apparent institution of rigid rules for diagnosis rather than clinical guides. And its length, definition of certain diagnoses, and social consequences were also criticized.

In 1987, the DSM-III-R was published. It included many changes that the author considered to be too much of a revision so soon after initial publication of DSM-III. Soon after the appearance of the revised edition, the American Psychiatric Association began work on the DSM-IV.

In this revision, decisions must be substantiated by explicit statements of rationale and review of empirical data. Thus, it attempts to strike a balance between historical tradition and various clinical and empirical resources. The goal is to obtain a consensus of mental health professionals and attain compatibility with the International Classification of Diseases (ICD-10). It is hoped that the new edition of DSM will provide increased clinical utility and user friendliness.

The DSM-IV needs to be usable across settings and various professions. The manual must guide clinical practice. Thus, the objections of expanding categories into impractical diagnoses and accumulating marginal new diagnoses must be considered seriously by the DSM-IV task force. The DSM-IV will continue to employ one set of criteria for use in both clinical and research practice, unlike the ICD-10 approach which separates the two.

Significant issues that are now being decided about the form of the new edition include such issues as: core features of mental disorder versus discriminating symptoms; the level of clincal inference in the criteria; polythetic versus monothetic criteria; and the utility of diagnostic test results in diagnosis. The authors conclude that no single diagnostic system will completely satisfy all professionals. Empirical evidence should take a front row in the changes for DSM-IV. Only with the evidence of various sources of data will changes be included in the DSM-IV. Thus, expect to see few new diagnoses and simple clinical utility in the coming revision.

Questions for Discussion

1.   How important is the DSM series in the practice of psychology?
2.   What contributes to the need for revising the DSM?
3.   How much input into the revision process should various mental health professionals have?

FOCUS ON RESEARCH 4

Zook, A., and Walton, J. M. (1989). "Theoretical Orientations and Work Settings of Clinical and Counseling Psychologists: A Current Perspective." Professional Psychology: Research and Practice, 20, 23-31.

What are the theoretical orientations of practicing psychologists? This is one of the questions reviewed by the authors. In addition, they investigated how practitioners interpret the term "eclecticism", and tried to determine if clinical psychology is merging with counseling psychology in terms of similarity of practice. The question of a merger between clinical and counseling psychology has been debated by many professionals. If a merging of fields has taken place, a new name for the entity may be coined. The authors examine the possibility that a "human service psychology" is emerging.

To examine the research questions, the authors completed a survey of 600 clinical and counseling psychologists who are members of the American Psychological Association. The questionnaire completed by the respondents (66.5% rate of return) sought information describing their orientation and work setting.

Results of the survey revealed a wide variety of theoretical orientations in the sample. A move toward behavioral approaches was evident among young respondents of both specialty areas. The cognitive-behavioral perspective was the most common one listed. Although psychodynamic approaches continue to be strong among clinicians, it does not appear to be favored by younger psychologists. Rogerian person-centered methods were listed as most preferred by counseling psychologists. This popularity showed a dramatic drop when young counseling psychologists were considered.

Few practitioners listed eclecticism as their major orientation. The authors did not provide a category of eclecticism on their questionnaires. To be classified under this theoretical orientation, the person had to check "other" and fill in the term. This suggested to the authors a lack of a clear-cut definition for eclecticism among psychologists.

Concerning the work setting of clinical and counseling psychologists, the majority indicated working at two settings. Counseling psychologists were more likely found in academic settings while clinicians were in private practice or Veterans Administration hospitals. Compared to earlier studies, a decline in the number of psychologists working in community mental health centers was found.

In examining similarities between clinical and counseling psychologists, the authors found significant differences between the two groups. Counseling psychology maintains a core humanistic approach toward its clientele that is less apparent among clinicians who emphasize psychodynamics and behavioral viewpoints. Behavioral approaches have garnered increased usage partly because of client approval for the procedures.

Questions for Discussion

1. Are undergraduates aware of differences in clinical and counseling psychology?
2. Why would some counseling psychologists desire a merging with clinical psychology?

READINGS

1. Bauer, M., Calabrese, J, and Post, R. (1994). "Multisite Data Reanalysis of the Validity of Rapid Cycling as a Course Modifier for Bipolar Disorder in DSM-IV." American Journal of   Psychiatry, 151, 506-515.

2. Carson. R. (1991). "Dilemnas in the Pathway of the DSM-IV. Journal of Abnormal Psychology, 100, 302-307.

3. Cervantes, R., and Arroyo, W. (1994). "DSM-IV: Implications for Hispanic Children and Adolescents." Hispanic Journal of Behavioral Sciences, 16, 8-27.

4. Chapman, T., Mannuzza, S., Klein, D., and Fyer, A. (1994). "Effects of Informant Mental Disorder on Psychiatric Family History Data." American Journal of Psychiatry, 151, 574-579.

5. First, M., Frances, A., and Vettorello, N. (1994). Hospital and Community Psychiatry, 45, 18-20.

6. Frances, A., Pincus, H., and Widiger, T. (1995). "DSM-IV and International Communication in Psyuchiatric Diagnosis." In, Y. Honda and J. Mezzich (Eds.), Psychiatric Diagnosis: A World Perspective. New York: Springer.

7.   Grant, I., Gutierrez, R., and Atkinson, J. (1994). "DSM-IV: Mild Neurocognitive Disorder, a Reply." Journal of Neuropsychiatry and Clinical Neuroscience, 6, 60.

8.   Gross, H., Schiltz, K, and Herndon, C. (1994). "DSM-IV: Mild Neurocognitve Disorder." Journal of Neuropsychiatry and Clinical Neurscience, 6, 59-60.

9.   Hafner, H., and Maurer, K. (1994). "The Contribution of Epidemiology to the Study of Diagnosis." European Psychiatry, 9, 3-12.

10. Henry, G. (1994). "DSM-IV: Proposed Criteria for Postconcussive Disorder." Journal of Neuropsychiatry and Clincial Neuroscience, 6, 58.

11. Matthysse, S. (1993). "Genetics and the Problem of Causality in Abnormal Psychology." In, P. Sutker and H. Adams (Eds.), Comprehensive Textbook of Psychopathology. pp. 47-56, New York : Plenum.

12. Mezzich, J., Fabrega, H. and Kleinman, A. (1995). "On Enhancing the Cultural Sensitivity of DSM-IV." Journal of Nervous and Mental Disease, 183, 234-250.

13. Mohl, P., Lomax, J., Tasman, A., and Carlyle, H. (1990). "Psychotherapy Training for the Psychiatrist of the Future." American Journal of Psychiatry, 147, 7-13.

14. Pincus, H. A., Fances, A., Davis, W., and First, M. (1994). "Diagnostic Categories: Holding the Line on Proliferation." American Journal of Psychiatry, 151, 123-141.

15. Robins, W., and Barrett, J. (1989). The Validity of Psychiatric Diagnosis. New York: Raven Press.

16. Spitzer, R., Williams, J., and First, M. (1990). "A Proposal for DSM-IV: Solving the Organic/Nonorganic Problem." Journal of Neuropsychiatry, 1, 126-127.

17. Szasz, T. (1987). Insanity: The Idea and Its Consequences. New York: John Wiley and Sons.

DISCUSSION AND LECTURE IDEAS

1.   Students can be introduced to the numerous definitions of abnormality by trying to formulate a definition of what is abnormal. The question "How would you define abnormal behavior?" can be used to initiate the discussion. A number of different answers will be generated, and these should be recorded on the blackboard. The instructor will have to challenge each of the answers in order to illustrate the concepts expressed in the text. The responses generated by the students can then be categorized into the different areas identified in Chapter 1--for example, the view that abnormality is always dangerous or that mental disorder is something to be scorned. Through the course of the discussion, students should come to appreciate the problem in defining abnormal behavior and gain an insight into factors affecting the labeling of abnormality.

2.   A useful follow-up discussion to the aforementioned exercise is to elicit student views on the causes of abnormal behavior. This information garnered during class discussion can be related to the research issues addressed in the latter part of Chapter 1. Once students have produced their ideas concerning the reasons for abnormal behavior, the question of how these ideas can be investigated experimentally should be addressed. Students should be encouraged to disclose the reasoning behind the development of their explanations. Once these have been recorded, the ideas can be related to such research issues as correlation versus education, sampling and generalization, and operational definitions. The students can also receive feedback in terms of how their popular notions of abnormality correspond to the paradigms expressed in the text. This discussion should help students understand how ideas about mental disorder evolve in our society and how researchers attempt to provide testable hypotheses about abnormal behavior and its development.

3.   The question of the adaptive or maladaptive qualities of abnormal behavior hinges on societal values and concerns. The process of social labeling determines what is considered abnormal in a particular culture. In order for a label of abnormality to occur, there must be some person or persons who make the judgment. Thus behavior does not occur in a vacuum but exists in the context of social labeling and the evaluation of others.

The concept of social labeling provides an excellent topic for a lecture-discussion session. Any number of cultural groups can be used as examples to provide contrasts in how societies label pathology. Students can be asked to generate their own examples of social labeling, using experiences with subcultural groups. The behaviors found among different age groups are often labeled as abnormal by the dominant age group in our society. For instance, street slang may be evaluated as maladaptive by the school system, yet it provides rich communication in the subcultural context. The behavior of adolescents may be labeled as pathological by adults who see the behavior as maladaptive (an example is the punk rock movement and the style of dress and behavior it produced).

Students should find the discussion of social labeling an interesting one, because they can contribute experiences from their own subcultural group. In-class lecture can illustrate that, although social labeling can be a powerful process, some behaviors (such as depression) are generally assumed to be maladaptive in all societies. Students can also be asked to try to identify those behaviors whose maladaptiveness transcends cultural boundaries. For further information see H. John (1990). "The Big-Five Factor Taxonomy: Dimensions of Personality in the Natural Language." In, Handbook of Personality Theory and Research. New York: Guilford.

4.   When a student enrolls in a course covering abnormal psychology, he or she has a number of reasons for taking the course. These reasons may range from satisfying a degree requirement to a desire for enhanced personal insight. The expectations of the students regarding the course and why they may or may not get out of it are significant factors to be explored in classroom discussion.

Students should be encouraged to volunteer their reasons for enrolling in the course. Common answers that usually arise include: to learn more about my own behavior, to understand

11

others, and to learn about the different mental health professions. Students can be asked to record their own ideas about abnormal behavior in terms of what it is and what it isn't. These records can be reviewed at the conclusion of the course to determine how their attitudes may have changed. This discussion can provide a good opportunity to present the rationale involved in studying abnormal psychology and how the scientific tradition assists in increasing our understanding of behavior and its determinants. After this discussion students should have a clear understanding of the demands and expectations of this course and how they, as individuals, fit into the course design.

5.	To permit a presentation of the stigma of mental disorder, it is often useful to encourage a discussion during class of personal problem behaviors. Encourage students to self-disclose concerning habits or actions that could be considered maladaptive. Such commonplace habits as fingernail biting, chewing gum, smoking cigarettes, and knuckle-cracking can all be considered maladaptive for one reason or another. Once a list of these common behaviors is generated, students can be directed toward describing how such actions can be maladaptive. For example, knuckle-cracking can irritate others and cause relationship problems.

This discussion can be expanded to a review on the stigma of labeling and the social isolation that often results from an unfavorable diagnosis given to a person. The reasons why certain maladaptive behaviors are maintained in a person's behavioral repertoire can be discussed. Self-disclosures centering on reasons why students are unable to break undesirable habits can enliven the discussion.

6.	Are there forms of abnormal behavior that could be considered universal? Different cultures apparently encourage different styles of psychological disorder, but are the major DSM-IV categories apparent in all cultures? If a disorder can be found in numerous cultures, what are the implications for the prevention and treatment of abnormal behavior? J. Tooby and G. Cosmides (1990) address the issue of how culture influences the style of psychopathology (Journal of Personality, 58, 17-68).

ACTIVITIES AND PROJECTS

1.	The manner in which our society portrays mental disorder through the media has an impact on the attitudes of individuals. Television and the movies consistently use psychological labels to describe unfavorable and dangerous characters. The written media likewise often use lurid descriptions of crimes, including psychological diagnoses and terms.

An informative project for students is to gather evidence of the often-biased presentation of psychological disorders in the visual and print media. Different groups of students can be assigned varied popular publications in order to collect material discussing mental conditions. This project should encompass publications of differing quality and orientation, such as Newsweek versus The National Enquirer. The student groups would be required to categorize and assess the portrayals of mental disorder in the varied publications. What biases can they identify? Are common psychological terms or labels used? Are the discussions of mental disorder done in a manner sympathetic toward the afflicted person? What general attitudes toward mental health are described in popular magazines?

A similar project can involve the visual media. Groups of students can be assigned to watch popular television programs and record the manner in which mental disorder is pictured. Or a paticular movie may be assigned. Discussion can center on the stereotypes that are reinforced when movies and television use psychological ideas.

2. The evidence derived from the scientific method varies in usefulness and credibility. One of the problems affecting many early research efforts was the question of how systematic the research approach was. The case study approach can be integrated into a useful class project. The students can be required to selectt a person they know as a subject. The individual, while remaining anonymous, could be the focus of a case study. A particular target behavior is the focus of the investigation.

The students, choosing a relative, friend, or roommate for study, are given a particular behavior to investigate (such as social behavior, dating behavior, or study behavior) and then required to compile a brief case study of that individual over a predetermined period of time. Once the student completes the case study, he or she needs to generate meaning from the collected data and complete a coherent picture of the case.

Once the case studies are completed, a discussion is needed to illustrate the value and shortcomings of this research strategy. Limitations concerning the method of data collection, subjectivity of the observers, and lack of control available in the procedure can be discussed in terms of how other methods (such as controlled experimentation) supplement and improve on the case study procedure. After having experience in attempting to construct a case study, students should appreciate the contribution of varied scientific procedures to the investigation of abnormal psychology.

3. The definitions of abnormality are affected by numerous factors. Students can be assigned to determine whether age or cohort group influences the perception of abnormality in our society. Students acting in groups can be assigned the task of interviewing people in order to create a definition of abnormal. The students are required to question persons from childhood through old age. The students ask the subjects for a definition of abnormal and, using age as a factor, attempt to see whether the definitions vary with age group. The students shall look for similar ideas and terms that people use to define abnormality. Useful questions include: "Do males and females suggest different definitions?" "Does aging change attitudes?" "What terms appear at all ages to describe abnormality?" "What factors may contribute to the differences found (if any)?" "What type of behavior toward persons with mental disorder would these attitudes predict?" "Should attempts be made to modify the attitudes of others toward mental disorder?" "How do children develop their attitudes toward mental disorder?"

CHAPTER 2

Historical Views of Abnormal Behavior

CHAPTER OUTLINE

I. Abnormal Behavior in Ancient Times
    A. Demonology, gods, and magic
        1. Abnormal behavior attributed to demonic possession
            a. Differentiated good vs. bad spirits
            b. Religious significance of possession
            c. Treatment for possession was through exorcism
        2. Shamans originally treated the possessed
            a. Priests assumed the role of exorcist
            b. Many priests showed the beginning of humane care
    B. Early philosophical and medical concepts
        1. Hippocrates
            a. Insisted mental disorders due to natural causes
            b. Classified all varieties of mental disorders
                1) Mania
                2) Melancholia
                3) Phrentis
            c. Treatments were designed for the specific classifications
            d. Many misconceptions were perpetuated
                1) Hysteria caused by a wandering uterus
                2) Four bodily fluids out of balance
        2. Plato and Aristotle
            a. Criminal acts examined by Plato
                1) Suggested humane treatment
                2) Addressed issue of insanity as a legal defense
            b. Plato proposed that behavior was motivated by needs or appetites
            c. Aristotle described the content of consciousness
                1) People strive to eliminate pain and seek pleasure
                2) Followed Hippocrates' theory of disturbances in life
        3. Later Greek and Roman thought
            a. The Greek physician Galen contributed to describing the nervous system
            b. Roman physicians followed the principle of contrariis

contrarius (opposite by oppposite)
- C. Views during the Middle Ages
  1. Islamic countries preserved some scientific aspects of Greek medicine
  2. Avicenna, the prince of physicians, wrote the Canon of Medicine
  3. European attitudes toward mental disorder were characterized by superstition
     a. Mental disorders were prevalent in this period
     b. Sin was seen in only a minority of cases as a cause
  4. Mass Madness
     a. Tarantism episodes in Italy
     b. Lycanthropy affected many rural residents
     c. Oppression, disease, and famine maintained the mass hysterias
  5. Exorcism
     a. Attacks on Satan's Pride
     b. Some exorcisms continue in contemporary practice
- D. Witchcraft and mental illness: fact or fiction?
  1. Witchhunts during the fifteenth and sixteenth centuries
  2. Controversies concering extent of the witchhunts
     a. Schoeneman's contention that mental disorder was not viewed as witchcraft
     b. Problems in the historical record confused the issue

II. The Growth Toward Humanitarian Approaches
- A. Resurgence of scientific questioning in Europe
  1. Teresa of Avila provided a conceptual leap concerning mental disorder
  2. Paracelsus was an early critic of possession as mental illness
  3. Weyer's book, The Deception of Demons, refuted the Malleus Malefecarium used by witch hunters
  4. Reginald Scot denied the existence of demons in Discovery of Witchcraft
- B. Establishment of early asylums and shrines
  1. Early asylums
     a. Treatments were designed to restore the balance of body and brain
     b. Methods were powerful and aggressive
  2. The Geel Shrine provided humane care.
- C. Humanitarian reform
  1. Pinel's Experiment
     a. He removed chains from mental patients
     b. Treated patients with kindness and as sick people
     c. His Bicetre and Salpetriere hospitals were the first modern mental hospitals
  2. Tuke's work in England
     a. The York Retreat was established
     b. He helped change attitudes about demonic possession
  3. Rush and moral management in America
     a. He founded American psychiatry

b.   He invented the "tranquilizer"

c.   Stresses or moral causes of insanity were proposed

d.   Moral management was abandoned by the late nineteenth century

    1)   Mental hygiene movement condemned patients to dependency

    2)   An emphasis on physical basis of mental illness countered moral treatment

4.   Dix and the mental hygiene movement

a.   Aroused awareness of inhumane treatment for the mentally ill

b.   Contemporaries criticized Dix's work as leading to the warehousing of the mentally ill

III.   The Foundations of Twentieth-Century Views

    A.   Changing attitudes toward mental health

        1.   Beer's book, <u>A Mind That Found Itself</u>, describes the poor state of care

        2.   Stimulated the interest for reform among professionals and the public

IV.   The Growth of Scientific Research

    A.   The Roots of the Biological Viewpoint

        1.   General paresis

        2.   Milestones in the discovery process

    B.   The Establishment of brain pathology as a causal factor

    C.   The Beginnings of a classification system

        1.   Kraepelin

        2.   Recognizing symptom patterns

    D.   Advnces achieved a a result of early biological views

    E.   Advances in psychological understanding of mental disorders: The psychodynamic perspective

        1.   The roots of the psychodynamic viewpoint

            a.   Mesmerism

            b.   The Nancy School

        2.   The beginnings of psychoanalysis

    F.   Advances in psychological research

        1.   The behavioral perspective

        2.   Roots of the behavioral perspective

            a.   Classical conditioning

            b.   Watson

            c.   Skinner

V.   Unresolved Issues on Interpreting Historical Events

    A.   Retrospective analysis has limitations

        1.   There is an absence of direct observation

        2.   Written accounts may be incomplete

            a.   Historical articles are out of context of the times

            b.   A propaganda element may be present in them

    B.   Current viewpoints color our interpretation of past events

        1.   Conclusions are only working hypotheses

2. Need to search for "new" historical documents

LEARNING OBJECTIVES

1. Describe early beliefs in demonology and explain the reasons why exorcism was used as a cure.
2. Describe Hippocrates' system of classifying mental disorders in ancient Greece and indicate some of the treatments he advocated.
3. Describe some conclusions that Plato and Aristotle reached about mentally disturbed people and explain how both anticipated some of Freud's ideas.
4. List four Greeks and Romans who continued in the Hippocratic tradition after 120 B.C. and describe some of the contributions each made to the understanding and treatment of abnormal behavior.
5. Describe the treatment of mental patients in Islamic countries around 792 A.D. and list the mental disorders described by Avicenna in The Canon of Medicine.
6. Describe the dance manias that occurred widely in Europe and relate them to an earlier Greek tradition.
7. Describe the treatment for mental disorders used by the clergy during the Middle Ages known as exorcism, or the "laying on of hands."
8. Explain the supposed connection between mental illness and witchcraft and comment on the accuracy of this assumption.
9. Give several examples of people who, during the latter part of the Middle Ages, began to question whether witchcraft and demon possession were reasons for abnormal behavior.
10. Describe the treatment that mental patients received in early "insane asylums" in Europe and the United States.
11. Detail the events that led up to the founding of the Gheel Shrine in Belgium and describe its operation today.
12. Describe the humanitarian reforms in the treatment of mental patients that were instigated by Philippe Pinel, William Tuke, Benjamin Rush, and Dorothea Dix.
13. Describe the attitudes about mental health that existed near the end of the nineteenth century.
14. List some events beginning in the late nineteenth century that illustrate the increase of scientific research into the causes of mental abnormalities.
15. List and explain several weaknesses of the kind of retrospective research that attempts to produce an accurate history of mental illness and its treatment.

KEY TERMS

exorcism
insanity
St. Vitus's dance
asylums
mental hygiene movement
psychoanalytic perspective

psychohistory
tarantism
lycanthropy
moral management
mesmerism
psychoanalysis

18

psychodynamic perspective
catharsis
dream analysis
classical conditioning
instrumental (operant) conditioning

Nancy School
free association
behavioral perspective
behaviorism
biologial viewpoint

FOCUS ON RESEARCH 1

Maher, B. and Maher, W. (1994). "Personality and Psychopathology: A Historical Perspective." Journal of Abnormal Psychology, 103, 72-77.

The authors present an overview of the history of the understanding of the relationship between personality and psychopathology. This link has been examined in a number of ways. The central concept is for personality variables to be related to the premorbid phase of psychopathology development. The authors present an overview of the early historical viewpoints on this issue.

The best known early paradigm involved the concepts of the four humors which is usually associated with Hippocrates. The four elements of the world (earth, air, fire and water) had specific attributes (heat, cold, moistness, and dryness). These attributes combined to form the four essential fluids of the body: blood, phlegm, bile and black bile. These formed a balance within the person, with some becoming more dominant than the others. Temperament was determined by the dominant humor. Vulnerability to illness was determined by one's temperament.

During the Darwinian period, scientists placed an emphasis on the evoluationary process. The belief of the eventual superior organism appearing as the result of natural selection was evident in this period. The traits that favored survival were the ones in persons who produced offspring.

In the 19th century, the idea that mental illness was the result of degeneracy persisted for many years. Two versions of this concept appeared. The first placed focus on the environment of the city and was seen as unhealthy both physically and mentally. Researchers of the time pointed to the increases of mental illnesses among rural families who left their farms for the cities. The second version of degeneracy was that those who were obviously impaired were, by definition, lower on the evolutiolnary scale. Mental illness was claimed to be symptomatic of a basic, unitary, fundamental genetic inferiority. The epidemiological coincidence of poverty, rickets, tuberculosis, mental illness, alcoholism, high rates of infantile mortality, and limited adult expectations indicated that Nature was at work trying to remove these lower elements of the human race and preventing them from reproducing. Anyone trying to help the conditions of this class were acting against Nature's intentions. Extreme forms of degeneracy were considered to be evident in retardation and mental illness. Henry Maudsley was one of the chief proponents of this nineteenth century viewpoint.

An attempt to put a more enlightened interpretation to the role of evolution in mental illness than the degeneracy concept was made by the neurologist, J. Hughligs Jackson. His main point was that evolutionary development proceeded through the successive appearance of higher structures added to lower ones. Damage to the higher structures, such as the cortex, would permit the appearance of the lower brain structures. Thus mental illness may result from brain damage or the dissolution of higher centers of control. Regression was first presented as a concept related to mental illness in this viewpoint.

The double brain hypothesis developed when the nature of the two hemispheres of the brain was discovered. This idea posited that everyone has one good nature and one evil nature. Hallucinations, mood swings, and other mental illness signs were due to the "dialogue" between the two hemispheres.

In addition to these viewpoints that existed in the nineteenth century, the authors present good reviews of early twentieth century viewpoints including: Pavlovian concepts, Sheldon's Somatotyhpes, Kretschmer's work on body types, and early Freudian ideas. Overall the article is a very good supplement to the textbook material.

Questions for Discussion

1.   What would be the major implications for the degeneracy model if applied today?

2.   What are some of the current findings on hemisphere influences on behavior?

3.   What is needed to dismiss some of the theories once held as true?

4.   Discuss the role of research in the development and maintenance of theories.

FOCUS ON RESEARCH 2

Luckins, A. (1989). "The Rise and Decline of the American Asylum Movement in the 19th Century." Journal of Psychology, 122, 471-486.

This is an interesting review of the American public asylum from the 1840s to the late nineteenth century. It provides students with an overview of the factors contributing to establishing asylums and what led to their eventual decline. The author attempts to provide parallels to our current treatment of mental patients. Contemporary lawmakers are receiving pressure to reopen or build new mental hospitals as a means to remove the mentally disturbed from various communities. This attitude reflects the 1840s mentality of isolating the mentally disturbed from society. During the early part of the nineteenth century, numerous facilities were built with the stated purpose of providing meaningful care for the mental patient. Specially designed buildings were constructed as an "instrument of treatment." The asylum was seen as a place where patients could be transformed into productive people. Homelike environments were often created to provide a morale wholeness. A person was considered to be cured when freedom from symptoms was attained. The treatment procedures were comprised of activities reflecting on one's mental, physical, and social hygiene. The philosophies that guided the early to mid-nineteenth century asylum movement were pragmatism, Protestantism, British empiricism, and Scottish moral philosophy.

But the asylums became overcrowded because of the long stays required for chronic patients. As overcrowding became the norm, long work hours and low wages faced the staffs. This was particularly true for public asylums that buckled under the weight of increased immigration and urbanization. Also added to the chronic population were increased numbers of infirm and demented older persons. Cutbacks in funding necessitated less care for the patient population and cheap facilities being constructed. Critics of the asylums began to become visible both from within the system and without. The superintendents of many facilities were criticized for their lack of modern medical knowledge and experience. The moral environments constructed by the superintendents were seen as contradictory to "modern" medical practices. As criticism mounted and other political and economic factors evolved, the structure of the mental asylum was changed by the end of the nineteenth century.

Questions for Discussion

1. What factors contribute to abuse in a mental health system?
2. What qualifications are needed to work in a mental health facility?
3. Should local governments provide for the mentally disturbed?
4. Is funding for mental health popular with the public?

FOCUS ON RESEARCH 3

Fabrega, H. (1989). "An Ethnomedical Perspective of Anglo-American Psychiatry." American Journal of Psychiatry, 146, 588-596.

Ethnomedicine concerns the study of how disease problems are related to social factors in identification and treatment. Social and cultural factors including the beliefs, attitudes, and actions surrounding illness and treatment are examined. This approach considers the knowledge of illness and treatment to be an important element of culture. The ethnomedical approach is concerned with a number of topics including the following: what are the objects of concern?; how is illness conceptualized?; what values surround illness?; and what meanings are given to specific illnesses?

The author notes that the Anglo-American medical community is dominated by the biomedical theory of illness. The medical labels used in the Anglo-American culture have social, political, and moral implications. The psychiatric community attempts to utilize the same framework in the diagnosis and treatment of psychiatric disorders, but it is not yet possible to diagnose psychiatric disorders by using only technical procedures, or to describe specific underlying causes. Some diagnostic categories, including the anxiety disorders, do not have a clear disease base, and biomedicine may not be appropriate. Because of the influence of the biomedical approach in Anglo-American psychiatry, there exists a medicalization of social and psychological behavior. Since there is an intrinsic idea that illness needs some corrective action, psychiatric diagnosis and treatment becomes a form of social control.

The author contends that psychiatry strays outside the scope of other medical disciplines in the conceptualization and treatment of psychiatric disorder because it attempts to control the individual. Psychiatry becomes involved with numerous institutions which have social control functions.

These include the welfare system, the courtroom, the military, and prison system. This involvement leads to a conflict between the altruistic individual mode of providing psychiatric services and the institutional mode which may discredit the individual through labeling. Because of the cultural biases inherent in Anglo-American psychiatry, the author believes it is impossible to reach a truly universal science of psychiatry. In fact, the Anglo-American medical community is seen as exporting psychiatric illnesses throughout the world. This article provides some thoughtful information concerning the development of the psychiatric outlook in our Anglo-American society.

Questions for Discussion

1. What ethnic groups in the United States may have different perspectives on mental disorder?
2. Should psychologists be trained in cultural differences during graduate school?
3. What folk medicine remedies are you aware of?

FOCUS ON RESEARCH 4

Burket, R., Myers, W., Lyles, B., and Carrera, F. (1994). "Emotional and Behavioral Disturbances in Adolescents Involved in Withcraft and Satanism." Journal of Adolescence, 17, 41-52.

Although the connection between withcraft and psychopathology is usually related to historical references, there exist some current interest in the types of problems exhibited by individuals currently involved in Satanism. This article gives a good review of the current knowledge in this area of study.

The number of adolescents who are involved in withcraft and Satanism has appeared to increase in recent years. The authors have found that these adolesents call themselves "Satanic witches," and do not draw any distinction between witchcraft and Satanism. They believe that the Satanic powers derive from Satan worship. The authors suggest that the behavior is a reflection of one's psychological needs.

The authors present data from psychiatric admissions of adolescents who view themselves as Satanic witches. The authors found that identity disorder, alcohol abuse and hallucinations were more frequent in this group compared to other adolescent admissions. These adolescents also reported a high frequency of self-mutilation. Criminal behaviors were not found to be a significant factor in their sample.

The authors note that the phenomenon under investigation is not well researched. Their own sample was small and they caution against generalization to other samples, but they suggest that these issues are important to consider for the selection of treatment strategies.

Questions for Discussion

1. What are the experiences of students in this area? Have they known individuals similar to

those described in this article?

2. How would treatment be influenced by the factor of withcraft belief in the patients?

3. What are some of the commonly held beliefs about those who practice witchcraft?

READINGS

1. Adams, F. (1939). The Genuine Works of Hippocrates. Baltimore: Williams and Wilkins.

2. Ellenberger, H. F. (1974). "Psychiatry from Ancient to Modern Times." In S. Arieti (Ed.), American Handbook of Psychiatry. New York: Basic Books.

3. Fisher, H., and Greenberg, R. (1985). The Scientific Credibility of Freud's Theories and Therapy. New York: Columbia University Press.

4. Hankoff, D. (1985). "Ancient Egyptian Attitudes Toward Death and Suicide." Pharos, 38, 60-64.

5. Harrington, A. (1987). Mind, Medicine, and the Double Brain. Princeton, NJ: Princeton University Press.

6. Knoff, W. F. (1975). "Depression: A Historical Overview." American Journal of Psychoanalysis, 35, 41-46.

7. MacDonald, M. (1981). Mystical Bedlam: Madness, Anxiety and Healing in 17th Century England. Cambridge: Cambridge University Press.

8. Russell, J. B. (1980). A History of Witchcraft: Sorcerers, Heretics, and Pagans. New York: Thames and Hudson.

9. Shafter, R. (1989). "Women and Madness: A Social Historical Perspective." Issues in Ego Psychology, 12, 77-82.

10. Smith, W. D. (1965). "So-Called Possession in Pre-Christian Greece." Transaction of the American Philological Association, 96, 403-426.

11. Torrey, E., and Wolfe, S. (1986). The Case of the Seriously Mentally Ill: A Rating of State Programs. Washington, DC: Public Citizen Health Research Group.

12. Wilkins, K. (1974). "Attitudes to Witchcraft and Demonical Possession in France During the 18th Century." Journal of European Studies, 3, 349-362.

13. Wolberg, A. (1989). "Pilgrim's Progress Through the Psychoanalytic Maze."

Psychoanalysis and Psychotherapy, 7, 18-26.

14.   Wood, A. D. (1974). "The Fashionable Diseases: Women's Complaints and Their Treatment in 19th Century America." In M. Hartman & L. W. Banner (Eds.), Clio's Consciousness Raised. New York: Harper and Row.

15.   Woodward, W. E. (1969). Record of Salem Witchcraft. New York: DaCapo Press.

16.   Zucker, H. (1989). "Premises of Interpersonal Theory." Psychoanalytic Psychology, 6, 401-419.

DISCUSSION AND LECTURE IDEAS

1.   An interesting lecture entails a presentation of the legal documents related to mental disorder dating from the Middle Ages. A review of the legal aspects of mental disorder for this time period can be found in B. Neugebauer (1979, "Medieval and Early Modern Theories of Mental Illness," Archives of General Psychiatry, 36, 477-485). He examined the English legal system from the thirteenth century, and found that the monarchy assumed the right and responsibility for caring for the property and person of the mentally ill. If a person was thought to be mentally disturbed, a petition could be made to the monarch requesting guardianship be assumed. A hearing on the petition would then be held and testimony from witnesses was solicited. The legal system distinguishd two forms of incompetency: idiots and lunatics. The hearings used simple common sense type of tests to assess the competency of the persons investigated. These included simple memory and reasoning tasks. It should be noted that Neugebauer could not find evidence that demonological explanations were widely used to explain mental disorder. This article is particularly useful for class discussion as it presents sources for interesting examples.

2.   Changing attitudes about a behavior's acceptability or nonacceptability to society can induce an interesting class discussion. In the 1700s there was an attempt to develop a theory and treatment approach for mental disorder that could fit into the organic viewpoint. This viewpoint was gaining increasing acceptance among those in control of asylums. In 1758, a physician, Tissat, proposed that the loss of seminal fluid during masturbation resulted in a number of disorders including insanity. Tissat felt that a "life force" would be used up too soon if one masturbates frequently or engages in excessive sexual intercourse. Once the life force is depleted, insanity ensues. This theory produced an obvious treatment approach in which the goal was to stop excessive sexual activity. Benjamin Rush's tranquilizing chair was a form of restraint used for those exhibiting excessive masturbation. Severe forms of treatment were also developed and used including severance of the dorsal nerve in the penis, and removal of the clitoris. The popular acceptance of this viewpoint was due in part to the desire of psychiatrists to have a retractable behavior.

A discussion in class can center around how attitudes concerning masturbation have changed and not changed in our society. What other behaviors that have been previously labeled as abnormal are now gaining approval? What helps to maintain such beliefs? What can speed the change in societal approval of previously rejected behaviors in the area of sexuality?

3.   A number of authors have written books referring to psychiatrists and psychotherapists as modern day witchdoctors or shamans (e.g., E. Fuller Torrey (1976), The Mind Game. New York: Bantam Books). The rationale for success in treating abnormal behavior, according to books such as the one cited, is not specific techniques but the expectations of the clients. In order for therapists to be successful, Torrey concludes they must demonstrate certain characteristics including shared language with the client, self-confidence, a professional office, and certification of expertise in the field. Once the client perceives these factors, the expectations of change held by the patient will produce the desired change in behavior. These ideas can be related to the historical treatment procedures discussed in this chapter. What the client expects from the therapist is what gives the professional "power" to treat a particular disorder. The power enjoyed through history by witchdoctors and shamans was due to the attitudes of their respective client populations.

Once the viewpoint is presented in class, students can discuss the viability of this idea. Even if students have not had direct experience with psychotherapists or psychiatrists, they should have developed expectations about other professionals, and these can be shared during class discussion. The significance of the ideas suggested by Torrey on education and training can be discussed and outlined.

4.   Students will find a discussion of the conditions of contemporary mental health institutions to be an interesting one. A number of supplemental readings are available on this topic. Two good classic sources are E. Goffner's book Asylums, and an article by Alderidge, P. (1979), "Hospitals, Madhouse, Asylum: Cycles in the Care of the Insane." British Journal of Psychiatry, 134, 333-343. During discussion it should be pointed out that for decades there has been outrage expressed concerning conditions for treating persons with mental disturbance, yet change is slow in this field. The current economic climate in many states demonstrates how budget cutbacks are often made in mental health care. This leads to limited monetary resources available for mental health care and innovation. Discussion in class could focus on the reasons that mental health funding is often one of the first areas to be cut by politicians. This may point out how public attitudes toward mental disturbance have not changed dramatically in our society.

ACTIVITIES AND PROJECTS

1.   Since the early historical use of trephining, the person with some mental disturbance has often been subjected to harsh treatment at the hands of society. Once the students have read this chapter, they may form the impression that poor treatment of the mentally disturbed is only a thing of the past. A field trip to a mental health center with inpatient facilities is useful for students to gain first-hand exposure to current treatment practices. Such a visit can provide a fertile

ground for later classroom discussion. The students' attention can be focused on the general living conditions of the patients, and what privileges and/or opportunities exist for them. Students can be asked how they would feel living in an institution, and what improvements would they like to see take place. Also, the student should be sensitized to observe any present conditions that may still be influenced by attitudes and practices from the historical record.

2.   A small group exercise that enables students to review how attitudes affect the treatment of mental disturbance involves designing treatment strategies for disorders "caused" by different things. Once students have been divided into small groups, present them with the task of contrasting treatment approaches for (a) a mental disorder blamed on weakness of character, (b) a mental disorder blamed on sinfulness, (c) a mental disturbance caused by poor heredity, (d) a mental disorder developed because of poor and faulty learning situations, (e) a mental disorder due to some physical illness, and (f) a mental disorder created by a poor social environment. Students are not expected to develop professional types of treatment, but rather be able to identify those attitudes that could affect how one person with mental disturbance would be treated considering the "cause" of the condition. Following the group activity, discussion can focus on relating past and present activities concerning mental disorder to the student ideas.

3.   Although students may find some of the theories used to discuss abnormal behavior throughout history as being outlandish, there have been current investigations that rival early research in terms of novelty. Students often enjoy being acquainted with the more offbeat scientific literature in this field. Students can be assigned the task of searching the literature for scientific investigations that study unusual concepts. For example, the effect of the moon and its phases on behavior has gained attention from a number of researchers (e.g., Campbell, D. E., and Betts, J. L. (1978) "Lunacy and the Moon." Psychological Bulletin, 85, 1123-1129). Such research often reflects popularly held attitudes or ties into the superstitions held by a society.

Students can be assigned to small groups for the review of literature. Different periods in the twentieth century could be assigned the student groups. In this way popular beliefs during a time span can be identified by the type of topics reaching serious study. A class period used for sharing the groups' efforts, should generate interest and enthusiasm.

4.   The last century saw a number of physical treatment methods being used on mental disturbance. A group project could involve a more thorough investigation of these methods. Reports on the use of varied physical procedures often make intriguing reading for new students in psychology. Groups could be assigned to gather information on the various procedures developed in the 1800s. Bleeding, purging, and opium usage are areas for investigation that can provide the students with vivid descriptions of early treatment procedures. C. Zilboorg and J. Henry's book, A History of Medical Psychology, is one source of information.

CHAPTER 3

Casual Factors and Viewpoints in Abnormal Psychology

CHAPTER OUTLINE

I. What Causes Abnormal Behavior?
    A. Necessary, sufficient, and contributing causes
        1. Etiology is the causal pattern of abnormal behavior
        2. A condition that must exist for a disorder to occur is a primary cause
        3. Predisposing causes pave the way for a later occurrence
        4. The trigger for a disorder is the precipitating cause
        5. Maintenance of the abnormal behavior is due to a reinforcing cause
        6. Vulnerability is used interchangeably for predisposition
    B. Feedback and circularity in abnormal behavior
        1. When more than one causal factor is involved, a causal pattern is found
        2. Simple cause-and-effect sequences are rare in abnormality
            a. Self-regulating systems are usually present
            b. Complex systems of feedback produce circularity or vicious circles
    C. The diathesis-stress model
        1. A predisposition toward a given disorder is termed a diathesis
            a. Stresses upon the person with a diathesis produces a disorder
            b. Stress is a response to an adjustment demand
            c. Stressors are current challenges in a person's life
        2. The distinction between diathesis and external challenges

II. Models or Viewpoints for Understanding Abnormal Behavior
    A. Competing explanations can cause students confusing
    B. Professionals often utilize many theoretical perspectives

III. The Biological Viewpoint
    A. Mental disorders are viewed as medical diseases
    B. The biopsychological model is a less extreme viewpoint
    C. Conditions can disrupt the brain's information processing
IV. Biological Causal Factors
    A. Neurotransmitter and Hormonal Imbalances
    B. Genetic defects
        1. Chromosomal anomalies

        a.   Normal chromosomes versus abnormal arrangements
        b.   Down's syndrome produced by trisomy
    2.   Faulty genes
        a.   Structures of genes are examined with electron microscopes
        b.   Contrasts between dominant and recessive genes
        c.   Gene expression is the result of an intricate process
        d.   Polygenically transmitted disorders are now being identified
        e.   Methods for studying genetic influences
C.   Constitutional liabilities
    1.   Physical handicaps
        a.   Congenital defects are present at birth
        b.   Low birth weight is a risk factor
        c.   Emotional distress of mother can induce prematurity
        d.   Importance of prenatal development is documented
    2.   Primary reaction tendencies and temperament
        a.   Longitudinal studies show the enduring nature of reaction tendencies
        b.   Studies of Chess, Thomas, and Birch
        c.   Childhood disturbance is often followed by adult forms
D.   Brain dysfunction
    1.   Gross brain pathology causes 25percent of mental retardation
    2.   Increases in brain damage over time
E.   Physical deprivation or disruption
    1.   Basic physiological needs
        a.   Blocking survival needs can decrease coping resources
        b.   Sleep deprivation studies show psychological disorganization
        c.   Dietary deficiencies change psychological functioning
        d.   Studies of former POWs during WWII and the Korean War
    2.   Stimulation and activity
        a.   Hospitalism syndrome found by Spitz
        b.   Limits exist on optimal stimulation for the developing organism
F.   The impact of the biological viewpoint

V.   Psychosocial Viewpoints
A.   The psychodynamic perspective
    1.   Basics of pschoanalysis
        a.   Id, ego, and superego
            1)   Id as the source of instinctual drives
                a)   The life instinct is termed the libido
                b)   The death instinct is described as thanatos
                c)   Id operates on the pleasure principle
            2)   The ego mediates the id with reality
                a)   Secondary process
                b)   Reality principle
            3)   The superego is essentially one's conscience
        b.   Anxiety, defense mechanisms, and the unconscious

              1)   Three forms of anxiety causing psychic pain
                     a)   Reality anxiety
                     b)   Neurotic anxiety
                     c)   Moral anxiety
              2)   Repression of intrapsychic conflicts into the unconscious causes symptoms

        c.   Psychosexual stages of development
              1)   Each stage is briefly described
              2)   The role of fixation is discussed
              3)   The Oedipal complex, Electra complex, and castration anxiety dominate the phallic stage

    2.   Newer pschodynamic perspectives
        a.   The focus is on objects toward which impulses are directed
        b.   Mahler and Kernberg's emphasis is on object relations

    3.   Impact on our views of psychopathology
        a.   This was the first systematic approach.
        b.   Problems in coping associated with disorder
        c.   Critics have focused on the overemphasis on the sex drive

B.   The behavioral perspective
    1.   Basics of the behavioral perspective
        a.   Classical and operant conditioning
        b.   Generalization and discrimination

    2.   Impact of the behavioral perspective
        a.   Maladaptive behavior is the failure to learn competencies
        b.   Maladapive behavior may be the learning of ineffective responses
        c.   Therapy seeks to eliminate undesirable behaviors and learn desirable ones
        d.   Behavioristic approaches are precise and objective
        e.   Some behaviorists place value on thought processes

C.   The cognitive-behavior perspective
    1.   The basics of the cognitive-behavioral perspective
        a.   Bandura, an early pioneer
        b.   Kelly's personality theory owes much to the cognitive view
    2.   Therapists shifted the focus to underlying cognitions (Beck)
    3.   The impact of the cognitve-behavioral perspective

D.   The humanistic perspective
    1.   The roots of the humanistic approach
        a.   It emerged during the 1950s and 1960s
        b.   Concerned with issues usually not researched extensively
    2.   Basics of the humanistic perspective
        a.   The self as a unifying themes
        b.   Focus on values and personal growth
    3.   Impact of the Humanistic perspective
        a.   Emphasizes the capacity toward fully functioning individuals
        b.   Therapy fosters personal growth potential
        c.   This approach has been criticized for its diffuseness

E.   The Interpersonal Perspective
     1.   Roots of the interpersonal perspective
          a.   Alfred Adler saw people as seeking group participatio
          b.   Eric Fromm focused on the orientations we develop toward others
          c.   Erik Erikson's approach toward eight psychosocial stages is described
     2.   Sullivan's Interpersonal Theory
          a.   Personality only has meaning when defined in interpersonal terms
          b.   The anxiety-arousing aspect of interpersonal relations was a major focus
          c.   Socialization of children leads to labeling of "good-me" or "bad-me"
     3.   Features of the interpersonal perspective
          a.   Thibaut and Kelley's social exchange theory
          b.   Social roles provide another way to view interpersonal relationships
          c.   Communications and interpersonal accommodation
     4.   Impact of the interpersonal perspective
          a.   Unsatisfactory interpersonal relationships cause problems
          b.   Diagnosis includes interpersonal functioning
          c.   Ideas lack scientific support
F.   Summary

VI.   Psychosocial Causal Factors
     A.   Schemas and self-schemas
          1.   Schema serve as guides for understanding
          2.   Self-identity may evolve from our self-schema
          3.   The self as a set of rules
              a.   The role of accommodation to change our framework
              b.   Deficits or distortions in rules is a usual occurrence
          4.   Anxiety occupies a conceptual center in the domain of psychopathology
              a.   Barlow's arousal model of apprehension
              b.   The anxious person feels a lack of control due to the self-schemas
     B.   Early deprivation or trauma
          1.   Institutionalization
              a.   Provence and Lipton's study of infants in institutions
              b.   The reversibility of institutional deprivation
          2.   Deprivation and abuse in the home
              a.   Failure to thrive
              b.   Veiw world as untrustworthy
          3.   Childhood trauma
              a.   Childhood trauma causes lasting effects
              b.   Traumas are generalized to other situations
              c.   Effects of trauma are very resistant to cognitive reappraisal
     C.   Inadequate parenting
          1.   Parental psychopathology
              a.   depression
              b.   alcoholism

2. Parental warmth and control
   a. Parenting syles are described
   b. Restrictiveness can be protective in problem families
D. Pathogenic family structures
   1. Marital discord
      a. A lack of satisfaction can lead to frustration and negative effects on children
      b. Disturbed families have eccentricities or abnormalities present
      c. The marital schism is contrasted to the marital skew
   2. Divorced families
      a. Incomplete families are increasing due to divorce
      b. Effects of disruption can have long-term consequences
E. Maladaptive peer relationships
   1. A child's early peer relationships are developed primitively
      a. A lack of empathy exists
      b. Assessment of others is incomplete
   2. Socialization "casualities" often result from scapegoating of peers
   3. Peer relationships can be rewarding and count in the self-schemas
   4. Sources of popularity versus rejection
      a. Status invariance is found by the fifth grade
      b. Rejection by peers can have many causes and lead to social isolation
      c. Adult outcomes are negative for the child with inadequate peer relations

VII. The Sociocultural Viewpoint
   A. Uncovering sociocultural factors through cross-cultural studies
      1. Controlled experimentation is difficult in sociocultural investigation
      2. Cross-cultural research is plagued by technological and methodological problems
      3. Western-trained researchers bias observations
      4. Cultural relativism sees no universal standards of normality
      5. Sociocultural factors appear to influence the type of disorder and its course
         a. Swiss studies by Butcher show this
         b. Depression seen across cultures
   B. Sociocultural influences in our own society
      1. Socioeconomic status and schizophrenia admission in the United States
      2. Urban versus rural rates of mental disorder

VIII. Sociocultural Causal Factors
   A. The sociocultural environment
      1. Sociocultural groups systematically perpetuate basic personality types
         a. Similarity in child rearing
         b. Education is similar for children
      2. Feminine and masculine traits illustrate cultural influences
         a. Development of androgyny in recent years

31

             b.   Low masculinity is associated with maladaptive behavior
    B.   Pathogenic societal influences
             1.   Low socioeconomic status
                      a.   Correlation between psychopathology and low socieconomic status
                      b.   Stressors are common
             2.   Disorder-engendering social roles
                      a.   Reactions of soldiers to the demands of war
                      b.   Militaristic regimes foster problematic social roles
             3.   Prejudice and discrimination
                      a.   Stereotypes are demoralizing
                      b.   Women have been the target of discrimination and disabling social
                               roles
             4.   Economic and employment problems
                      a.   Chronic anxiety is produced by unemployment and recession
                      b.   Economic problems hit the lowest social strata hardest

IX.   Unresolved Issues on Theoretical and Causation Viewpoints
       A.   Adherence to a systematic viewpoint has strengths and weaknesses
                1.   The viewpoint orients practice and research within guidelines
                2.   May limit a professional's practice and research outlook
       B.   Corrective interpretations attempt to update theoretical perspectives
       C.   Eclecticism has become increasingly popular among practitioners
                1.   Works best in practice rather than theory
                2.   Critics view this as a "crazy quilt" approach.

LEARNING OBJECTIVES

1.   Summarize the events that led to the discovery that brain pathology could cause mental
       disorders and explain the difference between its answers to the "how" and "why" of
       causation.
2.   Explain how Emil Kraepelin's Lehrbuch der Psychiatric contained the forerunner of
       today's DSM-IV classification system.
3.   Compare some positive and negative consequences of the medical model of abnormal
       behavior and show how it was carried over into some nonbiological viewpoints on the
       nature of mental disorders.
4.   Compare and contrast modern biological views of mental disorders with the early "brain
       pathology" point of view.
5.   Summarize **some** of the findings of behavior geneticists that have increased our
       understanding of the causes of mental disorders.
6.   Describe two types of biophysical therapy that arose in the 1930s and 1950s that have had
       a great impact on abnormal behavior.
7.   Explain how mesmerism and the "Nancy school" became the early roots of psychoanalysis.
8.   Describe several events in Sigmund Freud's professional career that moved him toward the
       development of psychoanalysis.

9. Describe the interaction of the id, ego, and superego in Freud's conception of personality.
10. Describe three sources of anxiety described by Freud, and explain the function of the ego-defense mechanisms.
11. List and describe Freud's five stages of psychosocial development and their effects on personality.
12. Summarize some of the newer psychodynamic perspectives developed by Anna Freud, Melanie Klein, Margaret Mahler, and Otto Kernberg.
13. Describe two of Freud's most outstanding contributions to our understanding of normal and abnormal behavior, and list several criticisms of his approach.
14. Show how the discoveries of Ivan Pavlov, John Watson, and B.F. Skinner gave rise to the behavioral perspective on abnormal behavior.
15. Define each of the following and explain its importance for abnormal psychology: classical conditioning, operant conditioning, reinforcement, generalization, discrimination, modeling, shaping, and learned drives.
16. Contrast the focus of cognitive-behavior clinicians with that of the behavioristic therapists.
17. Explain three themes underlying the humanistic view of psychopathology, and summarize its impact on the field.
18. Explain how the work of Alfred Adler, Eric Fromm, Karen Horney, and Erik Erikson became the roots of the interpersonal perspective on psychopathology.
19. Describe the major features of Harry Stack Sullivan's interpersonal theory of personality.
20. List and describe several recent contributions of the social sciences and psychiatry to the interpersonal perspective, and evaluate its impact on our views of psychopathology.
21. Explain the difficulties encountered in sociocultural research and summarize some findings that have helped us understand the impact of sociocultural forces on psychopathology.
22. Explain what is meant by an interdisciplinary approach to psychopathology, and list three sets of determinants that may be considered.
23. Compare the advantages and disadvantages of adherence to a given theoretical position in the fact of new viewpoints on psychotherapy, and evaluate the adoption of an eclectic stance as a solution to such problems.

KEY TERMS

etiology
libido
primary process
secondary process
superego
ego-defense mechanisms
Oedipus complex
Electra complex
necessary cause
operant (or instrumental) conditioning
extinction

id
pleasure principle
ego
reality principle
intrapsychic conflict
psychosexual stages of development
castration anxiety
introjection
classical conditioning
reinforcement
generalization

discrimination
cognitive-behavior perspective
humanistic perspective
self-actualizing
neurotransmiters
social exchange
hormones
genotype
phenotype
spontaneous recovery
schema
assimilation
psychic trauma

sufficient cause
contributory cause
diathesis-stress model
interpersonal perspective
protective factors
resilience
interpersonal accommodation
cultural relativism
temperament
attributions
self-schemas
accommodation

FOCUS ON RESEARCH 1

Vaillant, G. E. (1994). "Ego Mechanisms of Defense and Personality Psychopathology." Journal of Abnormal Psychology, 103, 44-50.

This article is a discussion of the role of defense mechanism in the development of psychopathology. Defense mechanisms refer to innate involuntary regulatory processes that permit the person to diminish cognitive dissonance. These defenses minimize sudden changes in internal and external environments through the alteration of the perception of the events. The defenses alter the perception of self, object, idea, and feeling. The selection of the defenses is a determinant of how successful a person is with handling stressful events. Defenses have been included in the glossary of the DSM.

Research efforts over the last ten years have shown how defenses can be organized in a hierachy of relative psychopathology. Four classes of defenses are presented by the author in a hierachy format.

Psychotic defenses are denial and distortion. Next are the immature defenses of passive aggression, acting out, dissociation, projection, and autistic fantasy. The neurotic defenses would be the following: intellectualization, isolation, repression, reaction formation, displacement, somatization, undoing, and rationalization. The final category is the mature defenses: suppression, altrusim, humor, and sublimation.

These defenses are related to specific mental disorders. For example, projection and fantasy is related to paranoid schizophrenia and the schizoid personality. Acting out and dissociation is related tothe development of antisocial personality or borderline personality. The author presents interview data to support many of the contentions presented in the article connecting defense mechanisms with psychopathology. The use of multiple observations and multiple observers is a method that is suggested to study this phenomenon.

Overall, the author concludes that the validity of defenses makes them a valuable diagnostic tool in the understanding of the casual factors of psyhcopathology. They are also very useful in selecting strategies for treatment.

Questions for Discussion

1. What are alternative explanations for some of the defenses mentioned by this author?

2. How can an understanding of defenses be used in treatment situations?

3. Coping strategies are considered to have a greater component than the ego defenses. Discuss the differences.

FOCUS ON RESEARCH 2

Reiss, D., Plomin, R., and Hetherington, E. (1991). "Genetics and Psychiatry: An Unheralded Window on the Environment." American Journal of Psychiatry, 148, 283-291.

The role of genetics in the development of psychopathology remains a topic of some controversy. These authors present a very thorough discussion that supports the significant role of environmental factors in the development of psychopathology. First, they present genetic data that support the importance of environmental mechanisms. The genetic data suggest that the important environmental factors are those which are different from siblings in the same family. These include how they are treated by the same parent, differences in peer relationships, differences in school environments, and later marital and occupational differences. These influences are termed "nonshared environmental effects."

Second, the researchers examine how the nonshared environmental factors can best be studied. And third, they present implications of the genetic data for diagnosis and treatment.

This article addresses the position psychiatry has been in for the past century that of straddling biomedicine and the social sciences. Attempts to reduce the ambiguity of this situation has led psychiatry to look toward molecular biology as an answer to the conflict. The authors note that recent reviews of the genetic data have omitted evidence that behavioral genetics support environmental causes for abnormal development, as much as they support genetic causes. Psychiatry needs to move toward a discipline that contains an equal partnership of the social sciences and molecular biology in order to reconcile itself to the data reviewed by these authors.

The exploration of nonshared environments is relatively new. Twin and stepfamily studies are examining the correlates of psychopathology and nonshared characteristics of children, adolescents, and adults. Some factors that have been identified as significant include dyadic conflict resolution, marital conflict, self-perceptions, expression of affection, jealousy, alcoholism, and peer relationships.

The authors provide a good contrast to the research that attempts to identify discrete genetic lesions which predispose family members to the same disorder and the principle that genetics will define disease entities. The authors show that psychiatric disorders are probably produced by some balance of monogenic or polygenic genetic effects and environmental effects.

Some advocates of a purely genetic perspective would constrict the role of psychological therapeutics to handling only the stresses associated with genetic testing. These authors suggest that the data reflects the need to modify environmental factors. The nonshared environmental effects operate through marital, parenting, sibling, and peer influences.

Questions for Discussion

1.   How would genetic counseling be used by specialists to "treat" psychological disorder?
2.   What is the advantage or disadvantage to viewing schizophrenia as a genetic disorder?
3.   How can a psychologist work best in conjunction with a psychiatrist?

FOCUS ON RESEARCH 3

Howard, G. S. (1991). "Culture Tales: A Narrative Approach to Thinking, Cross-cultural Psychology, and Psychotherapy." American Psychologist, 46, 187-197.

Narrative approaches to understanding human behavior have taken an enhanced importance in a number of areas of psychology. Using a broad definition of storytelling, the author sees cultural differences as rooted in the preferred stories related to various groups. This report is relevant to the study of abnormal psychology since the author argues that psychopathology illustrates life stories of a culture that have gone awry.

From the author's perspective, the practice of psychotherapy is a repair of the cultural stories. When a therapist asks a patient to describe the problems that brought the individual to treatment, this is a request for the person's story. The patients usually understand that their task is to tell the part of their life story that reflects on their presenting problem. The storytelling provided to the therapist by the patient yields an orientation toward life, personal goals, and events surrounding the presenting problem. The therapist must decide if the problem is a minor deviation from an otherwise healthy life story, or is it a pervasive aspect of the person's story. The goals of treatment vary depending upon the answer. The work between patient and therapist can be viewed as life story elaboration, adjustment, or repair.

The author notes that many researchers have conducted therapist-patient match outcome research with the goal of identifying the critical "matching variable." Weak or equivocal results have been obtained when using personality factors as the basis for patient-therapist matching. Using storytelling as a sign of human thought, may yield appropriate matching between patient and therapist. Similarities between the storytelling cultural perspective of patient and therapist may be needed to enable the appropriate repair of dysfunctional life stories. Treatment becomes effective when the participants close the gap of stories between them. Therapy is viewed as a cross-cultural experience where two life stories come together in the "repair" process.

Questions for Discussion

1. Examine how personal values inhabit one's life stories.
2. What type of training and educational experiences would be beneficial for therapists using this author's perspective?
3. What objections would some therapists have concerning the importance of "matching" their life story to their patient's?
4. How would a person's life story be influenced by the environment?

FOCUS ON RESERCH 4

Russo, R. F. (1990). "Overview: Forging Research Priorities for Women's Mental Health." American Psychologist, 45, 368-373.

Recent government reports have documented the inadequacy of existing scientific knowledge for understanding gender differences in mental disorder. The need for a national agenda has been pursued by various advocacy organizations. This article provides a good review of the inadequacies in the research record, and proposes an agenda of research to deal with the current shortcomings.

Some gender differences that have been identified by researchers have included the predominance of women in the diagnostic categories of major depression, agoraphobia, and simple phobia. Males are found in great numbers in the antisocial personality disorder and alcohol abuse categories. Diagnosticians have produced a pattern in which women receive diagnoses of major depression, dysthymia, and obsessive-compulsive disorder more commonly than men. Marked differences are found in the utilization of mental health facilities. Women more frequently enter inpatient services than men in nonfederal general hospitals and private mental hospitals. The reverse is true for state, county, and VA hosptials. Also, women predominate in the care received at outpatient facilities.

Gender differences in diagnosis also vary by marital status and ethnicity. These differences cannot be explained by biomedical models. The importance of understanding the complex relationships among gender, ethnicity, sex roles, and mental health is needed to promote adequate mental heath policies. There is a need to go beyond narrow biomedical approaches in building a research knowledge base. The author questions current treatment as underserving females because it overlooks the multitude of problems impacting upon them.

Major issues that the author suggest as significant for a women's mental health agenda include the following. First, women's multiple roles in the work and family arena must be assessed for their advantages and disadvantages to mental health. Second, poverty is often concentrated among women and children. As poverty increases among women, this becomes a critical area to the development of mental disorder.

Third, the issue of violence against women and its aftereffects must be addressed. There has been a traditional bias toward focusing on the perpetrators of violence rather than on the impact violence has upon women. Fourth, with the aging of the population, new services need to be provided to the expanding female population in later life. Fifth, research must be designed to remove traditional biases in research approach, selection of variables and subjects, and formulation of hypotheses. With the promotion of a research agenda considering these issues, an enhanced understanding into the causal factors of mental disorder among females can be achieved.

Questions for Discussion

1. What factors have contributed to the apparent bias against women in research?
2. Who should be responsible for promoting the research agenda described by the author?
3. How can similar events affect men and women differently in terms of their mental health?

READINGS

1. Baldwin, S. (1989). "Applied Behavior Analysis and Normalization: Reason, Rhetoric, and Rationality." Behavioral Psychotherapy, 17, 314-315.

2. Callahan, J., and Saskin, J. (1990). "Predictive Models in Psychoanalysis." Behavioral Science, 35, 60-76.

3. Clark, L. and Watson, D. (1994). "Temperament, Personality, and the Mood and Anxiety Disorders." Journal of Abnormal Psychology, 103, 103-116.

4. DeVellis, B., and Blalock, S. (1992). "Illness attributions and hopelessness depression: The role of hopelessness expectancy." Journal of Abnormal Psychology, 101, 257-264.

5. Dewsbury, D. A. (1991). "Psychobiology." American Psychologist, 46, 198-205.

6. Enns, C., and Hackett, G. (1990). "Comparison of Feminist and Nonfeminist Women's Reaction to Variants of Nonsexist and Feminist Counseling." Journal of Counseling Psychology, 37, 33-40.

7. Fossi, G. (1989). "New Prospects in the Relationship Between Psychoanalytical Theory and Technique." International Review of Psycho-Analysis, 16, 397-411.

8. Hill, C., and Stephany, A. (1990). "Relation of Nonverbal Behavior of Client Reactions." Journal of Counseling Psychology, 37, 22-26.

9. Marshall, G., Wortman, C., and Vickers, R. (1992). "Distinguishing Optimism from Pessimism: Relations to Fundamental Dimensions of Mood and Personality." Journal of Personality and Social Psychology, 62, 1067-1074.

10. Moos, R. H, and Ruhr, R. (1982). "The Clinical Use of Socio-ecological Concepts: The Case of an Adolescent Girl." <u>American Journal of Orthopsychiatry</u>, <u>52</u>, 111-122.

11. Patterson, C. J. (1989). "Foundations for a Systematic Eclectic Psychotherapy." <u>Psychotherapy</u>, <u>26</u>, 427-435.

12. Perry, S., Cooper, A., and Michels, R. (1987). "The Psychodynamic Formulation: Its Purpose, Structure, and Clinical Application." <u>American Journal of Psychiatry</u>, <u>144</u>, 543-550.

13. Roberts, G. W. (1991). "Schizophrenia: A Neuropathological Perspective." <u>British Journal of Psychiatry</u>, <u>158</u>, 8-18.

14. Vaillant, G. (1992). "The Beginning of Wisdom is Never Calling a Patient a Borderline." <u>Journal of Psychotherapy Practice and Research</u>, <u>1</u>, 117-134.

15. Watson, D., Clark, L., and Harkness, A. R. (1994). "Structures of Personality and Their Relevance to Psychopathology." <u>Journal of Abnormal Psychology</u>, <u>103</u>, 18-31.

DISCUSSION AND LECTURE IDEAS

1. The psychoanalytic perspective suggests that our early relationships carry forward into our lives by influencing current friendships. Have students describe the characteristics of people influential in their early childhood; e.g., parents, grandparents, elementary school teachers. Next, have the students provide descriptions for recent friends. Do students select friends or dating partners based upon similarities with past significant others? Are friendship choices the result of <u>conscious</u> choices or is there some unconscious directive? Students can be asked to rate the similarity of current friends to past relationships using a numerical scale for dominant traits.

2. How does life style and its management influence psychological health? This question can be addressed in a classroom discussion. There is an instrument that can be used to facilitate discussion. The Lifestyles Appoaches Inventory can be administered to highlight concepts that relate to the management of lifestyle. R. Williams, J. Verble, and D. Price (1995) present some good information on this topic using this measurement device (<u>Journal of Personality</u>, <u>64</u>, 494-506). Students can be asked to develop strategies to management the stresses they are most familiar with in the academic environment.

3. The question of free will versus determinism can provide a good classroom discussion. This chapter lends itself to comparing and contrasting the views of Freud, Skinner, and humanism, using the issue of free will as a backdrop. It is appropriate to point out the breadth of this controverial issue and some of the implications derived from the different perspectives. Cultural issues can also be introduced into the discussion in order to broaden the issue to include sociocultural factors. When a society adheres to a deterministic perspective, does this lead to

extreme authoritarianism? How does the free will determinism dimension affect the development of moral and legal dictates? What does it mean to have free will? Are all guiding laws of behavior useless and irrelevant? Students could relate their own behavior to this discussion and attempt to identify areas of varying environmental or intrapsychic influence. What are potential outcomes when a person completely rejects the concept of free will?

4.   Can crime be considered a normal process? This question can be used for discussion in class. It is related to the classic value-conflict perspective of A. Davis (1975) in Sociological Constructions of Deviance (Dubuque, Iowa: Wm. C. Brown). Crime, according to this view, reflects a different set of values, rather than just conflicts with the more acceptable ones. When stressors such as poverty are present, these are not seen as causal agents of crimes. It is rather the values held by individuals that induce criminal actions. The values producing criminality are learned through association with others who hold such views. This perspective would equate crime with normal behavior, inasmuch as the person acts in a manner congruent to his or her learned value system. This viewpoint can lead to a discussion examining how attitudes toward crime prevention would need to be altered. This approach can be easily related to the different perspectives presented in the text. Would this view be acceptable to humanists? Are the ideas of cognitive behaviorism important when considering this issue? What are the general weaknesses of this model in explaining crime?

5.   Following presentation of the cognitive learning approaches, it may be useful to address the question of whether this perspective is behavioral. Many behaviorists have reacted negatively to the cognitive trend, because they feel it will lead to a loss of the scientific rigor of behaviorism. The empirical base of behavioristic methods is one of the factors separating it from other perspectives on abnormal behavior, so adherents to this approach are reluctant to see it diluted with cognitive issues. With cognitivistic methods there appears to be a return to talking cures in psychotherapy, rather than attempts to alter problem behaviors directly.

ACTIVITIES AND PROJECTS

1.   When reviewing the psychoanalytic perspective in the development of abnormality, Carlson (1989) suggests the use of "Psychosexual Pursuit" (Teaching of Psychology, 16, 82-84). She has found that this game situation which she describes with a game board has intrinsic appeal to students. The participants must learn several important psychoanalytic constructs in order to do well in the game. During the game students apply relevant knowledge about the operations of defenses, conflict resolution, fixation, and other factors related to the psychoanalytic perspective.

2.   The individual person learns particular preferences, and the result is a wide spectrum of likes and dislikes exhibited by the population. Different cultural practices provide good illustrations of the variations in human behavior produced by different learning situations. The flexibility in human nature can be demonstrated through a classroom project. Students can be questioned about their own personal methods of expressing attitudes and also about their particular likes and dislikes. In order to structure the task, four areas can be identified on the blackboard. Pain expression, affection, food favorites, and favorite odors can serve as areas that elicit personal preferences. Students can be asked to state how pain is expressed by themselves and their families.

How do they express affection toward another person? Their family can be compared to peers. What foods are perceived as delicious? What smells are desirable or unpleasant? The students should produce a vast array of responses, and discussion can explore cultural factors influencing learning. Are any of the students' behaviors "abnormal"?

3.   The humanistic perspective can be examined through a class project in which the students gather questionnaire data. To humanist theorists, people who do not think they have lived up to their potential may become anxious and experience stress. The class can interview persons of varying age groups and ask them for information concerning life goals and the attainment of these goals. Students should be directed to determine whether people have goals and how well they are defined. Do older persons feel that they have reached their stated goals? What evidence is there that people are upset when their goals are not achieved? Do people generally believe that they have lived up to their potential? Can people identify free choice in their lives, or do they see themselves as victims of enviromental factors? Humanists often report that society is limiting and inhibiting the native potential of individuals. What evidence for this idea can be found in the interviews? Students can complete this project either as individuals or in small groups.

4.   The students can review the concepts of the psychoanalytic approach through a small group exercise. The students should be divided into small groups, and each member should be given the "identity" of one of the Freudian concepts. One student becomes the id, another the ego, and so forth. The students assume these roles and play out their identities for different situations. A person's daily activities (e.g., going to work, eating dinner, etc.) serve as the script for the role-playing situations.
     Students acting the parts of the different Freudian concepts engage in dialogue appropriate for the particular identity they have been assigned. Conflicts between the id and superego are one example of interactions that are memorably demonstrated.

5.   In order to learn about the factors influencing individual theorists, students can be assigned to research life histories of the pioneers of psychology. The students complete reviews of appropriate biographies and report on them to the class. Students become sensitive to the environmental issues that may have affected the pioneers' perceptions of the world.

6.   The importance of dreams to the psychoanalytic perspective is central to the theory. A project involving dream interpretation can convey the central importance of dreams to this approach. Because unconscious conflicts are represented in dreams, the analysis of dreams can assist in alleviating problem behavior. Students can be required to record their dreams for a period of time and then attempt to identify symbols in them. Rather than trying to complete in depth dream analysis, this project has the goal of finding those recurring images in dreams. How these images are believed to reflect universal concerns can be discussed. A good resource book for this information that stimulate discussion is W. Stekels (1943), The Interpretation of Dreams (New York: Liveright Publishing Co.). Students can be shown how analysis takes place during psychoanalysis and how therapeutic benefit is believed to accrue. It is important to show that conscious associations to the recalled dream are also employed during the psychoanalytic process.

7.   It is possible to help students become familiar with the benefits of behavioristic

treatment approaches by having them identify potential areas of misuse and abuse. How would assertiveness training be adapted to produce negative outcome? If sex therapy using behavioristic methods can solve sex problems, could such methods be used to interfere with a person's private sex life? Students may want to determine whether there are areas wherein behaviorism offers potential dangers and whether these dangers are realistic in our society. Different student groups could be assigned a variety of behavioral areas to research and report on to the class.

CHAPTER 4

Stress and Adjustment Disorders

CHAPTER OUTLINE

I. Stress and Stressors
    A. Categories of stressors
        1. Frustrations
            a. Frustration often leads to self-devaluation
            b. External and internal obstacles can produce frustration
        2. Conflicts
            a. Approach-avoidance conflicts
            b. Double-approach conflicts
            c. Double-avoidance conflicts
        3. Pressures
            a. Pressures force a person to speed up
            b. External and internal sources for pressures
            c. Certain occupations exert numerous pressures
    B. Factors predisposing the individual to stress
        1. The nature of the stressor
            a. The impact of the stressor depends upon importance, duration, cumulative effect, multiplicity and imminence
            b. Mechanic's classic study of students and examinations shows how stress increases
            c. Traumatic events influence those closest to the situation
        2. A person's perception and tolerance of stress
            a. Perception of threat
                1) No ready made coping is available
                2) Realistic expectations for stressful events is helpful for adjustment
            b. Stress tolerance
                1) People vary greatly in overall vulnerability to stressors
                2) Early traumatic experiences can increase future vulnerability
        3. External resources and social supports
            a. Social and family relationships can modify effects of stress
            b. One's level of adjustment may be related to that of a spouse
        4. Intense stress and the experience of crisis

    a. Chronic stressors are long-lasting difficult life situations
    b. Acute stress is sudden and intense
    c. Life event scales provide <u>general</u> indicators of distress

II. Coping Strategies
    A. General principles of coping with stress
        1. Challenges faced when coping with stress
            a. Trying to meet the requirements of the stressor
            b. Protecting the self from psychological damage
        2. Task-oriented responses are usually directed toward the stressor
        3. Defense-oriented responses are designed to protect the self from disorganization
            a. Damage repair responses such as crying and mourning
            b. Ego defense mechanisms include repression and denial
                1) These are often combined with task-oriented actions
                2) They become maladaptive when used in extreme
    B. Decompensation under excessive stress
        1. Effects of severe stress
            a. Lowering of adaptive efficiency
            b. Depletion of adaptive resources
            c. Wear and tear on the system
                1. The work of Selye
                2. Three Mile Island residents
        2. Biological decompensation
            a. General adaptation syndrome
            b. Maintenance mechanisms try to repair and reorganize
        3. Psychological decompensation
            a. Alarm and mobilization
            b. Resistance
            c. Exhaustion

III. Adjustment Disorders: Reactions to Common Life Stressors
    A. Stress from unemployment
        1. Unemployment now occurs at all levels of employees
            a. Special hardships for the young and minority members
            b. Chronic unemployment attacks self-worth and feelings of belongingness
        2. Employee-based intervention programs assist displaced workers
            a. Transitional stress is reduced
            b. Provide strategies to overcome job loss stresses
    B. Stress from bereavement
        1. Grief over the loss of a loved one is a natural process
            a. It helps person free self for life without the other person
            b. Some people do not experience normal grief
        2. A survivor's adjustment may be affected for <u>months</u>
    C. Stress from divorce or separation

44

1. The loss of intimate relationship is a potent stressor
   a. The loss is a multifaceted event
   b. Readjustment to life has new demands and stresses
2. Even when divorce is relatively agreeable, coping is necessary

IV. Acute Stress Disorder and Posttraumatic Stress Disorder: Reactions to Severe Life Stressors
   A. Reactions to catastrophic events
      1. "Shock reactions" or transient personality decompensation is found after disaster strikes
         a. Coconut Grove nightclub disaster
         b. Evaluation of Santa Cruz de Tenerife Island plane collision
      2. The disaster syndrome
         a. Shock stage
         b. Suggestible stage
         c. Recovery stage
         d. Illustrated in the Tenerife disaster
      3. Casual factors in Posttraumatic stress
         a. Some people successfully handle disasters
         b. Preexisting personality factors influence outcome
   B. The trauma of rape
      1. Stranger rape vs. acquaintance rape
      2. Age and life circumstances of victim are involved in reactions to rape
         a. Conflicts over independence
         b. Regression can take place in the young
         c. Vulnerability is enhanced
      3. Husband and boyfriend reactions may signal rejection and blaming
      4. Empirical evidence of five problem areas following rape
         a. Physical disturbances
         b. Anxiousness
         c. Cognitive dysfunction
         d. Atypical behaviors including aggression
         e. Interference in social relations
      5. Coping behavior of rape victims
         a. Anticipatory phase
         b. Impact phase
         c. Posttraumatic recoil phase
         d. Reconstitution phase
      6. Counseling rape victims
         a. Long-term effects depend upon past coping skills and level of psychological functioning
         b. Rape victims usually wish to talk with another woman
   C. The trauma of military combat
      1. WWI traumatic reactions were termed "shell shocked"
         a. Considered to be organic conditions

45

b.   Resulted from the general combat situation
2.   During WWII, 10 percent experienced combat exhaustion
    a.   Figures were greater than officially reported
    b.   Produced greatest loss of personnel
3.   Vietnam veterans saw a high incidence of posttraumatic stress disorder
4.   Clinical picture in combat stress problems
    a.   Various dimensions have been identified
    b.   Uniformity in clinical picture is apparent
    c.   Wounds were seen as an escape from stressful situation
5.   Causal factors in combat stress problems
    a.   Biological factors
    b.   Psychosocial factors
    c.   Sociocultural factors
6.   Long-term effects of posttraumatic stress
    a.   The story of Dwight Johnson and his robbery attempt
    b.   Follow-up studies show continued disturbances

D.   The trauma of being a prisoner of war or in a concentration camp
1.   Nazi concentration camps produced numerous residual organic and psychological damage
2.   Returning POWs show relief and numerous long-term negative effects
    a.   Long-term care provided by military psychologists
    b.   Differences in characteristics of current war POWs from earlier conflicts

E.   The trauma of being held hostage
1.   Hostage taking is increasing in frequency
2.   Intense symptoms of anxiety and distress last for months

F.   The trauma of forced relocation
1.   Uprooted from home in a PCB fire
2.   Refugee hardships from such countries as Vietnam, Cuba, Poland, and Cambodia
    a.   Many experience problems in acculturation
    b.   Adjustment problems continue after ten years in the United States

V.   Treatment and Prevention of Stress Disorders
A.   Treatment after severe trauma
B.   Stress prevention or reduction
1.   Janis's work with surgery patients
2.   Worrying can serve a function similar to mourning
C.   Treatment of posttraumatic stress symptoms
1.   Medications
2.   Crisis intervention therapy
3.   Direct therapeutic exposure

VI.   Unresolved Issues on the Politics of Posttraumatic Stress Disorder
A.   Posttraumatic stress disorder is used as a defense in civil and criminal cases
1.   Establishing legal justification for the stress defense is tenuous

        2.   Conflicts in expert testimony are commonly found
    B.   This legal use of stress as a strategy will probably continue
        1.   Stress is not uniform in its effects
        2.   The symptoms of stress are often difficult to define

LEARNING OBJECTIVES

1.   List, describe, and illustrate three categories of stressors that make demands on us.
2.   Describe and illustrate three factors which influence the severity of stress.
3.   Differentiate between *chronic* and *acute* life stressors and indicate one way these have been measured.
4.   Differentiate between *task-oriented* and *defense-oriented* reactions to stress and describe two ego-defense mechanisms that are examples of the latter.
5.   Describe two major effects of severe stress and explain biological, psychological, and sociocultural decompensation.
6.   Describe some adjustment disorders which are reactions to unemployment, bereavement, divorce, and forced relocation.
7.   List three stages of the "disaster syndrome" and explain the causes and treatment of chronic or delayed posttraumatic stress that may develop in the last stage.
8.   Symonds (1976) has described the paralytic effects which fear often produces. What emotion often follows this and what should the victim know about this reaction?
9.   Summarize the statistics on combat exhaustion and psychiatric discharges in World Wars I and II, the Korean War, and cite three reasons why these traumatic reactions were markedly decreased in the Vietnam War.
10. List and illustrate some of the clinical symptoms of combat stress and describe some of the biological, psychosocial, and sociocultural factors responsible for this disorder.
11. Describe some of the reactions of concentration camp survivors and explain why the validity of many of these reports is questionable.
12. Summarize Janis's research on psychologically preparing patients to undergo dangerous surgery and describe a three stage type of stress inoculation used by cognitive-behavioral therapists.
13. Describe ways in which the post-traumatic stress syndrome has been used in both criminal and civil court cases.
14. State the legal precedent that has been established thus far for a "stress defense" and give some illustrations which show that considerable room for interpretation still exists.

KEY TERMS

stressors   stress
coping strategies   eustress
distress   stress tolerance
crisis   crisis intervention

47

task-oriented response
decompensation
adjustment disorders
disaster syndrome
acute stress disorder

defense-oriented response
general adaptation syndrome
posttraumatic stress disorder (PTSD)
stress inoculation training

FOCUS ON RESEARCH 1

Caselli, L. and Motta, R. (1995). "The Effect of PTSD and Combat Level on Vietnam Veterans' Perception of Child Behavior and Marital Adjustment." Journal of Clinical Psychology, 51, 4-12.

This is an empirical investigation of the effects of post-traumatic stress disorder (PTSD) and combat level on marital adjustment and children's behavior. Combat level is considered to be an important variable in the study of Vietnam veterans. It has been related to the manifestation of PTSD in previous research. Traditionally research on PTSD has focused on the individual effects of the disorder. This research is focused on the effects of war and combat on family members. The authors hypothesized that veterans with more PTSD symptomatology and greater combat exposure would perceive their marital relationships as less well-adjusted than those with fewer symptoms. A similar pattern was expected for the veterans' perceptions of their children's behavior and adjustment.

The subjects were Vietnam War veterans recruited from several veteran centers. They received a battery of assessment instruments including: Mississippi Scale for Combat Related Posttruamatic Stress Disorder, Military Stress Scale, Dyadic Adjustment Scale, Achenbach Child Behavior Checklist, and a demographic questionnaire.

The authors found that only PTSD emerged as an important consideration in the prediction of either marital or children's adjustment. PTSD also showed as a more potent variable than level of combat for reported interpersonal adjustment problems. Overall, the subjects with PTSD reported marital adjustment "much below average". PTSD veterans perceived their children's behaviors as more problematic than veterans without this disorder. The authors suggested that the PTSD veterans may be passing their symptoms on to their children. The family environment dominated by the preoccupation with the war trauma may foster problems in their children. The authors suggest that combat level may not have emerged as a significant variable in their study because the range of combat experienced was limited in their sample. But they concluded that family intervention is needed to enable the Vietnam veteran to achieve stable relationships with both spouses and children.

Questions for Discussion

1. What type of environment promoted by the PTSD veterans in their families could trigger similar problems in their children?

2. What type of family interventions would be helpful for these subjects?

48

3.   The mean age for these subjects was 44.7 years. Discuss the long term effects found in PTSD for both family members and veterans.

FOCUS ON RESEARCH 2

Palikas, L., Russell, J., Downs, M. and Petterson, J. (1992). "Ethnic Differences in Stress, Coping, and Depressive Symptoms after the EXXON Valdez Oil Spill." Journal of Nervous and Mental Disease, 180, 287-295.

This study reports on a follow-up to the 1989 oil spill when the supertanker the EXXON Valdez ran aground on the rocks in Prince William Sound, Alaska. The authors assessed the levels of depressive symptomatology of Alaskan Natives and Euro-Americans in a number of Alaskan communities near the oil spill. The researchers were interested in identifying possible ethnic differences in the expression of symptoms. Further the investigators examined the possible family factors that served as moderator variables to the stress resulting from the oil spill and its aftermath.

The researchers found that level of exposures was related to depressive symptoms for both of their targeted ethnic groups. But the Alaskan Natives were more likely to report greater exposure than the Euro-Americans. The Alaskan Natives were found to be involved in the clean-up activities following the spill in a more direct fashion than the Euro-Americans. For the Euro-Americans their exposure to the spill was related primarily to damage to fisheries, restricted use of the damaged areas, and proximity of their residences to the affected areas. For the Euro-Americans, the family was found to be an effective support and buffer for the negative exposure effects of depressive symptoms.

This is an interesting study than can be used to illustrate ethnic differences that can be involved in the outcomes of a disaster related stress. The authors present a detailed analysis of their samples and demonstrate how distinct traditions and social environments are important factors when considering ethnic groups.

Questions for Discussion

1.   What are some of the outcomes from the oil spill that would serve as stressors for residents of local communities?

2.   What can family members provide each other to assist with the stress associated with a disaster described in this article?

3.   What are the potential stressors associated with cleaning up after a disaster? Give examples that may have taken place following the oil spill.

FOCUS ON RESEARCH 3

Landau, S. F. (1990). "Subjective Social Stress Indicators and the Level of Reported Psychopathology: The Case of Israel." American Journal of Community Psychology, 18, 19-39.

The author proposes that Israel is an ideal natural laboratory for the study of stress and psychopathology. In addition to the usual stressors found in modern societies, Israel's current situation adds others. The continuous state of war with its neighbors, terrorist activities, and prolonged army duty have been identified as significant stressors. Previous investigations have found increased psychological distress associated with the various wars and mobilizations confronting Israel's residents.

Israel has also faced economic hardships due to recession, inflation, and unemployment. Both physical and psychological health has suffered from this second major source of stress. Criminal activities also increase as these economically based stressors become apparent. But, the author notes that an alternative explanation to these outcomes can be the uncovering hypothesis. External stress may bring forth existing psychopathology because the stressors diminish family and social supports.

For this study the author used a theoretical framework which included external stress factors and social support systems. The social support systems were examined from the macrolevel of national solidarity to the microlevel found in networks of friends. Social support systems can act as mediators between the stressor and the potential mental disorder. The author assumed that the level of psychopathology would be positively related to stress factors and negatively related to social support systems.

The data was collected over a period of twelve years considering fifteen stress variables with a dependent measure of inpatient admissions to psychiatric hospitals. Results showed that perceived social stress and social solidarity are significantly related to levels of psychopathology. These levels increased during periods of general stress and decreased when national solidarity rose. Unexpectedly, elevated economic stress was associated with decreased admission. It was suggested that during periods of economic stress, only disorders requiring outpatient treatment may increase. Concerning the "uncovering" hypothesis, the author supports this explanation for the results. Thus, he argues against the provocation hypothesis. Stressors may serve to influence the timing of when psychiatric assistance is sought by the person.

Questions for Discussion

1. What stressors exist in the American society that can be related to levels of psychopathology?
2. What situations delay seeking help for psychological problems?
3. Is Israel's situation so unique that this study's findings do not generalize to our society?
4. Did psychiatric disorders increase during our involvement in the Vietnam war?

FOCUS ON RESEARCH 4

Brooks, G. R. (1990). "Post-Vietnam Gender Role Strain: A Needed Concept?" Professional Psychology: Research and Practice, 21, 18-25.

The continued adjustment problems of Vietnam era veterans has attracted numerous investigations. This study reports on one aspect of adjustment that has been overlooked by many professionals. Many veterans are believed to have difficulties in adopting gender roles that are in harmony with current cultural expectations. The author provides a conceptualization of the Vietnam veterans' adjustment problems that includes this critical variable of gender role strain.

The men's studies literature describes gender role strain as a potential outcome of being heavily socialized in the traditional masculine gender role. This role strain has been generally ignored by treatment agencies. Basic to the Vietnam experience was continuous and pervasive exposure to violence. From basic training the recruit is indoctrinated into a value system in which 1) violence is revered, 2) the world is categorized into good and evil, and 3) enemies are depersonalized and justifiable targets of maximum aggression. Vietnam veterans also were exposed to "abusive violence" which is the systematic and intentional killing of others even when one's life is not threatened. Overall, the Vietnam veteran was socialized into the "warrior" role which exalts a moral violence.

The Vietnam experience of moral violence produced a number of consequences. Emotional numbing, paranoia, mistrust, excessive camaraderie, substance abuse, anger, and resentment were found to develop in the Vietnam veteran. Additionally, attitudes toward women emphasized the denigration of them. Sexuality expressed by the veterans during Vietnam was often marked with hostility and aggression. The author points to the conclusion that traditional masculine gender role expectations were amplified by the veteran's Vietnam experiences.

Once returning from the Vietnam war, contemporary women found the veterans to be sadly anachronistic and unable to understand the new sensitivities. The rejection felt by veterans produced feelings of intense resentment, frustration, and anger. Usually the veteran interpreted the rejection from women as being caused by political ideology rather than gender role strain.

The author finishes his article by suggesting ways for mental health agencies to deal with the veteran's gender role strain. Programs need to be developed that are sensitive to gender role changes. Gender role must be a focus of therapy and treatment must move the client toward psychological and behavioral androgyny.

Questions for Discussion

1. Discuss ways to make gender role a focus of treatment.
2. Would group therapy with other veterans be beneficial in treating gender role strain?
3. Should military training be modified to consider this problem?
4. Will increasing numbers of women in the military influence this problem?

READINGS

1. Brown, G. (1990). "A Causal Analysis of Chronic Pain and Depression." <u>Journal of Abnormal Psychology</u>, <u>99</u>, 127-137.

2. Fontana, A., Rosenheck, R., and Brett, E. (1992). "War Zone Traumas and Posttrraumatic Stress Disorder Symptomatology." <u>Journal of Nervous and Mental Disease</u>, <u>180</u>, 748-755.

3. Green, B., Lindy, J., Grace, M., Leonard, A. (1992). "Chronic Posttraumatic Stress Disorder and Diagnostic Comorbidity in a Disaster Sample." <u>Journal of Nervous and Mental Disease</u>, <u>180</u>, 760-766.

4. MacFarlane, A. C. (1992). "Avoidance and Intrusion in Posttruamatic Stress Disorder." <u>Journal of Nervous and Mental Disease</u>, <u>180</u>, 439-445.

5. MacFarlane, A. C. , and Papay, P. (1992). "Multiple Diagnoses in Posttruamatic Stress Disorders in Victims of Natural Disaster." <u>Journal of Nervous and Mental Disease</u>, <u>180</u>, 498-504.

6. Muehlenhard, C., Synspson, S., and Highby, B. (1994). "Are Rape Statistics Exaggerated? A Response to Criticism of Contemporary Rape Research." <u>Journal of Sex Research</u>, <u>31</u>, 144-146.

7. Orton, R. (1994). "Date Rape: Critiquing the Critics." <u>Journal of Sex Research</u>, <u>31</u>, 148-150.

8. Pargament, K., Ensing, D., Falgout, K., and Warren, R. (1990). "Religious Coping Efforts as Predictors of the Outcomes to Significant Negative Life Events." <u>American Journal of Community Psychology</u>, <u>18</u>, 793-824.

9. Safran, J. (1990). "Towards a Refinement of Cognitive Therapy in Light of Interpersonal Theory: Practice." <u>Clinical Psychology Review</u>, <u>10</u>, 107-121.

10. Schwarz, E., and Kowalski, J. (1992). "Malignant Memories: Reluctance to Utilize Mental Health Services After a Disaster." <u>Journal of Nervous and Mental Disease</u>, <u>180</u>, 767-772.

11. Shalev, A. (1992). "Posttraumatic Stress Disorder among Injured Survivors of a Terrorist Attack." <u>Journal of Nervous and Mental Disease</u>, <u>180</u>, 505-509.

12. White, S. (1991). "Hidden Posttraumatic Stress Disorder in the Mother of a Boy with Traumatic Limb Amputation." <u>Journal of Pediatric Psychology</u>, <u>16</u>, 103-116.

DISCUSSION AND LECTURE IDEAS

1.   Many theorists examining the developmental stages of life have placed importance on forming a meaningful philosophy of life to guide oneself through adulthood. Cohort groups demonstrate different philosophies that reflect on changing social mores and goals. In this group exercise, first have students develop a philosophy of life, which they view as reflecting attitudes of college students in the 1940s, 1950s, 1960s, 1970s, 1980S and 1990s. Next have one group take each cohort group's philosophy of life and describe how certain anxiety-based disorders may appear more readily in one cohort than another. For example, guilt over disappointing parental wishes may cause emotional distress in the 1950s group but not in the 1960s cohorts who tried to do "their own thing." This exercise may assist in the understanding of personal dynamics and reactions to stressors.

2.   Students can be asked to relate information from their own lives that relates special stressors with emotional reactions, or physical manifestations. Have they noticed any reoccurring cycles of stress and reactions? Students should be encouraged to bring forth experiences that may have strengthened them for later problems. Personal accounts of how growth occurred following crisis can demonstrate the value of crisis intervention.

3.   What methods can communities and businesses use to help prevent disabling emotional reactions to disasters? When a disaster strikes a community, what factors should the officials be aware of to overcome the negative effects of the calamity? Industrial accidents can have detrimental effects on employees. How should business officials prepare for crises that may hit employees? How sensitive are community leaders to the problems of stress and crisis intervention?

4.   The question of how sex role orientation may influence the use of defense mechanisms can provide a good lecture-discussion. The assessment of individuals on the Bem Sex Role Inventory has shown that depending on sex role orientation certain defense strategies are chosen by individuals. Females low in masculinity experience conflict with regard to aggression expression. They present themselves to frustrators in a manner not at all consistent with their own feelings. Males low in masculinity apparently utilize fantasy to cope with stress far more often than direct actions. Students can be encouraged to relate their own defense strategies when confronted with stress. This can be related to their perceived sex role orientation. Patterns in the class may emerge from such a discussion. Students may be encouraged to suggest how these patterns may have changed since the date of the study. What factors may change the outcomes?

5.   A lecture that can promote discussion can involve the stress produced by sexual harassment associated with employment. Women have often experienced a level of stress that challenged their coping capabilities. Verbal harassment is the most common type with physical forms accounting for 20 percent of the incidents. The incidents of sexual harassment can threaten their job security and violated their privacy. Discuss how a person can show a variety of physical and mental stress symptoms as well as reduced productivity on the job. One's self-confidence can also be detrimentally affected. Students' own work experiences which are shared in discussion can provide examples. This topic is relevant to students soon to enter the job market and shows how harassment can lead to stress reactions.

ACTIVITIES AND PROJECTS

1.   Recent military actions undertaken by the U. S. have created different sources of stress for the returning participants. Students can be asked to identify the unique type of stressors experienced by military personnel who were involved in Desert Storm, Somalia, and Haiti.

2.   People differ in their capacity to handle emotions in a constructive fashion. The Emotional Self-Disclosure Scale measures people's willingness to discuss both positive and negative emotions with others. This scale provides useful information for the willingness of both men and women to discuss their emotions with significant others and therapists. William Snell (1989) provides some useful information on the use of this scale and cultural differences he has identified (Sex Roles, 21, 467-486). Students can be administered the scale to assess their tendencies toward disclosure. It is a scale that can stimulate meaningful classroom discussion on the development and treatment of anxiety disorders.

3.   A project can center around the issue of how some stress is self-induced. Depending on the expectations of an individual, the stress from a particular event may be influenced. Have the students interview a number of their friends just prior to an examination in one of their courses. The students will be required to ask the friends how well they expect to do on the exam and how sure they are that they will do well or poorly. Once the exam is completed, the students need to observe the friends to see if the expectations of performance influenced the reactions to the exam feedback. How would the students explain their observations? Some students may be assigned other activities to assess instead of exam performance. Sporting competitions are one example of the type of activity that participants could be questioned on to determine their performance expectations.

4.   Students may gain a better insight into the stresses of military combat by hearing first-hand descriptions. Local veteran organizations can be contacted to supply a person willing to speak about combat-related stresses. The speaker could also provide valuable information concerning the problems in adjusting to civilian life after combat experience. The special stresses associated with the Vietnam war could then be related to those described for previous conflicts. With the use of such a speaker, students could discuss how the real-life experience of military combat compares to the way it is portrayed in films and television.

5.   Crisis intervention services are usually available in most communities. Some may have twenty-four hour crisis emergency services. Some universities sponsor and provide such services to the student population. Students can be assigned the task of collecting information about the crisis intervention centers and services available. What are the nature of services provided, who handles the requests for assistance, and what are the treatment rationales employed by the various groups, are questions that students should focus on.

6.   How well a person deals with the unexpected can relate to his/her ability to deal with stress. Students can conduct experiments testing the ability of others to handle the unexpected. For example, students can arrange to lose a purse or billfold in a hallway and see

how people react to finding it. The stress related to picking up the purse and if anyone is watching should reveal to students a number of coping strategies.

7.   Have students identify the major stressors associated with modern life. What stressors can be avoided or the negative impacts lessened? Should people attempt to secure a life style with limited stressors, or are more modern day stressors advantageous?

8.   Have students interview some Vietnam veterans. What were the major sources of stress in their experiences? Do they know of friends who experienced a posttraumatic stress disorder? What do they believe causes the disorder?

9.   Students can interview different community organizations to determine how prepared the community is for disasters. The recent earthquakes in Japan demonstrated the problems cities have when confronted with natural disasters. What type of disasters has the local community considered? Can outside agencies easily coordinate their services with the local ones?

CHAPTER 5

Panic, Anxiety, and Their Disorders

CHAPTER OUTLINE

I. The Fear and Anxiety Response Patterns
    A. Anxious behavior signaled by exaggerated avoidance behaviors and defenses
    B. Fear or panic activates the "fight or flight" response
    C. There are problems in defining anxiety
        1. Anticipation and apprehension are often used to describe anxiety responses
        2. Biological, psychological, and environmental events promote anxiety
        3. Avoidance-defensive behaviors are developed and are maladaptive

II. Anxiety Disorders
    A. Phobic disorders
        1. Specific phobia
            a. Psychosocial causal factors
            b. Biological causal factors
        2. Social phobia
            a. Interaction of psychosocial and biological causal factors
            b. Increased attention being paid to cognitive factors
    B. Panic disorder and agoraphobia
        1. Definition of panic disorder includes brevity and intensity of reaction
        2. Definition of agoraphobia
        3. Agoraphobia and panic disorder often are seen together
        4. Biological causal factors
        5. Cognitive and behavioral causal factors
    C. Generalized anxiety disorder
        1. The symptoms include motor tension, vigilance, scanning, and autonomic hyperactivity
        2. A constant state of worry is experienced
            a. Numerous physical complaints are seen
            b. Vague fears and fantasies are present
        3. Mild depression can be seen with this disorder
        4. Axis II personality disorders can precede the anxiety disorder
        5. Psychosocial causal factors
        6. Biological causal factors

D. Obsessive-compulsive disorder
    1. Obsessions and compulsions are defined
        a. High levels of manifest anxiety coexist
        b. The behaviors cover a wide range
    2. Many people exhibit some obsessive thoughts or compulsive actions
        a. The obsessive-compulsive disorder represents irrational and exaggerated behavior
        b. A person feels inadequate and inferior
    3. Persons with this disorder cannot take direct action to stop
    4. Psychosocial causal factors
    5. Biological causal factors
    6. Sociocultural causal factors

III. Treatment and Outcomes
    A. Pharmacological (drug) therapies
        1. Tranquilizing drugs are prescribed
            a. Potential abuses in their use
            b. Side effects of the drugs are unpleasant
            c. Masking of symptoms may prevent person from seeking psychotherapy
        2. Antidepressant medication as a treatment for panics and agoraphobia shows promise
    B. Psychological therapies
        1. Traditional psychotherapies
            a. Persons must lower their defenses
            b. A person learns new ways of coping
            c. Learning is transfered to real-life situations
            d. A person can modify their environment
        2. Behavior and cognitive-behavior therapies
            a. Controlled exposure to anxiety-provoking situations is involved
            b. Removal of maintaining reinforcements is sought
            c. Cognitive mediators are a center of focus in current behavioral methods
        3. Multimodal therapy

VIII. Unresolved Issues on the Anxiety Disorders
    A. One focus of research has been on the biological aspects of the disorders
        1. Genetic vulnerabilities
        2. Biochemical and sturctural abnormalitis
    B. Cognitive-behavioral vulnerabilities are being identified
    C. Interdisciplinary research is needed in this field of study

LEARNING OBJECTIVES

1. Describe the principal manifestation of anxiety disorders and summarize their relative occurrence among men and women.
2. Describe the symptoms of panic disorders and agoraphobia and explain why they are

considered together.

3. List and define several simple phobias and describe the major manifestations of phobias as a class.
4. Sumarize the major manifestations of obsessive-compulsive disorders and explain why they are considered maladaptive.
5. Compare and contrast symptoms of a generalized anxiety disorder and a panic disorder. Explain why the former is sometimes difficult to distinguish from a personality disorder.
6. Describe the major manifestations of somatoform disorders and explain why your text does not describe dysmorphic somatoform disorders in this section.
7. Describe the major manifestations of somatoform disorders and distinguish it from hypochondriasis.
8. Describe the major manifestations of hypochondriasis and explain why it may be viewed as a certain type of interpersonal communication.
9. Characterize a somatoform pain disorder and explain why patients with this disorder often become physically disabled.
10. Describe the major manifestations of a conversion disorder and describe some sensory, motor, and visceral symptoms that often appear.
11. Compare the psychological functions of conversion disorders and dissociative disorders and explain why the text's coverage of the latter is brief.
12. List and describe four types of psychogenic amnesia and explain why fugue is considered in the same section.
13. Describe the symptoms of multiple personality and explain why some may be considered genuine and others fraudulent.
14. Describe the symptoms of a depersonalization disorder and distinguish it from feelings of depersonalizaton that sometimes occur with personality deterioration.
15. Define *neurotic style* and give two reasons for discussing it here rather than with "personality disorders."
16. Describe three related characteristics of persons adopting a neurotic style and explain how three types of inhibition may be involved.
17. Explain why people with neurotic styles often have difficulties interacting with others and show how mutually neurotic couples may get along quite well.
18. Explain and illustrate how biological, psychosocial, and sociocultural factors cause and maintain anxiety-based disorders.
19. Describe some biological and psychological therapeutic approaches that have been successful in treating anxiety-based disorders.
20. Explain why your authors are only "loosely committed" to the anxiety-defense model for explaining anxiety-based disorders.
21. Explain why your authors are surprised that anxiety-based disorders don't cure themselves and indicate their speculation about the reason.

KEY TERMS

neurotic behavior
anxiety
anxiety disorder

neurosis
specific phobia
panic

agoraphobia
panic disorder
obsessions
obsessive-compulsive disorder
fear

blood injury phobia
social phobia
compulsion
generalized anxiety disorder
interoceptive fears

FOCUS ON RESEARCH 1

Taylor, S. (1994). "Klein's Suffocation Theory of Panic." <u>Archives of General Psychiatry</u>, <u>51</u>, 505-506.

This article presents the viewpoint of Donald Klein concerning the nature of panic, and critiques the concept. This explanation of panic suggests that many panics take place when the brain is experiencing an erroneous message from the suffocation monitor. This signal indicates that a lack of useful air is available to the person and the suffocation alarm system activates.

Klein's proposal that a physiological mechanism is involved in spontaneous panic attacks can apparently be triggered by psychosocial cues to suffocation that are salient or when the alarm threshold is pathologically lowered. Klein terms his viewpoint "physiocentric" in that it makes a disrupted physiological control system central to a range of symptomatic manifestations. He does indicate that some of the false alarms are triggered by experiences.

The author of this study tested the assumption that suffocation alarm hypersensivity is a risk factor for panic disorder. Alarm hypersensitivity was operationally defined through the use of a measure of suffocation fear. He administered the measure to a group of university students. He reasoned that people with hypesensitive alarms would be more likely to have their alarms activated and show a strong fear of suffocation.

The subjects were exposed to a suffocation provocation test which necessitated breathing through a straw for an extended period of time. It was found that high fear of suffocation participants reported more panic attacks than participants with a low suffocation fear.

The participants were interviewed by the experimenter for information concerning experiences with panic attacks in the past. The high suffocation fear individuals reported a significantly greater incidence of panic in enclosed spaces and other situations than low fear persons. The author suggests that his results show support for Klein's concepts, but disagrees with Klein concerning the extend of physical versus enviromental factors in triggering the alarm. The author states that psychological factors play a more central role than is conceded by Klein. He points to the successful use of cognitive therapy with panic disorder as supporting his claim.

Questions for Discussions

1. What are situations that may trigger a suffocation alarm in daily activities in hypersensitive persons?

2. How adequate was the author's assessment of suffocation fear?

3.   How can the outcomes of this study be useful for clinicians and diagnosticians?

FOCUS ON RESEARCH 2

Lucey, J., Butcher, G., Clare, A., and Timothy, D. (1994). "The Clinical Characteristics of Patients with Obsessive Compulsive Disorder: A Descriptive Study of an Irish Sample." Irish Journal of Psychological Medicine, 11, 11-14.

Weissman, M., Bland, R., Canino, G., and Greenwald, S. (1994). "The Cross National Epidemiology of Obsessive Compulsive Disorder: The Cross National Collaborative Group." Journal of Clinical Psychiatry, 55, 5-10.

The increased sensitivity of the DSM-IV to sociocultural factors makes these two articles of paticular interest. They report on the manifestation of one of the anxiety disorders in the following countries: Ireland, Canada, Puetro Rico, Germany, Taiwan, Korea, New Zealand, and the US.

The first study studied the characteristics and demographic details of a sample of persons in Ireland with obsessive-compulsive disorder. The majority of clients showed a lifetime history of at least one type of mental disorder. Medication was found to reduced significantly the symptoms of the sample.

The second study examined the lifetime and annual prevalence rates, age at onset, symptom profiles, and comorbidity of persons with obsessive-compulsive disorder. They found the prevalence rates to be consistent in the counties under study. Taiwan was found to have the lowest rates. Age of onset and comorbidity with depression was also found to be consistent in each country, but the predominance of the obsessions and compulsions varied from country to country.

These studies provide important information concerning the "robustness" of the obsessive-compulsive disorder diagnosis in diverse parts of the world. But the variations in symptom presentations points to the cultural factors that affect this disorder. The importance of increasing the awareness of the professional community of this diversity was noted.

Questions for Discussion

1.   How can culture or ethnic background influence the content of obsessions and compulsions? Provide examples.

2.   Can a clinician trained in the U. S. be effective in diagnosis and treatment in foreign countries? Give reasons for both pro and con positions.

3.   What factors may hamper cooperation among professionals in such studies as described above? How could they be overcome?

FOCUS ON RESEARCH 3

Weissman, M. M. (1991). "Panic Disorder: Impact on Quality of Life." Journal of Clinical Psychiatry, 52, 6-9.

This article reports on a probability sample of over 18,000 adults which was from the Epidemiologic Catchment area study. The social and health consequences of panic disorder are described by the author. The data from this study showed a prevalence of panic disorder in the United States similar to that found in Puerto Rico, New Zealand, Canada, and Germany. A third of the panic disorder patients felt they were in poor physical health, and this was significantly higher than those without the condition.

Alcohol abuse was identified to be a problem for 27 percent of the panic disorder patients, and marital problems were found to be a problem for 12 percent of this group. Concerning financial problems, 27 percent of persons with panic disorder reported receiving welfare or some form of disability compensation. Nearly 42 percent of this group had used minor tranquilizers in the preceding six months, and 28 percent had used the emergency room for emotional problems. All of these figures were higher than what was found in a nonpatient population.

The author concludes that panic disorder is associated with the self-perception of poor physical and emotional health, alcohol abuse, marital conflicts, financial problems, medication use, and suicide attempts. These impairments should be addressed during the treatment of panic disorder.

Questions for Discsussion

1. What type of treatment of panic disorder would include the necessary concern with one's quality of life?
2. What manifestations in one's life would the panic disorder produce?
3. Can a disorder be treated successfully and the patient still have a poor quality of life?

READINGS

1. Baer, L. (1994). "Factor Analysis of Symptom Subtypes of Obsessive Compulsive Disorder and their Relation to Personality and Tic Disorder." Journal of Clinical Psychiatry, 55, 18-23.

2. Ballenger, J. C. (1991). "Long-Term Pharmacologic Treatment of Panic Disorder." Journal of Clinical Psychiatry, 52, 18-23.

3. Clark, D., Turner, S., Donovan, J., and Beidel, D. (1994). "Reliability and Validity of the Social Phobia and Anxiety Inventory for adolescents." Psychological Assessment, 6, 135-140.

4. Clark, D., Beck , A. and Beck, J. (1994). "Symptom Differences in Major Depression , Dysthymia, Panic Disorder and Generalized Anxiety Disorder." Amerian Journal of Psychiatry, 151, 205-209

5. Enright, M., and Blue, B. (1989). "Collaborative Treatment of Panic Disorders by Psychologists and Family Physicians." Psychotherapy in Private Practice, 7, 85-90.

6. Fisman, S., and Walsh, L. (1994). "Obsessive Compulsive Disorder and Fear of AIDS Contamination in Childhood." Journal of the Amerian Academy of Child and Adolescent Psychiatry, 33, 349-353.

7. Friedman, S. and Chernen, L. (1994). "Discriminating the Panic Disorder Patient from the Patient with Borderline Disorder." Journal of Anxiety Disorders, 8, 49-61.

8. Kaspi, S., Otto, M., Pollack, M., and Eppinger, S. (1994). "Premenstrual Exacerbation of Symptoms in Women with Panic Disorder." Journal of Anxiety Disorders, 8, 131-138.

9. Keller, M., Yonkers, K., and Warshaw, M. (1994). "Remission and Relapse in Subjects with Panic Disorder and Panic with Agoraphobia: A Prospective Short Interval Naturalistic Follow-up." Journal of Nervous and Mental Disease, 182, 290-296.

10. King, D., and King, L. (1991). "Validity Issues in Research on Vietnam Veteran Adjustment." Psychological Bulletin, 109, 107-124.

11. Lotufo-Neto, F. and Valentim, G. (1994). "Alcoholism and Phobic Anxiety: A Clinical Demographic Comparison." Addiction, 89, 447-453.

12. Merz, W. (1994). "Placebo Response in Panic Disorder: A Review." European Psychiatry, 9, 123-127.

13. Ohman, A. and Soares, J. (1994). "Unconscious Anxiety: Phobic Responses to Masked Stimuli." Journal of Abnormal Psychology, 103, 231-240.

14. Salkovsis, P. and Mills, I. (1994). "Induced Mood, Phobic Responding, and the Return of Fear." Behaviour Research and Therapy, 32, 439-445.

15. Starcevic, V., Fallon, S., and Uhlenhuth, E. (1994). "Generalized Anxiety Disorder, Worries about Illness, and Hyupochondriacal Fears and Beliefs." Psychotherapy and Psychosomatics, 61, 93-99.

16. Stein, M. and Forde, D. (1994). "Setting Diagnostic Thresholds for Social Phobia: Considerations from a Community Survey of Social Anxiety." American Journal of Psychiatry, 151, 408-412.

18. Wiseman, E. (1994). "Alcohol Dependence May be the Missing Link between Posttraumatic Stress Disorder and Panic." Archives of General Psychiatry, 51, 429-430.

19.   Whisman, M. A. (1990). "The Efficacy of Booster Maintenance Sessions in Behavior Therapy: Review and Methodological Critique." Clinical Psychology Review, 10, 155-170.

20.   Willett, J., Ayoub, C., and Robinson, D. (1991). "Using Growth Modeling to Examine Systematic Differences in Growth: An Example of Change in the Functioning of Families at Risk of Maladaptive Parenting." Journal of Consulting and Clinical Psychology, 59, 38-47.

DISCUSSION AND LECTURE IDEAS

1.   As the mass media exposes the public to potentially fearful information, can individuals react to the messages of fear with the development of a anxiety disorder? Irwin Perr (1994) investigated the occurrence of a cancer phobia among individuals who had been exposed to information concerning the relationship of asbestos to cancer (Journal of Forensic Sciences, 39, 808-814). The author found that cancer phobia was a misused phenomenon among person who experienced minor pulmonary symptoms. A class discussion concerning the different types of phobias that may be promoted in persons by increasing amounts of information about disease risks. What predisposing factors in the individual contribute to the development of these form of phobia?

2.   The class can discuss when it is normal to experience anxiety. Why is it normal for some to experience anxiety on some occasions but not for others? Can a person exist in life without anxiety? What would life be like without anxiety? Class members may contribute their own "phobias" and "compulsions." How did these behaviors enter the students' behavioral repertoire? How and why are they maintained?

3.   A number of scales have been developed to identify obsessive-compulsive disorder. Such instruments as the Maudsley Obsessional-Compulsive Questionnaire and the Self-Rating Obsessional-Compulsive Inventory permit the quantification of symptoms. A recent study (1988) by G. Padua on the development of the Padua Inventory (Behavioral Research and Therapy, 26, 169-177) provides some interesting information on the development of such scales and their use in both normal and clinic populations. The article includes a copy of the Padua Inventory and can be used for class discussion.

4.   The person who experiences an accident may maintain some sequelae for years after the experience. A classroom discussion could focus on the experiences of students or persons they may know who were in accidents. K. Kuch, B. Cox, and I.Shulman (1994) presented some information that could be useful in a classroom discussion on the topic of anxiety after accidents (Journal of Anxiety Disorders, 8, 181-187). They investigated survivors of road vehicle accidents who experienced only minimal injuries and pain. The survivors were assessed in clinical interviews for panic, phobia,and anxiety sensitivity. Nearly half of the their sample met diagnostic criteria for simple phobia, and over 10 percent met the criteria for posttraumatic stress disorder. Considering these findings the class discussion can examine the connection between stressful

experiences and the development of psychological disorders.

5.   The DSM-IV Task Force made an effort to consider cultural and ethnic factors in the revision. What are some of the culturally related disorders and how are they related to mental disorders recognized in the DSM-IV? An article by Leibowitz, Salman, and Garfinkel (1994) describes a condition found in the Hispanic community called "ataque de nervios". This attack of nerves was seen as overlaping panic disorder. This disorder was identified primarily in females and was also related to depression. This could form a lecture on the role of culture in the expression of symptoms.

ACTIVITIES AND PROJECTS

1.   One film that can stimulate class discussion on a number of topics related to mental disorder is Rebel Without a Cause. This film vividly portrays the influence of family and perceived alienation on emotional adjustment. The "fifties" look and presence of star James Dean adds to its appeal for today's students. Following the film, students can be directed in a discussion of neurotic styles and the various factors influencing them. Why did the James Dean character and his friends attempt to create a "family"? What motivated their delinquent actions? What role did family and society play in the characters' behavior and emotional reactions? How could the outcome of the film have been changed by family or societal interactions? Were the James Dean, Natalie Wood, and Sal Mineo characters suffering from anxiety-based disorders? Why or why not?

2.   Students can be asked to introspect about the three major components of anxiety: thinking, feeling, and behavior. Thinking can consist of thoughts about oneself that contribute to anxiety; one's perceptions of worry and apprehension involve the feeling dimension; and nervous pacing or bodily movements may involve behavioral signs of anxiety. Once in small groups, give the students some common anxiety-provoking situations that they are familiar with in their own lives (e.g., the day of a difficult exam). Have the groups provide a profile of how they respond in the three areas to the anxiety-inducing situation. During discussion of the group answers, the instructor can expand on the topic by informing the students how the thoughts/feelings we have may interfere with effective action to handle one's anxiety.

3.   Some of the anxiety disorders have different rates of prevalence for males and females. Survey results of males and females may demonstrate areas of concern that can evolve into specific disorders. Have students develop a questionnaire to be administered to other college students. The questions could cover a range of interests from bodily concerns, cleanliness, achievement, fear of failure, competition, and numerous others. The students could produce a scale to rate the level of concern for the various areas. Once the students survey fellow students, the results would be differentiated into male and female areas of concern. If differences are found in the survey, do they reflect on the incidence of mental disorder of various types? What contributes to differences in the areas of concern between men and women? Would the results support one theoretical perspective explaining the development of mental disorder over another? Explain.

4.   To achieve some understanding of how anxiety may be experienced in the elderly population, students could be assigned the task of interviewing older persons. They could recruit volunteers in senior centers or interview an older relative. A research study by A. Flint (1994) can provide guidance about the nature of anxiety experience among the elder population (American Journal of Psychiatry, 151, 640-649). He discusses the most common anxiety disorders that are found in the elderly population. The project could also show how pre-existing anxieties can relate to the development of disorders in later life.

5.   Students are confronted with an array of symptoms in Chapter 5, and they may begin to identify with some of the conditions. The students may recognize certain symptoms in themselves and diagnose themselves as having some of the anxiety manifestations. This phenomenon can occur easily in relationship to anxiety; it is very often experienced. Have students confront this issue directly and have them individually record the symptoms reflected in their life. How do they cope with these "problems," and what separates the ordinary manifestations of anxiety from the conditions discussed in the textbook?

6.   Superstitious behavior can develop from receiving reinforcement in a chance fashion. How can superstitious rituals develop into compulsions? Why are superstitious actions not extinguished quickly in a person's life? Professional athletes often exhibit such superstitious rituals. Students can contribute reasons for the develoment of personal compulsions or superstitions. How could they eliminate the superstition? How do "popular" superstitions spread to numerous persons?

CHAPTER 6

Mood Disorders and Suicide

CHAPTER OUTLINE

I. Unipolar Mood Disorders
   A. Normal depression
      1. Grief and the grieving process
         a. The person will "turn-off" to everyday events
         b. The person becomes involved in fantasies depicting the loss
         c. The capability of response to the external world returns within one year
      2. Other normal mood variations
         a. Postpartum depression can be a reaction to birth
         b. College students experience normal depressions with three variables
            1) Dependency
            2) Self-criticism
            3) Inefficacy
   B. Mild to moderate mood disorders
      1. Dysthymia
         a. A depressed state exists without a cycle of elevated mood
         b. The person calls forth reactions from the environment that support the depression
      2. Adjustment disorder with depressed mood
         a. A disorder with shorter duration than cyclothymia or dysthymia
         b. An external precipitating event must be identified
         c. Depressions usually occur with anxiety being present
         d. Sufferers are unlikely to seek treatment from psychological/psychiatric practitioners
   C. Major depressive disorder
      1. Intense symptoms marked with sadness, insomnia, diminished
      2. cognitive capacity, and low self-esteem
      3. Two subcategories of major depression are specified
         a. Single episode
         b. Recurrent
      4. DSM-IV uses melancholic type

5. This diagnosis can be used without severe current symptoms if a history of severe depression is found
6. A seasonal pattern can be identified
7. Recovery from a major depression is usually not "complete"

II. Bipolar disorder
    A. Cyclothymia
        1. Mania involves excessive levels of excitement and elation
        2. Hypomania is a milder form of mania
        3. Cycles between hypomania and depression are signs of cyclothymia
        4. This disorder may be a mild form of major bipolar disorder
        5. Cycles do not have any external precipitating event
    B. Bipolar Disorder
        1. One episode of mania is needed for diagnosis
        2. Mania shows elevated mood, irritability, increases in activity, and a "flight of ideas"
        3. Medication serves to reduce excitement of manic phase
        4. Three subcategories of bipolar disorder exist
            a. Mixed
            b. Manic
            c. Depressed
        5. A full recovery only occurs in a minority of cases
        6. Gender differences are found in prevalence
        7. Bipolar II disorder
            a. Full blown manic episodes are not seen
            b. Considered to be a distinct disorder
    C. Schizoaffective disorder
        1. Mood disruption occurs with deranged mental processes
        2. Recovery to full capacity is doubted by recent researchers
        3. Some professionals do not accept this classification

III. Causal factors in mood disorders
    A. Unipolar Disorders
        1. Biological factors
            a. Hereditary factors
            b. Biochemical factors
            c. Neurophysiologic and neuroendocrine factors
            d. Sleep and bioogical rhythms
        2. Psychosocial factors
            a. Stress as a causal factor
                 1) Long term changes in brain functions may occu.
                 2) Interaction with biochemical approaches is seen
                 3) Beck has provided a classification of precipitating circumstances
                 4) Research on identifying precipitating events has been equivocal
            b. Types of diathesis-stress models for unipolar depression
                 1) Constitutional weakness

2)   Predispositions to depression
3)   Dysfunctional beliefs
4)   Pessimistic attributional style
5)   Early parental loss
- c.   Psychodynamic theories
- e.   Behavioral theories
- f.   The helplessness and hopelessness theories of depression
- g.   Interpersonal effects of mood disorders

B.   Biploar Disorders
1.   Biological factors
- a.   Hereditary factors
- b.   Biochemical factors
- c.   Other biological causal factors

2.   Psychosocial causal factors
- a.   Stressful life events
- b.   Psychodynamic views

C.   General sociocultural factors
1.   Cross-cultural studies have found that the incidence of mood disorders varies
2.   Depression can take different forms in other cultures

IV.   Treatment and Outcomes
A.   Pharmacotherapay and Electroconvulsive Therapy
1.   Lithium carbonate is widely used in the treatment of manic disorders
- a.   Blood levels must be monitored
- b.   Some unpleasant side effects can be seen

2.   Antidepressants are the treatment of choice for depression
- a.   Tricyclics and MAO inhibitors
- b.   Prozac and the controversy surrounding its use

3.   Electroconvulsive therapy (ECT) can produce quick results

B.   Psychotherapy
1.   Treatments are often combined with medication therapy
- a.   Cognitive-behavioral approaches attempt to re-educate the patient
- b.   Interpersonal therapy is a relatively new method with limited research backing

2.   Behavioral approaches manipulate reinforcement contingencies

V.   Suicide
A.   Clinical picture and causal pattern
1.   Who attempts and who commits suicide?
- a.   The peak age is 24-44 years with twice as many men as women
- b.   Methods of suicide vary between the genders
- c.   Child and adolescent suicides are increasing
- d.   College students are susceptible to developing suicidal motivations
- e.   High risk groups include the depressed, alcoholics, divorced, certain professionals, and people living alone

2. Other psychosocial factors associated with suicide
   a. A variety of situational factors can trigger suicide
   b. "Success suicides" can be seen following positive life events
   c. Oblivion is a positive goal in the mind of the suicidal person
3. General sociocultural factors
   a. Rates vary from one society to another
   b. Religious beliefs are important determinants of suicide rates
   c. Japan is one culture that sanctions certain suicides
   d. Subgroup differences exist within societies
   e. Durkheim's view of group cohesiveness as a factor in suicide

B. Suicidal ambivalence
1. Degree of intent
   a. The "To be" group wish to communicate a message to others
   b. The "Not to be" group are seemingly intent on ending their lives
   c. The "To be or not to be" group are ambivalent and leave death to chance
   d. Following an attempt there is a reduction in emotional turmoil
2. Communication of suicidal intent
   a. Some people who threaten suicide do, in fact, take their lives
   b. Some people use indirect threats
   c. Threats are a cry for help and are expressing distress
3. Suicide notes
   a. Analysis of suicide notes show a pattern of self-blame, hatred, and vengeance
   b. The desire to communicate after the fact is related to demographic and cultural variables
   c. Most notes do not provide significant insights into the suicidal mind

C. Suicide prevention
1. Crisis intervention
   a. The goal is to help people deal with an immediate life crisis
   b. Suicide prevention centers try to avert an actual suicide attempt
      1) Maintenance of contact with person is necessary
      2) Distress is impairing a person's judgment
      3) Helps person seek alternatives
      4) Provides emotional support for person
      5) Increases awareness that distress will end naturally
   c. People who attempt suicide are likely to try again
      1) Long-range aftercare has been introduced
      2) Evaluation of the effectiveness of prevention centers shows success
2. Focus on high-risk groups and other measures
   a. Broad-based programs are needed to alleviate life problems
   b. Samaritans offer support to the suicidal person
   c. Psychological autopsies provide profiles of successful suicides
   d. Suicide prevention training is extended to a variety of professionals

III.   Unresolved issues on mood disorder and suicide
    A.   Ethical issues in suicide prevention
        1.   Should people be allowed to take their own lives?
        2.   Terminally-ill people are asking for the "right to commit suicide"
        3.   Suicide intervention is a neutral moral stance
    B.   Moral problems associated with involuntary hospitalization
        1.   Practitioners take a cautious and conservative path
        2.   Some people are institutionalized based upon limited clinical justification

LEARNING OBJECTIVES

1. Know the symptoms associated with the milder forms of depression and list three psychological losses that may trigger depression.
2. List the dimensions customarily used to differentiate the mood disorders and give examples of mood disorders from mild to moderate.
3. Describe the clinical manifestations of major depression.
4. Describe the symptoms of a bipolar disorder and discuss research studies on the manifestations of this disorder.
5. Describe the symptoms of a schizoaffective disorder and explain why some psychologists find this diagnosis controversial.
6. Describe the biological and psychosocial factors that are causally-related to mood disorders.
7. Discuss how sociocultural factors affect the incidence of some of the mood disorders.
8. Describe several biological and psychosocial therapies that have been successful in treating mood disorders.
9. Characterize the people who are most likely to commit suicide. List some of their motives for ending their lives, and explain how sociocultural variables influence the likelihood of suicide among depressed persons.
10. Discuss the ethical dilemma surrounding a person's right to end his or her own life. Differentiate between cases which involve the terminally ill and those whose wish to die is based on temporary depression.
11. Summarize what we know about why people commit suicide with reference to degrees of intent, communication of intent, and suicide notes.
12. List five emphases that guide the counselor who is talking to a person contemplating suicide. Describe the long-range outcomes of crisis intervention.
13. Describe the "befriending" approach to people in high-risk groups, and list three other methods of broadening the approach of suicide prevention programs.

KEY TERMS

mood disorders	disthesis-stress
mood-incongruent	mood-congruent
mania	depression

major depressive disorder	bipolar disorder
hypomania	cyclothymia
dysthymia	adjustment disorder with depressed mood
unipolar disorder	schizoaffective disorder
suicide	severe major depressive episode with psychosis
rapid cycling	melancholic type
recurrence	relapse
seasonal affective disorder	pessimistic attributional style
dysfunctional beliefs	negative cognitive triad
negative automatic thoughts	learned helplessness
attributions	

FOCUS ON RESEARCH 1

Ogler, B., Lambert, M. and Sawyer, J. (1995). "Clinical Significance of the NIMH Treatment of Depression Colloborative Research Program. Journal of Clinical an Consulting Psychology, 63, 321-326.

How useful are research studies for practicing clinicians? This is a question that is continually raised by practitioners who make a conscientious effort to make useful applications of treatment research. Empirical research has traditionally focused on group means and statistical sigfnificance in research reports. This often overlooks the variety of meaningful individual responses to treatment strategies.

Responding to these shortcomings, attempts have been made to address these issues through the reanalysis of previously reported data. This article reports on the reanalysis of the NIMH collaborative depression study. The participants of this study were randomly assigned to four treatment conditions: cognitive-behavioral therapy, interpersonal therapy, antidepressant therapy, and a placebo. A number of assessment instruments were used in the project including: Beck's Depression Inventory, Hamilton Rating Scale for Depression, and Hopkins Symptom Checklist.

The authors found significant improvements in depression on self-report measures and clincial judges following treatment. The authros reported substantial agreement of improvement across the measurements. A small group of subjects showed reliable deterioration despite experiencing treatment. This coincides with previous outcome research showing the potential of harm for a small minority of therapy participants.

This article can be useful in discussing the problems in assessing depression, differences in treatment strategies, and how to make research useful for therapists.

Questions for Discussions

1.   Would case studies be more useful for therapists then studies similar to this one? Explain.

2.   What is the purpose of the placebo group? Are there problems using this condition?

FOCUS ON RESEARCH 2

Isometsa, E., Henriksson, M., Aro, H., Kuoppasalmi, K., and Lonnquist, J. (1994). "Suicide in Major Depression." <u>American Journal of Psychiatry</u>, <u>151</u>, 530-536.

This is an extensive study of lifetime risk of suicide in major mood disorders in Finland. The risk during a person's life who is experiencing depression of suicide has been estimated to be 19 percent. Major depression is considered to be one of the central risk factors for suicide. The clinical features of depression that have been associated with suicide risk include: insomnia, impaired memory, self-neglect, anhedonia, anxiety symptoms, difficulty concentrating, alcohol abuse, hopelessness, and mood cycling. The authors found that only a minority of individuals who were suicide victims had received psychiatric treatment for their depression.

The authors examined a sample of all suicide victims within a one year period. They were searching for clincial history, comorbidity, treatment history, suicide methods, and communication of suicide intent among the victims. They used the psychological autopsy method in their investigation.

They found that the majority of suicide victims were complicated with comorbid diagnoses. Yet only 45 percent were receiving treatment at the time of the suicide. The majority had not received treatment for their underlying depression. They concluded that only 3 percent were receiving antidepressant medication in adequate doses. Overall males had received less treatment for depression than women. The majority of males used violent means for their suicide, while only 8 percent used an overdosage of antidepressant medication.

The authors concluded that the suicide victims in general were not receiving adequate treatment for their depression. They recommend improved prevention strategies for major depression, and careful follow-up of patients. Males were identified as needing particular attention for their depression which was significantly overlooked in treatment.

Questions for Discussions

1. What benefits do these large scale studies have for assessment and treatment of mood disorders?

2. How can using one's medication for the means of suicide be prevented?

3. Are the gender differences reported here similar in the United States?

FOCUS ON RESEARCH 3

Roy, A., Segal, N., Centerwall, B., and Robinette, D. (1991). "Suicide in Twins." <u>Archives of General Psychiatry</u>, <u>48</u>, 29-32.

What are the possible genetic components in suicidal behavior? This study sought to determine if a predisposition for suicidal behavior is genetically transmitted independently of psychiatric disorder. The author studied a sample of twins who had experienced suicidal behavior. Brief case descriptions are provided for the twins and are useful for class illustration.

Their results suggest that genetic factors may be implicated in suicidal behavior. They propose that suicide clusters in families, and it may represent the genetic transmission of psychiatric disorder known to be associated with suicide. An inability to control impulsive behavior may be genetically transmitted in families. Depression and stress may serve as mechanisms which foster or trigger the impulsive suicidal behavior. Monozygotic twins demonstrated greater concordance than dizygotic twins in this study. Psychiatric disorder was found to be associated with suicide in their sample. They finish the article by signaling the need for future research, with surviving twins of suicide victims and their family members, to search for the suggested genetic predisposition.

Questions for Discussion

1. How could the acceptance of genetic transmission of suicide tendencies influence a person's adjustment to suicidal behavior clusters in his/her family?
2. What could be done in terms of treatment if suicidal behavior is genetically transmitted?
3. Are all suicides the result of impulsive behavior?
4. Does depression cluster in family groups?

FOCUS ON RESEARCH 4

Akiskal, H., Maser, J., Zeller, P., Endicott, J., Coryell, W. and Goodwin, F. (1995). "Switching from Unipolar to Bipolar II." Archives of General Psychiatry, 52, 114-122.

This study reports on the clinically significant process of predicting which patients will become bipolar subsequent to a diagnosis of major depressive disorder. They sought to identify the profile of the major depression patient who converts to the more subtle bipolar II subtype. They studied a population of 559 patients who had been extensively evaluated for depression.

They found a small percentage of major depressive disorder patients to convert to either bipolar I disorder or bipolar II disorder. These patients were essentially found to be similar except for the following contrasts. Bipolar II converters showed a protracted and tempestuous couse with short period of wellness. Temperamental instability gained through self-report measures were identified among bipolar II patients. Mood liability was the most specific predictor of switching.

The authors view bipolar II disorder as a condition with lability intruding into and accentuating major depressive episodes. They contend that the DSM-IV profile for bipolar II disorder which emphasizes hypomanic episodes should be directed toward the more fundamental condition of affective dysregulation.

Questions for Discussion

1. What are the clinical reasons for knowing who may switch to bipolar II disorder from major depressive disorder?

2. What are the symptoms associated with bipolar II disorder?

3. How are the symptoms of major depressive disorder different?

READINGS

1. Baron, M., Endicott, J., and Loth, J. (1994). "A Pedigree Series for Mapping Disease Genes in Bipolar Disorder." Psychiatric Genetics, 4, 43-55.

2. Bauer, M., Kurtz, J., Rubin, L., and Marcus, J. (1994). "Mood and Behavioral Effects of Four-week Light Treatment in Winter Depressives and Control." Journal of Psychiatric Research, 28, 135-145.

3. Clark, D., and Fawcett, J. (1994). "The Relation of Parenthood to Suicide." Archives of General Psychiatry, 51, 160-161.

4. Goodwin, G. (1994). "Recurrence of Mania After Lithium Withdrawal: Implications for the Use of Lithium in the Treatment of Bipolar Disorder." British Journal of Psychiatry, 164, 149-152.

5. Grayson, P., Lubin, B., and Van Whitlock, R. (1995). "Comparison of Depression in the Community-Dwelling and Assisted Living Elderly." Journal of Clinical Psychology, 51, 18-21.

6. Kato, T., Shioiri, T., Murashita, J., and Hamakawa, H. (1994). "Phosphorus-31 Magnetic Reonance Spectroscopy and Ventricular Enlargement in Bipolar Disorder." Psychiatry Research Neuroimaging, 55, 41-50.

7. Lacy, O.W. (1990). "Nonthreatening, Objective Psychometric Identification of Students at Risk for Depression and/or Suicidal Behavior." Journal of College Student Psychotherapy, 4, 141-163.

8. Levy, S., Jurkovic, G., and Spirito, A. (1995). "A Multisystem Analysis of Adolescent Suicide Attempters." Journal of Abnormal Child Psychology, 23,. 221-234.

9. McDonald, D. H., and Rang, L. M. (1990). "Do Written Reports of Suicide Induce High School Students to Believe that Suicidal Contagion Will Occur?" Journal of Applied Social Psychology, 20, 1093-1102.

10. Riesenny, K., Lubin, B., and Van Whitlock, R. (1995). "Psychometric Characteristics of the Trait Version of the Depression Adjective Check Lists in Adult Psychiatric Outpatients." Journal of Clinical Psychology, 51, 13-17.

11. Sheehan, T., Fifield, J., and Tennen, H. (1995). "The Measurement of Structure of the Center for Epidemiologic Studies Depression Scale." Journal of Personality Assessment, 64, 507-521.

12. Shiquing, Z, and Guang, Q. (1994). "The Sex Ratio of Suicide Rates in China." Crisis, 15, 44-48.

13. Symonds, R. (1994). "Psychiatric and Preventative Aspects of Rail Fatalities." Social Science and Medicine, 38, 431-435.

14. Tohen, M., Castillo, J., Harrison, P., and Herbstein, J. (1994). "Concommitant Use of Valproate and Carbamazepine in Bipolar and Schizoaffective Disorders." Journal of Clinical Psychopharmacology, 14, 67-70.

15. Westefeld, J. S., Whitchard, K. A., and Range, L, M. (1990). "College and University Student Suicide: Trends and Implications." Counseling Psycholologist, 18, 464-476.

DISCUSSION AND LECTURE IDEAS

1. What vulnerbilities in personality contribute to suicide? Students may find the research by J. Bartelstone and T. Trull (1995) to be of interest on this issue (Journal of Personality Assessment, 64, 279--294). They identified two distinct categories that produced a predisposition to depression and suicide. The conditions were a dependent style and a self-critical style. The study provides information on how assessment instruments were used in identifying these dimensions, and could be used for classroom illustration.

2. The majority of studies examining bipolar persons have emphasized observational and assessment data. Eleanor O'Leary and her colleagues (1991, Psychology: A Journal of Human Behavior, 28, 42-47) gave a brief report on the attempt to focus on the patient's view of manic episodes. They were able to identify thirteen categories that can be described through self-statements that classify the personal experience of mania. A classroom project can involve students role-playing a bipolar person and recording personal statements that coincide with the experience. These statements can be compared to the categorization provided by O'Leary (1991). Discussion can develop around any discrepancies and the similarities between student perceptions and those found by the researcher.

3. Suicide rates have risen rapidly in the United States over the past few years, especially among the aged population. The rate for college students has been increasing as well. What explanations can students present for the rise? Have students discuss the stresses and changes associated with college life and how they could affect moods.

4.   How would students handle the situation if their roommate at college began to show signs of a major affective disorder? Of suicide? Would they be sensitive to the communication of suicide intention provided by the roommate? Who could they contact if they believed the person was suicidal? Would the student be intruding into the privacy and "rights" of the suicidal roommate?

5.   Attempts to predict suicide potential have examined numerous risk factors. One test instrument that has been repeatedly used for this purpose is the Rorschach. Usually investigators have tried to link multiple signs on the test to suicidal individuals. Andrea Hanrell and her colleagues (1988) reported (Journal of Personality Assessment, 52, 658-669) an attempt to validate the using of a single response. They conclude that single sign indicators may be tapping some suicidal personality rather than a time limited proneness to suicide.

6.   Do males and females receive different amounts of emotional support from family, friends, and peers? J. Slavin and P. Rainer (1990, American Journal of Community Psychology, 18, 407-422) followed a large group of high school students in a prospective study to determine what types of emotional support they receive and how it may relate to depression. The girls reported more emotional support from outside sources than boys. Depressive symptoms in girls appear to lessen the family support they receive. The results show that young females establish social connectiveness among nonfamily members to a greater extent than males. Class disscussion can examine the way symptoms of depression may reduce family support. Should males and females receive different forms of treatment for depression? Are males' symptoms separate from social supports or less sensitive to relationships than women's?

7.   What constitutes an adequate follow-up treatment plan for a person who attempts suicide? Students can work in groups to develop a protocol for adequate follow-up of persons who have attempted suicide. What factors are important to consider?

ACTIVITIES AND PROJECTS

1.   Religious beliefs and dogma can have an impact on the suicidal actions of individuals. A student research project can involve the investigation of how suicide is viewed by different religions. Resource persons from various religious groups could be contacted and questioned about attitudes toward suicide and the individual who attempts it. What will happen to the person who commits suicide? Does suicide affect how the body is treated for burial? Do some religions condone this behavior?

2.   If a sibling during adolescence commits suicide, does this place the surviving siblings at greater risk for suicide? This question can be developed into an informative lecture-discussion session. Wagner and Cohen (1994) present extensive data on the topic as well as describing the importance of perceptions of parental behavior among adolescents(Journal of Abnormal Child Psychology, 22, 321-337). Students usually find this topic of interest since many are aware of classmates who have had a sibling commit suicide.

3.   The cognitive approach in the explanation of depression has wide appeal. Students can explore the cognitive aspects of depression through small group discussion. Have students

focus on personal thoughts associated with disappointments and failures which they may have recently encountered. How do their thoughts change when things are no longer going right for them? What experiences produce depressive thoughts? How can their thinking be modified to reduce depressive moods?

4.   Since depression is considered to be a normal reaction that everyone experiences, how do students deal with depression? In group discussion, students can focus on activities that alleviate mild depression. How did they learn to control their depressions? What procedures are most effective in controlling periods of depression?

5.   How dangerous can the work environment be for employees? Can the work place contribute to mental disorder? Recent news reports of job-related illness have questioned the protection employers provide their workers against toxic conditions or "sick" work environments. The microelectronics field uses many potentially harmful organic solvents. Donna Mergler (1991, Journal of Clinical Psychology, 47, 41-52) and her colleagues report on the prevalence of mood disorders in microelectronic workers. A project on this topic can require students to select an industry and try to assess it for potential psychological hazards. This article provides a good guideline for such a project, and contributes valuable discussion ideas.

6.   In order for students to gain first hand information about crisis intervention, a representative from a 24-hour crisis service can be invited to talk to the class. What type of services are provided? What type of training is given to personnel? Are volunteers used by the service? What are the common problems associated with suicide threats?

CHAPTER 7

Somatoform, and Dissociative Disorders

CHAPTER OUTLINE

I. Somatoform Disorders
    A. Somatization disorder
        1. Symptoms of the disorder are presented
            a. The disorder lacks widespread research scrutiny
            b. Briquet's syndrome was an early term
        2. Some similarities to hypochondriasis are apparent
    B. Hypochondriasis
        1. Characteristics of the disorder are described
            a. Vague symptoms are common
            b. A mental orientation of constant vigilance against illness
        2. Patients usually show a lack of anxiety
        3. Patients often show preoccupation with digestive and excretory functions
            a. The sick role can provide attention to the person
            b. The disorder may be an interpersonal communication
    C. Somatoform pain disorder
        1. Severe and lasting pain characterize the disorder
            a. The location of pain varies
            b. An invalid life-style can result
        2. No organic reason exists for the pain
    D. Conversion disorder
        1. Physical malfunction or loss of control is the central feature
            a. Hysteria was an early term for the disorder
            b. Freud's work with conversion hysteria
        2. A decreasing incidence in this disorder has taken place
        3. Range of symptoms in this disorder
            a. Sensory symptoms
            b. Motor symptoms
            c. Visceral symptoms
        4. Differentiation of conversion disorder from organic disturbances
            a. "la belle indifference"
            b. A lack of physical correctness
            c. Selective nature of the dysfunction
            d. Hypnosis can remove dysfunction.

5.   The phenomenon of mass hysteria or St. Vitus's dance
6.   Guilt and self-punishment can be found in this disorder
     a.   Once response is learned it is maintained by anxiety reduction
     b.   Interpersonal gains of sympathy and support reinforce the disorder

II.   Dissociative Disorders
   A.   Dissociative amnesia and fugue
     1.   A failure to recall is central to psychogenic amnesia
     2.   Four types are reported
       a.   Localized
       b.   Selective
       c.   Generalized
       d.   Continuous
     3.   Pschogenic amnesia is a fairly common reaction to trauma
       a.   Basic habit patterns are maintained
       b.   Neurotically functioning persons develop long-term amnesia
     4.   Fugue state is a defense by actual flight
       a.   New identities may be assumed
       b.   Fugue may last for days, weeks, or years
     5.   Patterns of defense for amnesia is similar to conversion disorder
       a.   Threatening information becomes inaccessible
       b.   Suppression is involved in memory loss
     6.   Characteristics of persons with psychogenic amnesia
       a.   Suggestibility is a central feature
       b.   They are usually egocentric and immature
   B.   Dissociative Identity Disorder
     1.   Two or more personality systems are created from stressful precipitating events
       a.   Personalities are dramatically different
       b.   Needs inhibited in one personality are displayed in another
     2.   The incidence of this disorder has dramatically increased in recent years
       a.   Increases may be artificial due to professional acceptance of disorder
       b.   Increases may reflect an increasingly "sick society"
         1)   Childhood sexual abuses have increased
         2)   Traumas from sexual abuse by adults precede disorder
       c.   Questions of malingering continue to influence perception of this disorder
         1)   Hypnosis can produce similar symptoms
         2)   Clinicians may encourage its appearance
   C.   Depersonalization disorder
     1.   Symptoms of the disorder are reviewed
       a.   A loss of self takes place
       b.   Aspect of self is changed or altered
       c.   Out-of-body experiences can occur
       d.   Acute stress triggers the reactions

2. Personal reactions to the symptoms
   a. The experience is usually frightening
   b. Anxiety about one's mental health increases
3. Differential diagnosis is important
   a. Depersonalization symptoms can signal decompensation
   b. Psychotic states often show early depersonalization symptoms

III. Causal Factors in Somatoform and Dissociative Disorders
   A. Biological factors
      1. What are the roles of genetic and constitutional factors?
      2. Ease of conditioning may play a role
         a. Extreme sensitivity and autonomic lability may produce excessive fears
         b. Some people may experience enhanced physiological disruptions
   B. Psychosocial factors
      1. Explanations for the origins of behaviors
         a. Anxiety leads to exaggerated use of ego-defense mechanisms
         b. Faulty learning causes the acquisition of maladaptive responses
         c. Blocking personal growth and meaning leads to anxiety and futility
         d. Pathogenic interpersonal relationships such as overindulgence or overprotection prevent effective coping techniques
      2. Psychosocial factors are interrelated and apply in varying degrees
   C. Sociocultural factors
      1. Cultural differences in terms of incidence in different disorders.
         a. Conversion disorders are found commonly in underdeveloped countries
         b. Obsessive-compulsive disorder is common in advanced societies
      2. Socioeconomics influence the appearance of certain disorders
         a. Somatic complaints and conversion symptoms have a high incidence in low socioeconomic groups
         b. Anxiety and obsessive-compulsive disorder are found at high socioeconomic levels

IV. Treatment and Outcomes
   A. Stabilization
   B. Working Through
   C. Postintegration Therapy

V. Unresolved Issues
   A. Disagreement over the separation of conversion and dissociative disorders diagnositic categories
   B. Treatment decisions can be influenced by categorizations

KEY TERMS

somatoform disorders	somatizaton disorder
hypochondriasis	malingering
pain disorder	conversion disorder
dissociative disorders	factitious disorder
secondary gain	fugue
dissociative identity disorder (DID)	depersonalization disorder
neuroticism	alexithymia
la belle indifference	implicit memory
dissociation	dissociation amnesia
host personality	alter personality
derealization	traumatic childhood abuse
false memories	

FOCUS ON RESEARCH 1

Apt, C., and Hurlbert, D. (1994). "The Sexual Atitudes, Behaior, and Relationships of Women with Histrionic Personality Disorder." Journal of Sex and Marital Therapy, 20, 125-133.

This study examined the sexual attitudes, behaviors, and intimate relationships of individuals with histrionic personality disorder. They used a sample of women fitting the criteria for histrionic personality disorder and matched them to a group of women without personality disorder. Persons with histrionic personality disorder are considered to be in constant need of reassurance and ego gratification. Behaviorally they exhibit helplessness and dependency while being extremely sensitive to criticism. They will show marked mood swings and identity disturbances. Their relationships are more problematic than found among non-histrionic individuals.

The authors assessed their participants using questionnaires which included a sexual history, demographics and the following formal measures: Hurlbert Index of Sexual Assertiveness, Sexual Opinion Survey, Index of Self-Esteem, Sexuality Scale, Index of Marital Satisfactin, and Hurlbert Index of Sexual Desire. Results on these measures revealed that the histrionic individuals evidenced low sexual assertiveness, negative attitudes toward sex, low sexual desire, orgasmic dysfunction, and sexual boredom.

Sexual activity is unsatisfying for these women because their emotional needs are so great. They are not adept at understanding and responding to their partner's needs. Sexual activity sets the stage for failure because of the histrionic's needs for ego gratification. Their physical needs are not satisfied because their emotional wants are so great. Since they tire of persons and situations easily, the reciprocal elements of sexuality are not identified nor acted upon. Flights of romantic fantasy were commonly seen as a way to avoid criticism.

Questions for Discussion

1. Explain the histrionic's failure at the reciprocal nature of satisfying sexual activity.

2.   What problems in assessment may exist in this study?

3.   The participants also showed high sexual esteem. How is this explained?

FOCUS ON RESEARCH 2

Golding, J., Smith, G., and Kashner, M. (1991). "Does Somatization Disorder Occur in Men?" Archives of General Psychiatry, 48, 231-238.

Previous researchers have concluded that somatization disorder is rare among men and is found most often in females. This present study expanded on early research by comparing diagnostic status, symptom patterns, functional impairments, self-reported health status, psychiatric comorbidity, and demographic characteristics among men and women with multiple somatic symptoms. The DSM criteria for diagnosis of somatization disorder were followed by the author.

Their sample of subjects consisted of 147 persons who were referred for multiple unexplained somatic complaints in the area of Little Rock, Arkansas. Following evaluation through clinical interviews and self-report measures, twelve men and sixty-eight women met the DSM-III-R criteria for somatization disorder. This represented 40 percent of the male subjects and 58 percent of the females. The males were not referred by primary care physicians. These men responded to media appeals for participants. The authors question if somatization disorder symptomology is more readily detected in women than men. Clinically, the male and female patients with somatization disorder showed more similarities than difference. The only gender differences were in sexual symptoms with women reporting pain during sexual intercourse, and dizziness occurring more frequently in women than men. Similarities were found in gastrointestinal, pain, cardiopulmonary, and pseudoneurologic symptoms.

The authors conclude that somatization disorder exists in both men and women yet is probably less common in men. There were no significant differences in demographic characteristics, functional impairment, self-reported health status, or psychiatric comorbidity. The need for prospective studies was noted by the authors.

Questions for Discussion

1.   The textbook has limited description of this disorder. How does this article clarify the text's material?
2.   What reasons may keep males from being identified as having somatization disorder?
3.   Will somatization disorder increase in frequency as the population becomes health conscious?

FOCUS ON RESEARCH 3

Kilhstrom, J., Glisky, M. and Angiulo, M. (1994). "Dissociative Tendencies and Dissociate Disorders." Journal of Abnormal Psychology, 103, 117-124.

The authors discuss the situation that although the dissociation disorders are fairly rare in clinical practice, dissociation experiences are somewhat common in everyday life. The dissociation disorders are syndromes in which an alteration in consciousness affects memory and identity. The diagnostic label for these disorders identifies the proposed underlying processes for the disorders.

When pathology is viewed on a continuum from minor dissociations of everyday life to major forms which require diagnosis, it's the quality of the symptom picture rather than the sign itself that signifies psychopathology. The Dissociative Experience Scale was developed to assess disturbances in awareness, memory, and identity. Usually persons with a formal diagnosis of a dissociative disorder score higher on the instrument than those without one.

Other instruments that have been developed to measure dissociative experiences include: Dissociation Questionnaire, Perceptual Alterations Scale, and the Questionnaire on Experiences of Dissociation. The authors expand the assessment tools to examine dissociative experiences by linking them to the construct of absorption. Thus, they propose the usefulness of using the Tellegen Absorption Scale for the assessment of dissociative experiences in the general population. The authors suggest that these dimensions in normal personality may be risk factors or diatheses for pathological dissociation.

Questions for Discussion

1. Should the general population be screened for vulnerability using the tests mentioned in this study?

2. What are some dissociative experiences found in everyday life?

3. What factors contribute to the development of this vulnerbility?

READINGS

1. Barsky, A., Wool, C., Barnett, M., and Cleary, P. (1994). "Histories of Childhood Trauma in Adult Hypochondriacal Patients." American Journal of Psychiatry, 151, 397-401.

2. Bell, I. (1994). "Somatization Disorder: Health Care Costs in the Decade of the Brain." Biological Psychiatry, 35, 81-83.

3. Brophy, J. (1994). "Monosymptomatic Hypchondriacal Psychosis Treated with Paroxetine: A Case Report." Irish Journal of Psychological Medicine, 11 21-22.

4. Hodges, J. (1994). "Semantic Memory and Frontal Executive Function During Transient Global Amnesia." Journal of Neurology, Neurosurgery, and Psychiatry, 57, 605-608.

5. Kirmayer, L, and Robbins, J. (1994). "Three Forms of Somatization in Primary Care." Journal of Nervous and Mental Disease, 179, 647-655.

6. Ostergaard, A. (1994). "Dissociations Between Word Priming Effects in Normal Subjects and Patients with Memory Disorders." Quarterly Journal of Experimental Psychology, 47, 331-364.

7. Paller, K., and Mayes, A. (1994). "New Association Priming of Word Identification in Normal and Amnesic Subjects." Cortex, 30, 53-73.

8. Pang, H, Pugh, K., and Catalan, J. (1994). "Gender Identity Disorder and HIV Disease." International Journal of STD and AIDS, 5, 130-132.

9. Roediger, H., and McDermott, K. (1994). "The Problem of Differing False Alarm Rates for the Process Dissociation Procedure." Neuropsychology, 8, 284-288.

10. Rosen, J., Reiter, J., and Orsoan, P. (1995). "Cognitive-Behavioral Body Image Therapy for Body Dysmorphic Disorder." Journal of Consulting and Clinical Psycholoy , 63, 263-269.

11. Smith, R. (1994). "The Course of Somatization and Its Effctson Utilization of Heath Care Resources." Psychosomatics, 35, 263-267.

12. Steinberg, M., Rounsaville, B., and Cicchetti, B. (1990). "The Structured Clinical Interview for DSM-III-R Dissociative Disorders." American Journal of Psychiatry, 147, 76-82.

13. Tomasson, K., and Kent, D. (1994). "Follow-Up Study Comparing Somatization and Conversion Disorders." Nordic Journal of Psychiatry, 48, 27-32.

14. Turk, D. (1994). "Perspectives On Chronic Pain: The Role of Psychological Factors." Current Directions inPsychological Science, 3, 45-48.

DISCUSSION AND LECTURE IDEAS

1. The question of the role of fantasy in dissociation can be used for a class lecture. S. Rauschenberger and S. Lynn (1995) report on a study relating fantasy-proneness and Axis 1 dissociation disorder (Journal of Consulting and Clinical Psychology, 104, 373-380). They used college students and found a number of individuals who met DSM criteria for this diagnosis, even though no formal diagnosis had been given them. They used the Inventory of Childhood Memories and Imaginings which could be adopted for classroom demonstration and discussion.

2. The person experiencing somatoform disorders often receives secondary gain.. The

85

attention and sympathy received can be a powerful influence in the person's life. The individual may be generally experiencing limited satisfaction in life and may enter psychotherapy for change. During treatment the person may become unwilling to forego the secondary gain associated with the symptoms and refuse to give them up. How can this problem be handled in therapy? What may occur when the person experiences frustration after secondary gain is lost?

3. A good case study on depersonalization disorder is provided by D. Ordas and C. Ritchie (1994) who report on a twenty-four year old male patient (Journal of Neuropsychiatry and Clinical Neurosciences, 6, 67-69). The case can be presented to the class as part of a discussion on this disorder which is often difficult to describe to students.

4. A lecture can be developed on the topic of comrbidity in the dissociative disorders. R. Noyes and his associates (1994) present some useful information on the comorbidity among patients with hypochondriasis (General Hospital Psychiatry, 16, 78-87). They found major depression to be the most commonly found comorbid disturbance. A classroom discussion can examine the significance of comorbidity for treatment and diagnosis.

5. Ask students to report on any periods of forgetfulness that they may have experienced. What was related to the "amnesia" they experienced? A study by J. Wilson and his collegues (1994) discusses the phenomenon of post-traumatic amnesia (Journal of Neurology, Neurosurgery, and Psychiatry, 57, 198-201). This article can be used as a resource to encourage discussion and provide example of amnesia following trauma.

6. What are the common reactions to someone who complains constantly about pain? Does society encourage or discourage the expression of pain? What are possible misconceptions about pain disorders that the general public may hold? Are they related to society's views on the reporting of pain?

ACTIVITIES AND PROJECTS

1. A classroom activity can focus on the dissociative identity disorder. Have the students imagine what aspects of themselves could become isolated as unique personalities. Allow them to construct the type of situation that might produce the emerging personality. The students should construct their alternative personalities and detail the traits and emotions associated with them. The students can be asked to discuss their feelings in completing this task. What emotions emerged in isolating different parts of the personalities?

2. What is the level of awareness for somatization among health care professionals? Students may interview health care professionals at their university health center. Patients with somatization disorder tend to overuse health care resources and increase the costs of health care. How are these factors handled by student health centers?

3. To illustrate the concepts associated with hypochondriasis to the class, an illness

attitudes scale can be administered to students. A good resource is provided in an article by V. Starcevic and his associates (1994) who show how to distinguish hypochondriasis from generalized anxiety disorder (Psychotherapy and Psychosomatics, 61, 93-99).

4. Students can be asked to prepare themselves to role play patients experiencing dissociative identity disorder. Have students construct a group of identities that can be exposed during interviews. Other students can act as the inteviewer/therapist. What strategies or questions elicit the most identities in the role play situations? The class can vote on who was the most convincing patient and/or therapist.

CHAPTER 8

Psychological Factors and Physical Illness

CHAPTER OUTLINE

I. General Psychological Factors in Health and Disease
    A.   Health, attitudes, and coping resources
        1.   Attitudes of helplessness and hopelessness affect organic functioning
            a.   Preparation for surgery tries to promote optimism
            b.   A study of ex-athletes shows the role of attitude in health
        2.   Multiple life changes influence a variety of illnesses
            a.   The amount of adjustment may tax a person's resources
            b.   Even favorable changes can negatively affect health
        3.   Stress may aggravate and maintain specific disorders
            a.   Positive emotions seem to produce immunity
            b.   The placebo effect is attributed to attitudes
    B.   Autonomic excess and tissue damage
        1.   The "flight or fight" pattern as described by Walter Cannon
        2.   Other theorists who described the autonomic arousal role in behavior
            a.   Selye's alarm reaction
            b.   Franz Alexander reasoned that chronic internal threat had ill effects on health.
    C.   Psychosocial factors and the immune system
        1.   Elements of the human immune system
            a.   The immune system maintains bodily integrity
            b.   White blood cells are the core of the body's defenses
            c.   The immune function has two branches
                 1)   The humoral component includes B-cells and their antibodies
                 2)   The cellular function's T-cells mediate its response
        2.   Psychosocial compromise of the immune response
            a.   The functional status of the system can be influenced by stress and mental states
            b.   Psychoneuroimmunology examines psychological factors on nervous system functioning
                 1)   White blood cell reproduction is inhibited by numerous factors

2)   The neural pathways affected by stressors are being identified
     c.   Some theorists consider immunosuppression to be a learned phenomenon
   D.   Life-style as a factor in health maintenance
     1.   A growing awareness of the role of life-style and health is taking place.
       a.   Increasing exercise
       b.   Diets high in fiber
       c.   Restriction of alcohol and tobacco
     2.   How strong is the connection between life-style and physical illness?
       a.   Usually only correlational evidence exists
       b.   Many practitioners accept the relationships

II.   Psychosocial Factors in Specific Disease Processes
   A.   Coronary heart disease and the "Type A" behavior pattern
     1.   Type A behavior pattern coined by Friedman and Rosenman
       a.   Excessive competitive drive
       b.   Impatient and time urgent
       c.   Hostility expressed in manner and speech
       d.   Structured interview initially used for identification
       e.   Questionnaire-type approaches have been developed
     2.   Problems with the Type A assessment suggest continuing validity concerns
       a.   Not all components of Type A are equally predictive of heart disease
       b.   Recent studies have obtained contradictory results
     3.   Prospective studies have begun to examine A-B type status
       a.   Some aspects of the Type A pattern showing a negative effect have been implicated in heart disease risk
       b.   Results are being extended to female subjects
   B.   The anorexic/bulimic syndromes
     1.   Anorexia nervosa identified as a distinct disorder with central features
       a.   An intense fear of gaining weight is found coupled with a complaint of being fat
       b.   A refusal to maintain weight is seen with a loss of 15 percent of body weight
       c.   Overactivity accompanies the fear of obesity
       d.   Restricting or binge eating/purging subtypes in DSM-IV
     2.   The disorder is found primarily in females beginning in adolescence
       a.   Life changes often coincide with the onset of anorexia
       b.   Normal dieting often precedes its development
     3.   Bulimia involves seemingly uncontrollable binge eating with awareness of abnormality
       a.   The victim is preoccupied with fears of not stopping eating
       b.   Attempts are made to lose weight through extreme methods
       c.   Extreme weight fluctuations are common
     4.   Origins of the disorder are in psychological problems focused upon food

original

ingestion and bodily perception
- a. Social factors may promote thinness as an ideal
- b. Perfectionism and overachievement tendencies are present in both disorders
- c. Disturbed family dynamics may cause enmeshment
- d. Struggles with personal identity was proposed by Bruch as the core of the disorders

5. Outcomes for the disorders can be numerous
- a. Serious physical consequences and death can occur
- b. Autonomous dysregulation of both appetite and menstruation is found in advanced stages
- c. Bruch was a leading authority in this field of study

C. Essential hypertension
1. Essential hypertension is a risk factor for a number of physical ailments
2. The course of essential hypertension usually has no overt symptoms
3. Emotional stress may trigger the condition
4. Psychoanalytic interpretations focus on "suppressed rage" as a causal agent
- a. McClelland's variant explanation focuses on power motives
- b. An individual's propensities are at odds with societal proscriptions

D. Recurrent headaches
1. Migraines are intensely painful headaches
- a. A variety of stressors can cause vascular changes and pain
- b. Classic versus common migraines
2. Simple tension headaches are caused by different vascular events from migraines
3. A number of treatment strategies have been used for headache pain
- a. Analgesics
- b. Muscle-relaxants
- c. Biofeedback
4. Psychological predispositions to headache are still unclear
- a. Feelings of control are important to the headache-prone person
- b. Tension headache-prone persons show more psychopathological tendencies than migraine sufferers

III. Psychogenic Physical Disease: Additional Etiologic Considerations
A. Biological factors
1. Genetic factors.
- a. Twin studies show similar disease formation
- b. Interpretive complexities make decisions difficult in this research
2. Differences in autonomic reactivity and somatic weakness
- a. People can be classified on the basis of physical changes to stress
- b. Vulnerability of an organ may be due to heredity or trauma
3. Disruption of corticovisceral control mechanisms
- a. Homeostatic functions may fail
- b. Deficient hypothalamic regulation may be present
B. Psychosocial factors

1. Personality characteristics and inadequate coping patterns
   a. Everyone with a suspect pattern does not develop the disorder
   b. People vary in the capacity to deal with the aftermath of stress
2. Interpersonal relationships
   a. The effects of losing a spouse are examined
   b. Psychogenic family patterns can contribute to disease formation
3. The learning of illness
   a. Operant conditioning of autonomic reactivity can occur
   b. Secondary gain may maintain a disorder

C. Sociocultural factors
   1. Eating disorders and cultural factors
   2. Sociocultural factors may increase the stressfulness of certain conditions

IV. Treatment and Outcomes
   A. Biological measures
      1. Mild tranquilizers are usually employed
      2. Antidepressants are used to treat an expanding number of disorders
   B. Psychosocial measures
      1. Behavior therapy
      2. Cognitive-behavioral treatment
      3. Combined treatment measures
   C. Sociocultural factors
      1. Prevention is the core of sociocultural treatment strategies
         a. The public awareness of risk factors is increased
         b. Self-help programs are implemented
      2. Smoking cessation is used as an example

V. Unresolved Issues on Containing the AIDS epidemic
   A. AIDS is expected to continue accerlating geometrically
   B. Risk continues in different groups
   C. Behavioral compliance remains problematic

LEARNING OBJECTIVES

1. Give several examples of the close relationship between psychological factors and health.
2. Under what circumstances does excessive arousal of the autonomic nervous system cause actual tissue damage?
3. List and describe the two main divisions of the immune system, and explain the functions of each of their component parts.
4. Summarize the research findings that point to *some* psychosocial effects on the immune system, and describe some future directions such investigations may take.
5. List several aspects of the way we live that may produce severe physical problems, and explain why conclusive proof of these allegations is difficult to obtain.
6. Describe three clinical manifestations of coronary heart disease (CHD), and summarize the evidence linking it to the type A personality.

7. Describe anorexia and bulimia, explain some of the psychosocial factors that may be responsible for these disorders, and list some of the serious physical conditions that often result.

8. Define *essential hypertension*, list some physical diseases that it causes, and explain McClelland's variation of the suppressed-rage hypothesis about the cause of essential hypertension.

9. Describe the symptoms of peptic ulcers, and explain how dependency conflicts have been implicated as causal factors.

10. Differentiate between the physical causes of migraine and simple tension headaches, and summarize the research findings about psychosocial factors that may cause these dysfunctions.

11. Describe the sequence of events that appear to characterize the development of most psychogenic illness.

12. List and explain three types of biological factors that determine the adequacy of one's response to stressors.

13. List and explain three classes of psychosocial factors that may cause and/or maintain physical diseases.

14. Summarize the research results that show a link between sociocultural factors, physical disease, and other physical and mental problems.

15. List and describe three types of psychosocial measures that have been used to treat psychogenic diseases.

16. Explain why psychogenic illnesses must be treated by a combination of medical and psychological measures, and describe how such combinations have been used to treat anorexia nervosa.

17. Indicate the major objectives of sociocultural efforts to reduce psychogenic diseases, and describe the five-pronged North Karelia Project and some of its early results.

18. Describe three major problems that remain unresolved in our understanding of psychological influences on the physical body.

KEY TERMS

behavioral medicine
health psychology
immune system
psychoneuroimmunology
Type A behavior pattern
bulimia nervosa
essential hypertension
migraine
biofeedback

psychogenic illness
placebo effect
antigen
coronary heart disease (CHD)
anorexia nervosa
hypertension
secondary gain
"simple" tension headache

FOCUS ON RESEARCH 1

Collings, S., and King, M. (1994). "Ten-Year Follow-Up of 50 Patients with Bulimia Nervosa." British Journal of Psychiatry, 164, 80-87.

The authors long term follow-up of bulimia patients fills a void in the literature which generally lacks assessment past three years after diagnosis. They examined a group of fifty patients who were diagnosed at an eating disorder unit in London. They had recieved a number of assessment instruments at that time and during follow-up including: demographic data, psychiatric family history, Clinical Interview Schedule, Eating Attitudes Test, Hamilton Rating Scale for Depression, Hamilton Rating Scale for Anxiety, Social Problems Questionnaire and a semi-structured clinical interview.

At the time of follow-up twenty-three patients had fully recovered from the eating disorder. This marked an improvement over the five year follow-up when only 31 percent if the patients showed complete recovery. Those patient who recovered fully had developed the disorder at an early age, reported a family history of alcohol abuse, were married or cohabitating, and were of a higher social class.

Those who did not show recovery continued to demonstrate a range of psychological difficulties and abnormal eating attitudes. They found that the scores on the psychiatric scales were not predictive of outcome. The relationship of positive outcomes with family alcoholism was explained in the context of increased motivation to receive treatment for the eating disorder. They also suggest a connection between eating disorders and dependence disorders.

Questions for Discussions

1. What are the difficulties in completing long term follow-up studies?

2. What are possible long term negative outcomes for eating disorder patients?

FOCUS ON RESEARCH 2

Kearney-Cooke, A., and Striegel-Moore, R. (1994). "Treatment of Childhood Sexual Abuse in Anorexia Nervosa and Bulimia Nervosa: A Feminist Psychodynamic Approach." International Journal of Eating Disorders, 4, 305-319.

The authors enter the debate concerning the possible role of childhood sexual truama in the etiology of anorexia nervosa and bulimia nervosa. There exists disagreement concerning the specificity of risk among those who experienced child abuse. The authors expand on this debate by considering the issue of what are appropriate treatments for anorexia and bulimia. They suggest that the real issue should center on the identification of treatment strategies that best help the client deal with the sexual trauma that some clients had experienced.

They show the importance of a client moving through the three stages of recovery from a trauma: establishing safety, remembrance and mourning, and reconnection with life. The treatment components that are necessary to achieve this are: comprehenisve assessment of the abuse, developing clients' capacity for self-soothing, enabling clients to recall and work through the abusive event, dealing with shame and ending the cycle of victimization.

The therapeutic relationship best suited for providing these components is one in which the therapist forms a partnership on the journey of recovery. Thus the therapist should not be a silent expert or observer. Taking an active part in recovery is necessary and the therapist needs to show an empathic connection with the survivor and permit disagreement and conflict.

Recovery comes about when the client learns about the abuse and how it influenced their life. This understanding enables them to move into the next step of writing a new life story about one's self and body. Repeated victimization is prevented and the person claim their whole self in the world.

Questions for Discussion

1. How would a behavioral approach differ from the one in this article?

2. Should the majority of anorectics be treated by female therapists?

3. What would be the role of group therapy for the anorexia or bulimia client?

FOCUS ON RESEARCH 3

Kamarck, T., and Jennings, J. (1991). "Biobehavioral Factors in Sudden Cardiac Death." Psychological Bulletin, 109, 42-75.

This is a very thorough review of the literature on psychological factors and sudden cardiac death. Evidence suggests that several physiological precursors of sudden death may be enhanced by psychological challenge. These psychosocial stressors can tax or exceed the individual's adaptive processes. Life change units have been found to be elevated prior to sudden cardiac deaths. These events included loss events such as a death of a spouse or close friend, changes in work or living conditions, and social isolation. The authors warn that the majority of studies are retrospective and the life change stressors are reported by informants. The limited prospective studies are hampered by poor design and measurement issues.

The authors next discuss the research on environmental stressors as they relate to ventricular arrhythmia. Some studies have shown that prevailing psychological states and traits may be precipitants to arrhythmia. They suggest that ambulatory monitoring studies are needed in high-risk samples. This would permit examination of acute psychological precipitants in frequent or complex arrhythmia.

In the area of myocardial ischemia, evidence suggests that cognitive stressors play a role. Many ischemic changes produced by mental stress may not be identified because pain or electro-cardiographic change are not obvious. A new area of research has examined the potential effects of stress on platelet aggregation. Environmental challenges may vary platelet activity and impact on the risk of sudden cardiac death.

The authors conclude by recommending future research on life-style factors associated with long-term development of atherosclerosis. Follow-up programs for high-risk patients should include a research element. Extensive examination of autonomic variables and stress also need to be completed. This review demonstrated the complexities in researching and trying to connect psychological events to physical disease states.

Questions for Discussion

1. What are some of the popular notions about precursors to heart attacks and strokes?
2. What differences would long-term stressors have on cardiac functioning as opposed to short-term ones?
3. How can prospective studies be complemented to study cardiac risks?
4. Can psychological stressors be as easiy identified as such risk factors as smoking?

Focus on Research 4

Bornstein, R., and Greenberg, R. (1991). "Dependency and Eating Disorders in Female Psychiatric Inpatients." Journal of Nervous and Mental Disease, 179, 148-152.

These authors present data that suggests anorexia and bulimia are related to unresolved dependency issues. They focus on psychoanalytic theory which views overgratification or frustration during the oral stage as a cause of a dependent personality orientation. This should result in a preoccupation with food and eating as a means of obtaining security and nurturance. Food takes on strong symbolic qualities which recapture early feelings of security and connectedness to a primary caregiver.

The author examined fifty-one adolescent and adult females diagnosed with anorexia or bulimia. Two further groups were tested for comparison purposes. The first was a group of obese female psychiatric patients, and the second was a group of normal-weight, noneating disorder females. The Rorschach was employed to yield an oral dependency measure.

The results showed that anorectic and bulimic patients reported elevated rates of dependent imagery at two times the rate of control subjects, thus supporting the notion that dependency may be an important dynamic underlying anorectic and bulimic symptoms. The authors do not see dependency as the primary factor underlying eating disorders, but they believe its interaction with other variables needs to be examined.

The therapist who works with eating-disorder patients should be cognizant of the dependency issues. Relationship reactions would be affected by the dependency needs, and fears of abandonment would evolve when termination nears. Also, successful treatment may be associated with a reduction in dependent behavior and fantasy. Other personality traits such as perfectionism may interact with dependency needs to influence the course of the disorder. These results support the evidence that patients with anorexia and bulimia often report elevated levels of parental neglect, rejection, blame, and hostility.

Questions for Discussion

1. What are the potential shortcomings of the conclusions based upon correlational evidence?
2. The use of the Rorschach to yield an oral dependency measure has what limitations?
3. How should treatment progress for anorexia and bulimia, taking in account the patients' dependency needs?

READINGS

1. Adler, N., and Matthews, K. (1994). "Health Psychology: Why Do Some People Get Sick and Some Stay Well?" Annual Review of Psychology, 45, 229-259.

2. Bennett, P., and Carroll, D. (1994). "Cognitive Behavioral Interventions in Cardiac Rehabilitation." Journal of Psychosomatic Research, 38, 169-182.

3. Blaney, N. (1990). "Type A, Effort to Excel, and Attentional Style in Children." Journal of Social Behavior and Personality, 5, 159-182.

4. Bowers, M., and Greenfield, D. (1994). "Elevated Plasma Monoamine Metobolites in Eating Disorders." Psychiatry Research, 52, 11-5.

5. Bulik, C., Sullivan, P., and McKee, M. (1994). "Characteristics of Bulimic Women with and Without Alcohol Abuse." American Journal of Drug and Alchohol Abuse, 20, 273-283.

6. Cohen, S., and Williamson, G. (1991). "Stress and Infectious Disease in Humans." Psychological Bulletin, 109, 5-24.

7. Eisler, R., and Blalock, J. (1991). "Masculine Gender Role Stress: Implications for the Assessment of Men." . Clinical Psychology Review, 11, 45-60.

8. Etscheidt, M., Steger, H., and Braverman, B. (1995). "Multidimensional Pain Inventory Profile Classification and Psychopathology." Journal of Clinical Psychology, 51, 29-36.

9. Fornari, V., and Goodman, B. (1994). "Anorexia Nervosa: Thirty Something." Journal of Substance Abuse Treatment, 11, 45-54.

10. Gleaver, D., Williamson, D., Everenz, K., and Barker, S. (1995). "Clarifying Body-Image Disturbance: Analysis of A Multidemisional Model Using Structural Modeling." Journal of Personality Assessment, 64, 478-493.

11.   Lesem, M., Kaye, W., and Jimerson, D. (1994). "Cerebrospinal Fluid TRH Immunoreactivity in Anorexia Nervosa." Biological Psychiatry, 35, 48-53.

12.   Luzzatto, P. (1994). "Anorexia Nervosa and Art Therapy: The Double Trap of the Anorexia Patient." Arts in Psychotherapy, 21, 139-143.

13.   Norris, R., Carroll, D., and Cockrane, R. (1990). "The Effects of Aerobic and Anaerobic Training on Fitness, Blood Pressure, and Psychological Stress and Well-Being." Journal of Psychosomatic Research, 34, 367-375.

14.   Peterson, C., and DeAvila, M. (1995). "Optimistic Explanatory Style and the Perception of Health Problems." Journal of Personality Assessment, 51, 128-132.

15.   Pereira, M., and Calheiros, H. (1994). "Headaches in Medical School Students." Neuroepidemiology, 13, 103-107.

16.   Treasure, J., and Campbell, I. (1994). "The Case for Biology in the Aetiology of Anorexia Nervosa." Psychological Medicine, 24, 3-8.

17.   Waller, G. (1994). "Bulimic Women's Perceptions of Interaction with their Families." Psychological Reports, 74, 27-32.

DISCUSSION AND LECTURE IDEAS

1.   When studying the eating disorders of anorexia and bulimia nervosa, students often ask about contributing factors. A study by G. Leon, J. Fielkerson, C. Perry, and M. Early-Zadd (1995) provides interesting information about the precursors to the development of these disorders (Journal of Consulting and Clinical Psychology, 104, 140-149). This presents information from a prospective study and is an ongoing project.

2.   What is the possibility to predict which children are prone to coronary disease? Saundra Hunter (1991) and her colleagues provide some useful information on this topic. (Journal of Social Behavior and Personality, 6, 71-84). They identify Type A behavior in a sample of children.

3.   One of the symptoms associated with anorexia nervosa is a distorted body image. A classroom discussion using an objective measure of body image can be useful to illustrate this symptom. The Body Image Ideals Questionnaire developed by Thomas Cash and Marcela Szymanski (1995) can provide the basis for a class discussion (Journal of Personality Assessment, 64, 466-477). This measure evaluates attitudinal dimensions of the discrepancy between perceived and idealized physical charcteristics. A multitude of physical characteristics are considered in addition to those that are weight related.

4.   The role of positive emotions in the promotion of good physical health has been demonstrated most dramatically by Norman Cousins (Anatomy of an Illness). Following

diagnosis of a terminal illness, Cousins surrounded himself with stimuli to facilitate a positive affect. It was found that laughter was producing beneficial physiological effects in addition to psychological ones. His recovery began soon after his self-treatment was implemented. Cousins experienced a recovery from his illness. What physiological changes could have been affected by his positive mood and laughter? Were his changes a placebo effect or just luck?

5. What level of support does a cancer patient desire from family, friends, and health professionals? This question was examined by Julia Rose (1990) in her study of sixty-four nonhospitalized cancer patients (American Journal of Community Psychology, 18, 439-464). She found that emotional and instrumental functions of support were distinct and required separate examination. Family and friends were preferred sources for dealing with emotional concerns. A classroom discussion can center on the actual behaviors and situations that may be helpful to the cancer patient. What factors may contribute to the development and course of the disease? The author presents a good categorization of support functions that can guide classroom discussions.

6. What are the stresses faced by diabetic youngsters? How does a person cope with the disease process of diabetes? A number of developmental trends in coping approaches by diabetic children have been identified by L. Band (1990), (Journal of Pediatric Psychology, 15, 27-41). The children's level of cognitive development was found to determine the manner of doing exhibited by the diabetic. This study utilized the self-reports from diabetic children between the ages of seven to seventeen.

7. The problems of hypertension can be insidious as few, if any, symptoms are readily apparent. A study by William Dressler (1990, Journal of Psychosomatic Research, 34, 515-523) demonstrated how people are unaware of fluctuations in blood pressure, and attempted to identify which factors promote elevation in blood pressure. Lower education was found to be associated with high blood pressure when life-style incongruity took place. This article provides useful insights into the management of hypertension and the factors affecting blood pressure level.

ACTIVITIES AND PROJECTS

1. During small group discussion, students can examine the relationship between emotional reactiveness and physiological ailments. Students can look at their own lives for examples. Have the groups record various physical reactions they have experienced to times of stress. The students should attempt to identify the times and instigating events. Students may be able to find patterns in their own lives, and the group may show how people react with different physical reactions to similar stress experiences.

2. The use of transcendental meditation has been reported to deter physiological processes and could be useful to treat psychophysiological disorders. There has been evidence the TM can alter brainwave activity. Students can research the use of TM for physiologic disorders, and compare TM to deep muscle relaxation techniques. Relaxation methods often form a base for biofeedback techniques. Student research in these areas can provide insights into the therapy designed for the psychophysiologic disorders.

3. Many people suffer from migraine and tension headaches and ulcers. A student project can involve having the students interview people who experience such conditions. The students could focus questions on such issues as how long the people have experienced the symptoms. How do the symptoms affect their daily functioning? What treatment methods have been used effectively? Do physicians advise their patients of possible psychological factors when a diagnosis is made? Has the person been able to identify factors that aggravate the disorder? Are other family members affected with the same disorder?

4. Biofeedback techniques are widely used in the treatment of such psychophysiologic disorders as hypertension. If the instruments are available, present a portable biofeedback for classroom demonstration. An EMG or thermal unit would be most useful to demonstrate how biofeedback works. A student volunteer can be used for the illustration. Following the activity, a classroom discussion can focus on the applications and limitations of biofeedback for the psychophysiologic disorders.

5. Students can be assigned the task of collecting the different ways that body image distortions have been assessed among clients with anorexia nervosa. An article by M. Thompson and J. Gray (1995) reviewed the methods and found twenty-one different methods have been developed for this purpose (Journal of Personality Assessment, 64, 258-269). Once the different methods are presented in class, students can compare the strengthns and weaknesses of the different methods.

CHAPTER 9

Personality Disorders

CHAPTER OUTLINE

I. Personality Disorder
    A. Clinical features of personality disorders
        1. The personality disorders are classified according to the particular characteristics that are most prominent
            a. This feature may provide an unclear dividing line
            b. The feature predicts the kind of disordered relationship found in a person
        2. The definition of personality disorders in the DSM-IV
            a. The problems are long standing
            b. Axis II used to code disorders
            c. Misdiagnoses often occur in these categories
    B. Types of personaity disorders
        1. The disorders are grouped into three clusters based upon similarities
            a. Cluster A includes paranoid, schizoid, and schizotypal
            b. Cluster B includes histrionic narcissistic, antisocial, and borderline
            c. Cluster C includes avoidant, dependent, and obsessive-compulsive
            d. Depressive and passive-aggressive appear in the appendix of DSM-III-R
        2. Paranoid personality disorder
            a. Typical symptoms are suspiciousness, rigidity, and argumentativeness
            b. The person is constantly "on guard" for attacks from others
            c. This is not a psychotic condition
        3. Schizoid personality disorder
            a. Central symptoms are an inability to form social relationships and an indifference to them
            b. Early views saw this as a precursor to schizophrenia
            c. The need for love and belonging does not develop in these people
        4. Schizotypal personality disorder
            a. Seclusivity, oversensitivity, and eccentricity are the central features
            b. Oddities of thought, perception, and speech are also present

c. A genetic association with schizophrenia is widely suspected yet not conclusive

5. Histrionic personality disorder
    a. Immaturity, emotional instability, and self-dramatization are key features
    b. Sexual adjustment is usually poor
    c. Attention-seeking tactics are prominent

6. Narcissistic personality disorder
    a. An exaggerated sense of self-importance and need for attention are found
    b. There is a fragile ego and low self-esteem is present
    c. There is an inability to assume the perspective of others
    d. This disorder is found more commonly in men than women
    e. Psychodynamic treatments provide the most viable therapy for this disorder

7. Antisocial personality disorder
    a. Persons with this disorder violate the rights of others without remorse
    b. Intelligence and charm can be found in many antisocial personalities

8. Borderline personality disorder
    a. Common symptoms include impulsivity, anger, instability, and unpredictability
    b. These persons fail to complete the process of forming self-identity

9. Avoidant personality disorder
    a. These persons fear rejection and see disparagement everywhere
    b. They desire affection and are lonely
    c. This disorder is often confused with schizoid personality disorder or generalized social phobia
    d. Social skills training is usually insufficient in this disorder

10. Dependent personality disorder
    a. Extreme dependency on others and panic when alone are central symptoms
    b. Self-confidence is lacking
    c. They allow others to take over decision-making

11. Obsessive-compulsive personality disorder
    a. Overconcern with rules, a lack of warmth, and overconscientiousness are essential characteristics
    b. The behavior patterns are similar to the obsessive compulsive disorder

12. Passive-aggressive personality disorder
    a. This diagnosis is a source of controversy
        1) The ambiguity of the diagnosis leads to problems
        2) Empirical evidence is limited
    b. Hostility is expressed in indirect ways

13. Depressive personality disorder

        a.   Provisional category in DSM-IV

        b.   Persons show a pattern of depressive cognitions or behavior

14.   Overview of personality disorders

        a.   Overdeveloped sets of behavior patterns

        b.   Core dysfunctional beliefs

C.   Causal factors in personality disorders

    1.   The disorders are difficult to study thoroughly

        a.   Many of these disorders are not seen by clinicians

        b.   Retrospective studies have typically been used

        c.   The diagnosis of the disorders is often difficult

    2.   Biological factors have been proposed to predispose a person to a particular disorder

        a.   Early constitutions may be inherited

        b.   This relationship remains hypothetical

    3.   Psychological and sociocultural factors are seen as determinants for the disorders

        a.   Childhood interactions may be a factor

        b.   Speculation is still taking place

D.   Treatment and outcomes

    1.   These disorders are considered to be resistant to therapy

        a.   These people are seen as part of another person's treatment

        b.   Family therapy or child treatments often include a person with one of these disorders

    2.   The person with this disorder usually does not seek therapy

        a.   They lack motivation in treatment

        b.   They usually drop out of therapy

    3.   Traditional therapy methods are often inadequate

        a.   Antidepressants are used for some of the disorders

        b.   The therapist needs to be flexible

II.   Antisocial Personality and Psychopathy

A.   The clinical picture in antisocial personality and psychopathy

    1.   Common characteristics

        a.   Inadequate conscience development

            1)   They act out tensions

            2)   They often appear sincere

        b.   Irresponsible and impulsive behavior

            1)   They take what they want

            2)   They are prone to thrill-seeking actions

        c.   Ability to impress and exploit others and project blame on others

            1)   They are frequent liars

            2)   They understand and use the weaknesses of others

        d.   Rejection of authority

        e.   Inability to maintain good interpersonal relationships

            1)   They can easily win "friends"

            2)   They can be violent toward "friends" and family

2. Patterns of behavior in the antisocial personality
    a. They show a repetitive pattern as illustrated in the case of Donald
    b. The intelligence often found in this disorder can serve to protect one from criminality

B. Causal factors in psychopathy and antisocial personality
  1. Biological factors
    a. Genetic influence
    b. Deficient aversive emotional responsiveness and conditioning
      1) They fail to learn from punishment
      2) They may have constitutional deficiencies
    c. Stimulation seeking and delay of gratification
    d. Deficits in cognitive functioninging
  2. Family relationships
    a. Early studies pointed to early parental loss and emotional deprivation as causal agents
    b. Severe parental rejection and lack of parental affection appear related to its development
    c. Inconsistency in dispensing rewards and punishment may be a parental factor
  3. A developmental perspective on psychopathy and antisocial personality
    a. Childhood antisocial behaviors
    b. Oppositional defiant disorder is an early diagnosis
    c. Early neurophysiological vulnerabilities

C. Treatment and outcomes in psychopathic and antisocial personality
  1. Traditional psychotherapeutic approaches are not effective
    a. The inability to trust inhibits the therapeutic relationship
    b. Biological treatments have not been useful
  2. Behavior therapy has been the most useful
    a. Antisocial behaviors are targeted for modification
    b. Modeling is used to indicate desired behavior
    c. Inner controls are reinforced and external ones minimized
  3. Beck and Freeman recommend cognitive therapy
  4. Some antisocial personalities show improvement as they age
    a. They achieve insight into their self-defeating actions
    b. Social conditioning changes their behavior

III. Unresolved Issues on Axis II of DSM-IV
  A. Axis II diagnoses are often unreliable
    1. The personality processes are dimensional in nature
    2. Arbitrary decisions are used to define the degree of a trait
    3. The diagnoses are not based upon mutually exclusive criteria
  B. Clearer sets of classification rules need to be formulated
    1. The rules need to become exhaustive and incorporate non-overlapping behaviors
    2. This process may be beyond the current capabilities of researchers

LEARNING OBJECTIVES

1. Define *personality disorder*, and explain four special problems that may cause misdiagnoses in this category.
2. Describe six clinical features that all personality disorders seem to have in common.
3. List and describe the general characteristics of three clusters of personality disorders, and note two additional disorders that appear in DSM-IV.
4. Describe and differentiate among the following personality disorders in Cluster A: paranoid, schizoid, and schizotypal.
5. Describe and differentiate among the following personality disorders in Cluster B: histrionic, narcissistic, antisocial, and borderline.
6. Describe and differentiate among the following personality disorders in Cluster C: avoidant, dependent, compulsive.
7. Describe and differentiate between the following personality disorders in DSM-IV: depressive and passive-aggressive disorders.
8. Explain why we know comparatively little about the causal factors in personality disorders, and summarize what we do know about the biological, psychological, and sociocultural factors that seem implicated.
9. List several reasons why personality disorders are especially resistant to therapy, and describe Mulvey's treatment strategy for persons who are already too dependent.
10. Describe four criteria that must be met before an individual is diagnosed as an antisocial personality according to DSM-IV.
11. List and describe five characteristics that are typical of antisocial personalities in general.
12. List and explain several biological, family, and sociocultural factors that may cause the development of an antisocial personality.
13. Explain why most individuals with antisocial personalities seldom come to the attention of mental hospitals and clinics, and evaluate the success of traditional psychotherapy in treating this disorder.
14. List and describe three steps that Bandura recommends to modify antisocial behavior of individuals with antisocial personalities.
15. List three conclusions that Vaillant reached about the effective treatment of individuals with antisocial personalities.
16. Identify and explain two major problems that make Axis II diagnoses quite unreliable, and describe two solutions offered by the authors.

KEY TERMS

personality disorder

schizoid personality disorder

histrionic personality disorder

antisocial personality disorder

avoidant personality disorder

obsessive-compulsive personality disorder

sadistic personality disorder

paranoid personality disorder

schizotypal personality disorder

narcissistic personality disorder

borderline personality disorder

dependent personality disorder

passive-aggressive personality disorder

depressive personality disorder

psychopathic personality

FOCUS ON RESEARCH 1

Farmer, R., and Nelson-Gray, R. (1995). "Anxiety, Impulsivity, and the Anxious-Feaful and Erratic-Dramatic Personality Disorder." Journal of Research in Personality, 29, 189-207.

In recent years researchers have attempted to identify underlying dimensions associated with individual personality disorder. The research has typically utilized the concept of the Big Five personality dimensions. Factor analytic studies have derived these following personality dimensions which are termed the Big Five: Extraversion, Neuroticism, Openness to Experience, Agreeableness, and Conscientiousness. Personality research has found these characteristics to be the minimum number of broad trait characteristics necessary to explain variation in personality styles.

Previous research using the Big Five and the Axis II Personality Disorders has revealed no consistent evidence of distinct five-factor profiles to discriminate the seperate disorders. Yet, neuroticism appears to be a core factor of general personality disorder pathology. Conscientious and openness have been found to be least relevant in these investigations.

The authors suggest that extraversion and neuroticism may successfully differentiate a subset of personality disorders. Considering the substantial body of research on these dimensions, it is considered possible to apply existing empirical research to this question. Review of the work of Eysenck on the association between extraversion/neuroticism, biology, and response to the environment is presented. Introverts due to their enhanced cortical arousal would experience more fears and phobias than extroverts. The latter group should show impulsive, self-gratifying, and psychopathic behavior.

Extensions of Eysenck's ideas are provided by Gray who emphasized the dimensions of anxiety and impulsivity. Also, Cloninger added the concept of novelty-seeking, harm avoidance, and reward independence to the dimensions examined.

The present study considered Eysenck's concepts while adding the extensions of Gray and Cloninger for conceptualizing eight of the personality disorders using the Big Five. They concluded that two broad trait dimensions, rather than five, are sufficient for characterizing many of the personality disorders.

Questions for Discussion

1. What are the advantages of identifying core personality traits for personality disorders?

2. The researchers used existing questionnaires in their study. What are the advantages of using existing research instruments?

3. Would the information from this study be useful for clinicians in practice?

FOCUS ON RESEARCH 2

Widiger, T., and Spitzer, R. (1991). "Sex Bias in the Diagnosis of Personality Disorders: Conceptual and Methodological Issues." Clinical Psychology Review, 11, 1-22.

These authors explore the possibility of sex bias in the DSM personaity disorders. The personality disorders that receive the greatest criticism are the histrionic, self-defeating, dependent, and borderline diagnoses. Sex bias is considered to be a systematic deviation from an expected value associated with the sex of the subject. Differential sex prevalence of a disorder can result from biological differences and is not seen as a sex bias.

Sex bias can emerge from sociocultural factors and would be an arbitrary, unnecessary, and socially created differential of prevalence. A sampling sex bias takes place when one gender is overrepresented in a particular setting where a group of subjects is obtained. The third form of sex bias is a diagnostic sex bias which results from false positive or false negative diagnoses. Further categorization of diagnostic sex bias revolves around the two factors of criterion sex bias and assessment sex bias. The former is caused by the criteria used to define a disorder. The latter is produced by deficiencies in test instruments. It is diagnostic sex bias that forms the central criticism against certain DSM categories.

Females have been found to receive diagnoses of borderline, dependent, histrionic, and self-defeating personality disorders at greater frequencies than males. These results could point to a differential sex prevalence and not a diagnostic sex bias. The authors attempt to clarify the issue by examining a number of relevant variables. Previous research has shown the tendency of clinicians to provide different diagnoses for male and female subjets with identical symptoms. This has been demonstrated in numerous studies that found antisocial characteristics usually applied to males and histrionic ones attributed to females.

Other research has shown a tendency for clinicians to attribute healthy characteristics to males rather than females. The bias appears to be the result of interpretations and not the instruments of assessment. False negatives and false positives in diagnosis present a complex issue. The use of semistructured interviews can be one way to diminish the sex bias in false negatives and positives. The authors conclude that sex bias in the personality disorders of DSM is a secondary issue to the central question of the validity of that category of disorders. Research is needed to address the various complexities in the fundamental differentiation between normal and abnormal personality functioning.

Questions for Discussion

1. What sexist stereotypes contribute to sex bias in diagnosis?
2. What role have females had in the diagnosis and treatment of psychological disorders?
3. What training experiences can be used to counteract sex bias?
4. Are males victims of sex bias in such diagnoses as antisocial personality disorder?

FOCUS ON RESEARCH 3

Loeber, R. (1990). "Development and Risk Factors of Juvenile Antisocial Behavior and Delinquency." Clinical Psychology Review, 10, 1-41.

This is a very extensive report on the different risk factors affecting the development of antisocial behavior at different points in the life cycle. The term risk factor, as used by the author, implies that a child has been exposed to a situation that increases the likelihood that a negative outcome of antisocial behavior will occur. The author presents an ordering of the manifestations of antisocial behavior from childhood through adolescence. A preschooler with a difficult temperament may next show hyperactivity. Then in sequence the child develops conduct problems, poor peer relationships, academic problems, covert conduct problems, association with deviant peers, delinquent acts, and recidivism. The author tries to demonstrate the considerable continuity among disruptive behavior over time. With knowledge of this continual developmental pattern, interventions can be devised for specific points on the progression toward delinquency.

A number of risk factors at each point of the line of development toward delinquency are presented by the author. These include biological factors such as toxic substances, and combinations of problem behaviors. The interaction between certain risk factors magnifies the subsequent risk for antisocial behavior. Aggression and theft is one combination that appear to be a "keystone" antisocial behavior. Another significant factor relates to poor academic performance and drug use.

Next, the author identifies a number of social factors that promote juvenile delinquency. These factors include the following: poor supervision, parental uninvolvement, poor discipline, parental rejection, parental criminality, marital problems, and parental absence. These factors have received the greatest attention from researchers. But the list is not considered to be all-inclusive.

All delinquents do not follow the same develomental path toward antisocial acts. Three paths are presented in the article to demonstrate the variations that may occur in children. The children who follow the aggressive/versatile path become the "violent predators." What typifies these children is the large variety of conduct problems present early in life. Usually males are found in this path, and they run the risk of extensive drug use. The second path is called the nonaggressive path. These individuals develop antisocial behaviors late in childhood or early adolescence and usually confine themselves to lying, theft, or truancy. Females dominate in this group and are susceptible to substance abuse. White collar criminals are seen to evolve from this path. The third path is the substance abuse category. Eventual alcoholics and other drug abusers often come from this group.

The author discusses the importance of screening and early intervention. Although some critics warn of "false positives" when trying to screen for antisocial potential, the author justifies the need for intervention because of the seriousness of the problem. Delinquents do not appear suddenly in a community; rather, chronic problematic behavior precedes the antisocial actions by many years.

Questions for Discussion

1. What children are at great risk for the develoment of delinquency?
2. How can the results be used to prevent delinquency problems?

3. Can antisocial disorder be treated successfully?
4. What early interventions are indicated from this study?

FOCUS ON RESEARCH 4

Yager, J., Landsverk, J., Edelstein, C., and Hyler, S. (1989). "Screening for Axis II Personality Disorders in Women with Bulimic Eating Disorders." Psychosomatics, 30, 255-262.

With the advent of the DSM-III-R and its use of Axis II personality disorders, a number of studies have been done to identify personality disorders that are concurrent with other conditions. Little has been completed in correlating personality disorders with eating disorders. The authors of this report examined 628 women for a combination of personality disorders and bulimia.

Their results showed a high prevalence of personality disturbance among patients with eating disorders. The authors suggest further investigation to determine the relationships between the concurrent conditions. Issues of treatment effectiveness and long-term prognosis for bulimia may be influenced by certain personality characteristics present in patients.

READINGS

1. Andreoli, A., Gressot, G., and Aapro, N. (1990). "Personality Disorders as a Predictor of Outcome." Journal of Personality Disorders, 3, 307-321.

2. Arntz, A. (1994). "Treatment of Borderline Personality Disorder: A Challenge for Cogntive-Behavioural Therapy." Behaviour Research and Therapy, 32, 419-430.

3. Bleiberg, E. (1994). "Borderline Disorders in Children and Adolescents: The Concept, the Diagnosis, and the Controversies." Bulletin of the Menninger Clinic, 58, 169-196.

4. Curtis, J., and Susman, V. (1994). "Considerations in Misdiagnosis of Narcissistic Personality Disorder." Psychological Reports, 74, 408-410.

5. Frick, P. Lahey, B., Applegate, B., and Kerdyck, L. (1994). "DSM-IV Field Trials for the Disruptive Behavior Disorders: Syumptom Utility Estimates." Journal of the American Academy of Cyhild and Adolescent Psychiatry, 33, 529-539.

6. Goyer, P., Andreason, P., and Semple, W. (1994). "Positron-Emission Tomography and Personality Disorders." Neuropsychopharmacology, 10, 21-28.

7. Hirschfeld, R., and Holzer, C. (1994). "Depressive Personality Disorder: Clinical Implication." Journal of Clinical Psychology, 55, 10-17.

8. Klar, H., Siever, L., and Caccaro, E. (1988). "Psychobiologic Approaches to Personality and its Disorders: A Review." Journal of Personality Disorders, 2, 334-341.

9. Litvak, S. (1994). "Abrasive Personality Disorder: Definition and Diagnosis." Journal of Contemporary Psychotherapy, 24, 32-45.

10. Perris, C. (1994). "Cognitive Therapy in the Treatment of Patients with Borderline Personality Disorder." Acta Psychiatrica Scandinavica, 89, 69-72.

11. Skodol, An, and Oldham, J. (1994). "Validity of Self-Defeating Personality Disorder." American Journal of Psychiatry, 151, 560-567.

12. Runerson, B., and Beskow, J. (1991). "Borderline Personality Disorder in Young Swedish Suicides." Journal of Nervous and Mental Disease, 179, 153-156.

13. Shearin, E., and Linehan, M. (1993). "Dialectial Behavior Therapy for Borderline Personality Disorder." Acta Psychiatrica Scandinavica, 89, 61-68.

DISCUSSION AND LECTURE IDEAS

1. The use of the Personality Disorder Inventory by targets, spouses, and friends to validate the assessment of personality disorders is presented in a study by F. Cooleridge, and his colleagues (1995). This study discusses the importance of using significant others to supplement objective testing (Journal of Clinical Psychology, 51, 22-28). A class discussion can be focused on the concerns about confidentiality, truthfulness, and problems in reconciling differences in reports from family members and significant others. How can the potential problems be overcome?

2. When are behaviors considered to be abnormal? S. Gridley (1990) discusses the problem of including thrill-seeking behavior as one sign of a personality disorder. Interviews with rock climbers, high-speed motorcyclists, and road racers show they can exhibit considerable impulse control and concern for the safety of others, yet demonstrate thrill-seeking experiences. The author concludes that the extreme arousal attained by these groups is secondary to the sense of mastery over the environment. This source of mastery versus arousal as a major source of satisfaction is considered by the author to differentiate abnormality from normal behavior (Psychology: A Journal of Human Behavior, 27, 18-21).

3. Gardner, D., Leibenluft, E., O'Leary, K., and Cowdry, R. (1991. "Self-Ratings of Anger and Hostility in Borderline Personality Disorder." Journal of Nervous and Mental Disease, 179, 154-161) examined the prevalence of self-reported anger in borderline patients. Using the Buss-Durkee Hostility Inventory, they found borderline patients to have higher scores than normal volunteers. The hostility scores were pervasive throughout the disorder regardless of gender, treatment setting, and presence of depression. Hostility may need to be treated separately by biochemical means. What makes borderline patients difficult to treat? How can a therapist attempt to handle anger in a patient? What is more difficult to treat, a depressed patient or a hostile patient?

4. A good lecture discussion can be developed from an article by James Reich and

Alan Green (1991) on the topic of personality disorder symptoms as they may influence treatment (Journal of Nervous and Mental Disease, 179, 74-82). The recent literature was reviewed to identify what personality pathology may negatively influence therapy outcomes. After students have become familiar with the personality disorders, have them propose the characteristics that would make treatment difficult. How would Axis I disorders be affected by different personality disorders? This article then can be used to evaluate the discussion.

5.   The researchers K. Sher and T. Trull (1994) consider alcohol abuse and antisocial personality to be related concepts (Journal of Abnormal Psychology, 103, 92-102). A lecture can be developed using the concept of disinhibitory psyhchopathology to explain the connections. Personality factors are viewed as important casual variables and not merely static trait descriptions.

6.   Those who exhibit the antisocial personality do not respond to psychological treatment. How, then, should society treat them if they engage in violent or criminal acts? If people could be identified as antisocial before a crime was committed, should they be imprisoned as a preventive measure? Should punishment be assigned equally to antisocial personalities and to criminals without personality disorders? What alternatives are available for the treatment and prevention of antisocial personalities? What ethical problems are involved in treating someone who does not wish to change?

7.   The issues surrounding the antisocial personality can be addressed by asking the class whether there are any advantages in having an antisocial personality disorder. Does the antisocial personality act in his or her own best interests more than anyone else? Does everyone have some degree of antisocial tendencies? What prevents a person from behaving in an antisocial manner more often than typically occurs? How would society function if everyone had an antisocial personality? Could a government function in such a society?

ACTIVITIES AND PROJECTS

1.   The question of when abnormality begins in the personality disorder is often a difficult one to answer. Whether a person with a personality disorder will be viewed as abnormal or not depends on the circumstances in which the behavior is observed. Have students investigate this issue by selecting six or more careers or jobs and indicating how persons with the different personality disorder would perform in the different endeavors. Discussion could then evolve around how certain jobs have requirements that may actually fit certain traits found in the personality disorders. Which disorders do not fit well in almost any job? Which personality disorder has characteristic traits that would be useful in the largest number of careers? If a person's traits fit a particular career, will he or she experience a satisfying life even with a personality disorder?

2.   There continues to be a disagreement about whether personality disorders are distinct from each other and from normal personality. A student or group of students can be assigned the project of researching this issue for a debate. The students can present the debate to the class whose members could vote on which point of view was presented most persuasively. An article by Livesley, Schroeder, Jackson, and Jang (1994) provides important historical information

on this issue and could be a good first resource for the debating students (Journal of Abnormal Psychology, 103, 6-17).

3.	Students can be given the task of measuring narcissism among classmates or volunteers. H. Emmons (1987) provides a short scale for assessing narcissism (Journal of Personality and Social Psychology, 52, 11-17). A brief empirical study could be constructed using the narcissism measure to differentiate individuals, then test them on some task such as having to speak before the class extemporaneously. Other class members could rate the performance. These ratings could be compared to narcissism ratings.

4.	Have students select two people to observe in the course of a week. See if they can identify personality traits found in the diagnostic criteria for any of the personality disorders. This can lead to a discussion of what makes a trait "abnormal" or sufficient to make a diagnosis of personality disorder.

5.	Newman, J., Patterson, C., and Kosson, D. (1987, (Journal of Abnormal Psychology, 96, 145-149), studied prison psychopaths on their performance of card playing tasks involving monetary reward and punishments. Results indicated that psychopaths played significantly more cards and lost more money than the nonpsychopaths, except when the feedback was accompanied by a waiting period that prevented subjects from making another response. The authors consider this finding clinically significant in planning treatment strategies for psychopaths. How can a therapist prevent a patient from acting quickly? Ask students if they often ignore feedback and respond to situations impulsively. What is the outcome?

6.	The students can be assigned to view a movie or play that attempts to depict a personality disorder. Are the portrayals of this form of psychopathology realistic, or are liberties taken when showing a personality disorder in movies, TV, and the stage? What methods are used by writers to indicate to the audience that a character has personality problems? How would the students develop a character for a movie or play that would accurately show a type of personality disorder?

CHAPTER 10

Substance-Related and Other Addictive Disorders

CHAPTER OUTLINE

I. Alcohol Abuse and Dependence
    A.   The clinical picture of alcohol abuse and dependence
        1.   Chronic alcohol use and dependence
            a.   Alcohol is a potentially dangerous poison to our physical health
            b.   Cirrhosis of the liver is found in one of ten excessive drinkers
            c.   The high caloric intake of alcohol can be detrimental
            d.   White blood cell activity can be impaired
        2.   Psychoses associated with alcoholism
            a.   Alcohol withdrawal delirium (delirium tremens) can occur during prolonged drinking or at withdrawal
                1)   Its symptoms can include hallucinations, fear, and marked tremors
                2)   It can last from three to six days
            b.   Alcohol amnestic disorder (Korsakoff's psychosis) has memory defects as its main feature
                1)   Symptoms may be due to vitamin deficiency
                2)   They appear disoriented as they try to fill in gaps
    B.   Causes of alcohol abuse and dependence
        1.   Biological factors
            a.   A genetic vulnerability may cause a craving for alcohol
            b.   Researchers have attempted to identify a prealcoholic personality
                1)   Inherited a predisposition
                2)   Emotionally unstable
                3)   Impulsivity
                4)   Different physiological patterns from nonalcoholics have been found
            c.   Ethnic group research has studied the possibility of genetic influences
         2.   Psychosocial factors
            a.   Failures in parental guidance
            b.   Psychological vulnerability
                1)   Depression and antisocial personality are two disorders

                    commonly associated wih alcoholism
              2)   Not everyone with maladjustments becomes an alcoholic
       c.   Stress, tension reduction, and reinforcement
              1)   Alcoholism may be a learned maladapive response
              2)   Motivational models of alcohol use place responsibility on
                    the individual
       d.   Expectancy for social facilitation
       e.   Marital and other intimate relationships
              1)   Alcohol use may be related to crisis periods
              2)   Codependency is an important area of concern
    3.   Sociocultural factors
       a.   Social drinking has reinforcing properties
       b.   Social change and disintegration contribute to excessive drinking
       c.   Cultural attitudes toward alcohol influence the incidence of
              alcoholism
  C.   Treatment and outcomes
    1.   Biological approaches
       a.   Detoxification procedures focus on eliminating alcohol from the
              body
       b.   Tranquilizers may have more negative outcomes in treatment than
              positives
       c.   Antabuse causes vomiting when alcohol is ingested, and can disrupt
              the alcoholic cycle
    2.   Psychological treatment approaches
       a.   Group therapy
       b.   Environmental interventions
       c.   Behavior therapy
              1)   Aversive conditioning methods employ noxious mental
                    images
              2)   Skills training procedures are aimed at young drinkers
       d.   Alcoholics Anonymous
              1)   Affiliated movements bring family members together
              2)   Rehabilitation lifts the burden of personal responsibility
    3.   Results of treatment
       a.   Long-term studies show the intransigence of alcoholics
       b.   Favorable outcomes relate to personal motivation for change
    4.   Relapse prevention
       a.   The cognitive-behavioral view focuses on alcoholics' thought
              processes
       b.   The "abstinence violation effect" causes minor transgressions to
              be viewed as severe

II.   Drug Abuse and Dependence
  A.   Opium and its derivatives (narcotics)
    1.   Opium and morphine are defined, and how heroin is derived is explained
    2.   Effects of morphine and heroin

  a. Mainlined heroin causes euphoric spasm and a subsequent lethargic, withdrawn state

  b. Withdrawal occurs after extended use within eight hours of a dose

    1) Withdrawal is not always dangerous

    2) Symptoms of withdrawal decline by the fourth day

  c. The life-style of an addict centers around obtaining the drug

  d. Addiction has a number of adverse physical effects

 3. Causal factors in opiate abuse and dependence

  a. Neural bases for physiological addiction

    1) Endorphins are opium like substances in the brain

    2) Research has been inconclusive

  b. Addiction associated with the relief of pain

  c. Addiction associated with psychopathology

    1) Antisocial traits may be involved

    2) Lack of delaying gratification is a factor

  e. Addiction associated with sociocultural factors

 4. Treatment and outcomes

  a. Strategies are similar to those for alcoholism

  b. Methadone treatment was pioneered by a research team at Rockefeller University

B. Cocaine and amphetamines (stimulants)

 1. Cocaine

  a. Middle-to upper-income people have produced an epidemic

  b. Recent evidence shows a decline in usage

  c. A stimulation of the brain's cortex induces excitement

  d. Some tolerance may be found over time

  e. Follow-up studies show increased psychosocial problems over time

  f. Cocaine use can be fatal as in the case of Len Bias

  g. Crack is a "supercharged" variety of cocaine

 2. Amphetamines

  a. Causes and effects of amphetamine abuse

    1) Can cause paranoid thinking

    2) Can lead to lowered impulse control

  b. Treatment and outcomes

    1) Withdrawal is usually painless physically

    2) Depression is a psychological consequence of withdrawal

C. Barbiturates (sedatives)

 1. Effects of barbiturates

  a. Calm patients and induce sleep

  b. Excessive use leads to tolerance and dependence

  c. Brain damage may occur from prolonged ingestion

 2. Causal factors in barbiturate abuse and dependence

  a. Middle-aged persons are susceptible to dependency when used

as "sleeping pills"
    b.   Alcohol is commonly used with the barbiturates
   3.   Treatment and outcome
      a.   Withdrawal symptoms can be dangerous and severe
      b.   Withdrawal symptoms may be limited by other medications

  D.   LSD and related drugs (hallucinogens)
    1.   LSD.
      a.   Research has found it ineffective as a psychological treatment
      b.   "Trips" on the drug can be pleasant or extremel traumatic
      c.   Flashbacks are involuntary recurrences of hallucinations
      d.   Evidence is lacking to show a connection with creativity
    2.   Mescaline and psilocybin
      a.   Ceremonial uses among Indian groups
      b.   Perceptions are altered
  E.   Marijuana
    1.   Effects of marijuana
      a.   Mild euphoria is produced
      b.   Time distortions are often present
      c.   Depressant and hallucinogenic effects are found
      d.   Psychological dependence can occur
  F.   Caffeine and nicotine
    1.   Nicotine is a poisonous alkaloid
    2.   Caffeine
      a.   Withdrawal symptoms are minimal
      b.   Intoxication can produce negative effects
    3.   Treatment of nicotine withdrawal
      a.   Social support groups are commonly used to quit smoking
      b.   Self-help is preferred by smokers

III.   Other Addictive Disorders: Hyperobesity and Pathological Gambling
  A.   Hyperobesity
    1.   Causes of persistent overeating
      a.   Biological factors
        1)   Obesity is related to number of adipose cells
        2)   Endocrine anomalies can be invoked
      b.   Psychosocial factors
        1)   Psychodynamic viewpoints stress fixation at the oral stage
        2)   The externality hypothesis
        3)   Faulty learning may condition obesity
      c.   Sociocultural factors reinforce different standards of beauty
    2.   Treatment of hyperobesity
      a.   Weight-loss group programs
      b.   Fasting or starvation diets
      c.   Anorexigenic drugs

d.   Behavioral management techniques

e.   Outcome research demonstrating a return to obesity is common

    3.   Impact of failed weight-loss treatment programs

B.   Pathological gambling

    1.   Clinical picture in pathological gambling

    2.   Causal factors in pathological gambling

        a.   Limited systematic research exists on the topic

        b.   The condition appears very resistant to extinction

        c.   Pathological gamblers are immature, rebellious, thrill-seeking, and antisocial

        d.   Southeast Asians show extensive problems in this area

    3.   Treatment and outcomes

        a.   Gamblers Anonymous is modeled after AA

        b.   The Brecksville program utilizes inpatient treatment

        c.   This is an addictive disorder that appears on the increase

IV.   Unresolved Issues on the Genetics of Alcoholism

    A.   Genetic factors in alcoholism continue to be investigated

        1.   Adoption studies

        2.   Search for underlying mechanism for transmission of susceptibility

    B.   The current literature leaves the genetic interpretation of alcohol abuse as unproven

LEARNING OBJECTIVES

1.   Define *alcoholic* according to the 1978 President's Commission on Mental Health and summarize the statistics on the number of alcoholics and alcohol-related problems in this country.

2.   Describe three major physiological effects of alcohol and describe several symptoms experienced by individuals who are alcohol-dependent.

3.   Describe some physical ailments that can result from alcoholism and explain how these may lead to interpersonal problems.

4.   Describe four different types of alcoholic psychoses.

5.   Describe the withdrawal symptoms experienced by alcoholics who try to quit and summarize the evidence for genetic factors predisposing some to become alcoholics.

6.   List and describe three major psychosocial factors that may be partially responsible for the development of alcohol-dependence.

7.   Describe several sociocultural factors which may influence one's becoming alcohol-dependent.

8.   Describe several biological and psychosocial interventions that have been used to treat alcohol-dependent persons.

9.   Summarize the research findings on the results of treatment and relapse prevention for alcohol-dependent persons.

10.   Summarize the history of the use of opium and its derivatives over the last five thousand years.

11. Describe the major physical and psychosocial effects of ingesting morphine and heroin.
12. List and explain four major causal factors in the development of opiate-dependence.
13. Describe some psychosocial and biological treatments that have been used as therapy for opiate-dependent individuals and evaluate the success of using methadone hydrochloride.
14. Describe some of the effects of barbiturate abuse, list some of its causes, and summarize the dangers of withdrawal from this class of drugs.
15. Describe some causes and effects of amphetamine abuse and note some physical and psychological effects of withdrawal.
16. Describe some physical and psychological effects of ingesting cocaine and some symptoms that are experienced in withdrawal.
17. Describe the physical and psychological effects of using LSD and note the treatment used for the acute psychoses induced by its use.
18. Compare the effects of using mescaline and psilocybin with those of ingesting LSD.
19. Describe the physical and psychological effects of marijuana use and explain why it has been compared to heroin.
20. List five controversies that have arisen concerning the use of marijuana and summarize what we know about each.
21. Define *hyperobesity* and list some biological, psychosocial, and sociocultural factors that underlie its development.
22. Describe and evaluate several biological and psychosocial interventions that have been used to treat hyperobesity.
23. Define *pathological gambling* and describe its symptoms.
24. Summarize what is known about the causes of and treatments for pathological gambling.

KEY TERMS

addictive behavior
toxicity
psychoactive substance dependence
withdrawal symptoms
alcoholism
morphine
heroin
methadone
amphetamines
hallucinogens
flashback
psilocybin
hashish
nicotine

psychoactive drugs
psychoactive substance abuse
tolerance
alcoholic
opium
pathological gambling
endorphines
barbiturates
cocaine
LSD
mescaline
marijuana
caffeine
hyperobesity

FOCUS ON RESEARCH 1

Widiger, T., and Smith, G. (1994). "Substance Use Disorder: Abuse, Dependence, and Dyscontrol." Addiction, 89, 267-282.

This article reviews the changing diagnostic concepts of substance abuse and substance dependence as indicated historically in the DSM leading to the current DSM-IV. Initially the DSM provided a fairly clear conceptualization of substance dependence. The conceptual definition of substance abuse was defined by exclusion which included a pattern, impairment, and duration. When the concepts were revised it was initially in response to critiques of early definitions.

For the DSM-IV, a number of options for revision were considered. The criteria set is expanded representing the most likely impairments that would result from any dyscontrol in the use of a substance. One impairment is required but the criteria set attempts to differentiate dyscontrol from voluntary misuse by requiring the impairment be recurrent within a twelve month period.

The authors make a number of recommendations to enhance diagnosis in this area. They suggest collapsing the abuse and dependence criteria set into one, replacing the substance dependence with the term dyscontrol disorder, including physiological substance dependence as a separate diagnosis, and abandoning substance abuse as a meaningful distinction.

Questions for Discussion

1.   How useful are DSM classifications for substance abuse?

2.   What is the advantage of providing formal diagnoses for various substance abuse?

FOCUS ON RESEARCH 2

Alois-Young, P., Graham, J., and Hansen,W. (1994). "Peer Influence on Smoking Initiation During Early Adolescence: A Comparison of Group Members and Group Outsiders." Journal of Applied Psychology, 79, 281-287.

There exists a substantial research record showing peer influences to be at the heart of adolescent substance use. Because of these findings, prevention programs often try to assist adolescents in their resistance to peer pressure. Correlational evidence shows a strong relationship between adolescent smoking and alcohol use, and the use among friends. The authors suggest that teenagers may be influenced not only by their friends but by the behavior of future or desired friends. Thus, their conformity may be the result of trying to secure a desired friendship or entry into a targeted friendship group.

These authors examined behavior of adolescents in relationship to desired friends who they termed unilateral friends, and established friends which were identified as reciprocal friends. Persons without any reciprocal friends were classified as group outsiders, while those with these friends were considered to be members of a friendship group. They examined the smoking initiation behavior of seventh graders in the context of peer influences.

They found that adolescents who were not established members of a friendship group were influenced more by the smoking of their best friend than group members. Group outsiders were found to be twice as likely to begin smoking if their best friend was a smoker than if the person was a non-smoker. They concluded that desired friends exerted the most important influence on smoking initiation during adolescence. They viewed smoking as a conforming behavior related to keeping and making friends.

Questions for Discussion

1.   What other behaviors are influenced by the behavior of desired friends?

2.   What behavior among college students is dictated by peer pressures?

3.   How can this type of conformity be minimized or prevented?

FOCUS ON RESEARCH 3

Marin, G, Marin, B., Perez-Stable, Sabogel, F., and Otero-Sabogel, R. (1990). "Changes in Information as a Function of a Culturally Appropriate Smoking Cessation Community Intervention for Hispanics." American Journal of Community Psychology, 18, 847-864.

This is an extensive report on a community intervention program using the media and lasting for seven months to reduce smoking among a Hispanic population. Although Hispanics traditionally show slightly lower smoking rates than non-Hispanic whites, smoking rates of adolescent males are similar to non-Hispanics and may be increasing. Few prevention programs have targeted Hispanic populations, and fewer still are developed with a cultural sensitivity to the Hispanics.

This paper reports on a unique attempt to incorporate culture-specific attitudes, expectancies, norms, and values into an intervention program. Within a non-Hispanic white population, mass media smoking cessation community interventions are successful in creating the desired behavioral changes. Role models and the availability of written materials serve as mediators for success in mass media programs. The differences in the Hispanic culture from the non-Hispanic white one, required a special intervention program to be designed. For example, Hispanics appear more concerned about both short-term effects of smoking and social smoking than non-Hispanic whites.

Targeted at San Francisco Hispanics, the authors sought to lower smoking prevalence, increase awareness of the health consequences of smoking, and enhance awareness of smoking cessation services available to the Hispanic smokers. The materials used in the program reflected important Hispanic cultural values such as familialism, power distance, Respecto, and Simpatia (the value of smooth social relations). The authors designed messages to be presented on television, radio, posters, billboards, bus cards, bumper stickers, newspapers, pamphlets, and fliers. Free cessation clinics and a Spanish language self-help manual were also offered to the target population. The effectiveness of the intervention was determined through two preintervention surveys compared to a postintervention survey.

Results showed an increased level of awareness and information about the effects of cigarette smoking. The greatest effects were found among those Hispanics with the least acculturation. The authors do not report on changes in smoking prevalence since they view this as a slow change that requires later assessment. But they conclude that short-term effects were very positive and demonstrate the value of promoting culturally sensitive intervention programs.

Questions for Discussion

1. Is the white culture so similar that genetic prevention programs are appropriate?
2. What other cultural groups in this country would benefit from the approaches used by these researchers?
3. What other potentially harmful behaviors can be modified by a community-based intervention program?
4. Do advertisements reflect cultural issues when trying to sell products?

READINGS

1. Barnes, G., and Banerjee, S. (1994). "Family Influences on Alcohol Abuse and Other Problems Behaviors Among Black and White Adolescents in a General Population Sample." Journal of Research on Adolescence, 4, 183-201.

2. Blackson, T. (1995). "Temperament and IQ Mediate the Effects of Family History of Substance Abuse and Family Dysfunction on Academic Achievement." Journal of Clinical Psychology, 51, 113-122.

3. Bowen, A., and Trotter, R. (1995). "HIV Risk in Introveneous Drug Users and Crack Cocaine Smokers: Predicting Stage of Change for Condom Use." Journal of Consulting and Clinical Psychology, 63, 238-248.

4. Comings, D., Muhleman, D., and Gysin, R. (1994). "The Dopamine D-Sub-21 Receptor Gene: A Genetic Risk Factor in Substance Abuse." Drug and Alcohol Dependence, 34, 175-180.

5. Fals-Stewart, W. (1995). "The Effect of Defensive Responding by Substance Abusing Patients on the Millon Clinical Multiaxial Inventory." Journal of Personality Assessment, 64, 540-551.

6. Friedmanm, M, and Musgrove, J. (1994). "Perceptions of Inner City Substance Abusers About Their Families." Archives of Psychiatric Nursing, 8, 115-123.

7. Fergusson, D., and Lynskey, M. (1994). "The Comorbiditeis of Adolescent Problem Behaviors: A Latent Class Model." Journal of Abnormal Child Psychology, 22, 339-354.

8. Finn, P., and Kessler, D. (1994). "Risk for Alcoholism and Classical Conditioning to Signals for Punishments: Evidence for a Weak Behavioral Inhibition System." Journal of Abnormal Psychology, 103, 293-301.

9.   Hughes, J. (1994). "Protracted withdrawal." <u>American Journal of Psychiatry</u>, <u>151</u> 785-786.

10.   Moos, R. (1994). "Why Do Some People Recover From Alcohol Dependence, Whereas Others Continue to Drink and Become Worse Over Time?" <u>Addiction</u>, <u>89</u>, 31-34.

11.   Nicholson, T., Higgins, W., Turner, P., and James, S. (1994). "The Relation Between Meaning in Life and the Occurrence of Drug Abuse: A Retrospective Study." <u>Psychology of Addictive Behaviors</u>, <u>8</u>, 24-28.

12.   Pickens, R., Svikis, D., Lykken, D., and Clayton, P. (1991). "Heterogeneity in the Inheritance of Alcoholism: A Study of Male and Female Twins." <u>Archives of General Psychiatry</u>, <u>48</u>, 19-28.

13.   Prasher, V. P., and Corbett, J. A. (1990). "Aerosol Addiction." <u>British Journal of Psychiatry</u>, <u>157</u>, 922-924.

14.   Rodriquez, M. (1994). "Influence of Sex and Family History of Alcoholism on Cognitive Functioning in Heroin Users." <u>European Journal of Psychiatry</u>, <u>8</u>, 29-36.

15.   Swet, C., and Halpert, M. (1994). "High Rates of Alcohol Problems and History of Physical and Sexual Abuse Among Women Inpatients." <u>American Journal of Drug and Alcohol Abuse</u>, <u>20</u>, 263-272.

16.   Walters, G. (1994). "The Drug Lifestyle: One Pattern or Several?" <u>Psychology of Addictive Behaviors</u>, <u>8</u>, 8-13.

DISCUSSION AND LECTURE IDEAS

1.   Students can be assigned the task of developing the "ideal" treatment program for adolescent substance abuse clients. What factors do they consider to be important in the development of a program for this age group? How would they measure success for participants in their programs? An article by S. Brown and her colleagues (1994) can serve as a good resource for this exercise (<u>Applied and Preventive Psychology</u>, <u>3</u>, 61-73).

2.   Should employees be trained to detect substance abuse in follow workers? A classroom discussion or debate can be developed around this questions. What are the reasons for watching other workers for signs of substance abuse? Would this influence the work atmosphere? An article by M. Gossop (1994) can serve as a resources for this classroom debate (<u>Addictive Behaviors</u>, <u>19</u>, 127-134). The author describes a training program for staff recognition of substance abuse.

3.   When is drinking considered to be a problem? S. Heck (1991, <u>Journal of American College Health</u>, <u>39</u>, 227-231) provides a brief screening questionnaire to identify alcoholism. The author found many current screening instruments to be inadequate for detecting the less severe

pattern of problem drinking in college students. What are some of the factors that differentiate alcoholism from college student problem drinking? How useful is such a screening device for college students? Should all college drinkers be given such a screening instrument? How open are college students to receiving treatment for problem drinking?

4.   How do drugs become outlawed in our society? Some drugs that are now controlled were once freely available. Discuss the social, political, and religious issues surrounding the targeting of certain substances for legal control.

5.   The drugs described in this chapter are often used in conjunction with social and sexual behavior. Have the class discuss their impressions about the effects of alcohol, marijuana, and other drugs on sexual interaction and social activities. What effects do these drugs have on aggression? Have students share their views.

6.   How should local, state, and federal money and resources be used to counter drug abuse? Should attention be focused on the enforcement of laws? On changing the laws? On educating the public about drug effects? Should society be protected from drugs even though there is a ready market for them?

7.   Our society is currently emphasizing weight control. What are the attitudes of students regarding obesity? Do students accept the drug user more than the obese person? What stigmas exist among students regarding the addictions discussed in the text? Which disorder has the greatest stigma?

ACTIVITIES AND PROJECTS

1.   Students can be asked to investigate the connection between conduct problems in adolescence and substance abuse. Do they see a connection in college student behavior? What was their experience with children who showed conduct problems. They can interview teachers at a local elementary school for their thoughts on this matter. A research article by E. Maguin and H. Fitzgerald (1994) provides some interesting findings on this topic (Journal of Research on Adolescence, 4 249-269). This article also discusses ways of preventing conduct problems in dysfunctional families.

2.   A number of organizations have been formed to work for change in the laws governing drug use. Such organizations as NORML advocate the legalization of marijuana. Have students investigate such groups and report on their philosophies and methods to liberalize drug laws. Are the groups using up-to-date information concerning the substance discussed in the text?

3.   If possible, students may be able to atend a meeting of such groups as AA or Al-Ateen. They could report on the meeting and the dynamics observed. Representatives from a group designed to treat alcoholics may be invited to discuss alcoholism with the class.

4.   Before the substance abuse material is covered in the textbook, complete a classroom exercise in which students are asked to produce a profile of the young adult at greatest

risk for substance abuse. Select different drugs (e.g., alcohol, cocaine, crack) and have students prepare a risk profile for each. Students working in groups usually produce profiles reflecting their experience and perception of substance abusers. How similar are student perceptions of risk factors with those presented in the psychological literature? Are some drugs seen more negatively than others by the students (i.e., does a risk profile include more negative personal factors than another)? If the students can identify risk profiles for various drugs, can individuals benefit from prevention programs? What factors contributed most to the students' ideas about risk factors?

5.   The Adolescent Self-Efficacy Scale can be used to demosntrate the mediating processes in behavior change. This scale was developed by J. St. Mary and M. Russo (1991) to assess the perceptions of self-efficacy in potentially stressful situations for chemically dependent adolescents (Psychology: A Journal of Human Behavior, 28, 62-68). If substance abuse is related to situational stressors, coping behaviors to deal with the stress need to be enhanced. This scale can provide for discussion about appropriate treatment of adolescent substance abusers and identification of situations that could lead to chemical usage among adolescents.

6.   Because drug use on university campuses is a continuing concern, a representative from the student personnel services may be invited to speak before the class. What is the drug use situation on campus? What measures has the university administration taken to deal with any identified problems?

CHAPTER 11

Sexual Disorders and Variants

CHAPTER OUTLINE

I. Sociocultural Influences on Sexual Practices and Standards
    A. Case 1: Degeneracy and abstinence theory
        1. Early formation of degeneracy theory by Tissot
        2. Sylvester Graham and abstinence theory
    B. Case 2: Ritualized homosexuality in Melanesia
        1. Semen conservation
        2. Female pollution
    C. Case 3: Homosexuality and Amerian Psychiatry
        1. Homosexuality as a sickness
        2. Homosexuality as a nonpathological variation
II. Sexual Variants
    A. The paraphilias
        1. Fetishism
            a. Masturbation often accompanies the fetishistic behavior
            b. Antisocial behaviors and fire setting are often found with this condition
            c. Learning can be involved in its development
            d. Feelings of inadequacy may be controlled by the behavior
        2. Transvestic fetishism
            a. Males are usually found in this category
            b. Transvestites typically do not show other psychopathology
            c. Conditioning models are used to explain its development
        3. Voyeurism
            a. Curiosity is satisfied in shy and inhibited youngsters through this behavior
            b. Suspense and danger add to the experience
            c. A sense of power maintains the behavior
            d. Permissive pornography laws may provide alternatives for the voyeur
        4. Exhibitionism
            a. Exposure is consistent in type of situation and sex object
            b. A subtype with antisocial characteristics may be present

                c.   Three categories are found
                      1)   Personal immaturity
                      2)   Interpersonal stress
                      3)   Associated with other psychopathology

5. Sadism
   a. Bondage and discipline is a closely related pattern
   b. Sexual gratification can come from the sadistic practice alone
   c. Objects or animals can be targets of the sadism
   d. Causal factors include a conditioning of sexual arousal to pain, negative attitudes about sex, and other psychopathology

6. Masochism
   a. Pain is associated with sexual pleasure
   b. Complementary relationships are formed

B. Causal Factors for Paraphilias
   1. Usually found in males
   2. Typically more than one found in a person

C. Gender identity disorders
   1. Gender identity disorder of childhood
      a. Learning and psychosocial influences are of paramount importance
      b. Variants are probably not due to learning
      c. The gender identity disorders are fairly rare
   2. Transsexualism
      a. Surgery and hormone treatment are used
      b. Outcome studies show an approximate two-thirds success rate in treatment
      c. Trial periods are needed before surgery to identify the mentally disturbed
   3. Treatment

III. Sexual Abuse
   A. Childhood sexual abuse
      1. Prevalence of childhood sexual abuse
      2. Consequences of childhood sexual abuse
      3. Controversies concerning childhood sexual abuse
      4. Children's testimony
      5. Recovered memories of sexual abuse
   B. Pedophilia
      1. The manipulation of the child's genitals is usually involved
      2. Long-term negative effects on the victims have been documented
      3. Patterns are found in the victims and perpetrators of the abuse
      4. Subtypes of pedophiles have not proven to be reliable
   C. Incest
      1. Historical considerations about incest are presented
      2. The incidence may be under-reported in our society
      3. No single explanation is appropriate for understanding its cause
         a. Situational
         b. Associated with severe psychopathology

        c.   Associated with pedophilia
        d.   Faulty parental models
        e.   Disturbed marital relations
    4.   The effects on the victim are influenced by age and guilt
        a.   Heterosexual relations can be impaired
        b.   Risk for other emotional problems increases

D. Rape
1. Prevalence
2. Is rape motivated by sex or aggression
3. Psychological trauma is usually severe for the victim
4. Rapists

E. Treatment and recidivism of sexual offenders
1. These are difficult to treat successfully
    a. Aversive conditioning has been used successfully
    b. Ways to teach social skills effectively are needed
2. It is difficult to maintain therapeutic achievements

IV. Sexual Dysfunctions

A. Dysfunctions of Sexual Desire
1. Sexual desire disorder
    a. Hypoactive sexual desire disorder
        1) Little or no sexual drive is present
        2) What is "not enough" of sexual interest is debatable
    b. Sexual aversion disorder
        1) Sex is psychologically aversive

B. Dysfunctions of sexual arousal
2. Male erectile disorder
    a. Primary and secondary erectile insufficiency are the two subtypes
    b. Insufficiency before age sixty is usually due to psychological factors
    c. Aging can influence the reliability of the erectile response
    d. Differentiating psychogenic from organic insufficiency is a complex process
3. Female sexual arousal disorder
    a. This involves an absence of arousal and unresponsiveness to stimulation
    b. Primary nonresponsiveness to erotic stimuli is rare
    c. Various situational and previous experiences can produce this disorder

C. Orgasmic Disorders
1. Premature ejaculation
    a. Exact definition of this condition does not exist
    b. Self-treatment through masturbation can be effective
    c. Distraction and conscious control can be used to minimize the problem
2. Male orgasmic disorder
    a. Social concerns can prevent a person from seeking treatment for this condition

b.   The problem is usually one of psychological inhibition and overcontrol
3.   Female orgasmic disorder
    a.   "Extra" stimulation is required for orgasm
    b.   No amount of stimulation can produce orgasm in primary orgasmic dysfunction
    c.   What entails "extra" stimulation is very subjective
D.   Dysfunctions Involving Sexual Pain
    1.   Vaginismus
        a.   Muscles at the vaginal entrance appear to be conditioned toward intense contradiction at penetration
        b.   Multiple causal links can be associated with this distressing disorder
    2.   Dyspareunia
        a.   Painful sexual intercourse is more common in females than males
        b.   Infections or structural pathology maybe present
E.   Causal factors in sexual dysfunctions
    1.   Dysfunctional learning
        a.   Sexual techniques and attitudes are often learned informally
        b.   Social attitudes about sex may promote inhibitions and anxiety
        c.   Female sexual learning may have emphasized a passive role
        d.   Male's masturbatory experiences may be counter-productive to love relationships
    2.   Feelings of fear, anxiety, and inadequacy
        a.   Research evidence shows the importance of anxiety in dysfunctions
        b.   Fears of inadequacy can lead to pretending to have orgasms
        c.   Masters and Johnson focus on faulty learning and poor communication
    3.   Interpersonal problems
        a.   Lack of emotional closeness can lead to sexual dysfunctions
        b.   Hostility and antagonistic feelings are related to sexual functioning
    4.   Changing male-female roles and heterosexual relationships
        a.   The new female role has challenged many males
        b.   The female's active role in sexuality has stressful consequences
        c.   Sexually transmitted disease has produced anxiety
F.   Treatment and outcomes
    1.   New methods of treatment attack the dysfunction directly
    2.   Masters and Johnson's <u>Human Sexual Inadequacy</u> was a turning point
        a.   Relationships are often at the root of sexual dysfunctions
        b.   Success in treatment has approached 100 percent
    3.   Quality of therapy varies greatly
V.   Unresolved Issues: Long-term Consequences of Childhood Sexual Abuse
    A.   The Role of Abuse in the Development of Various Disorders
    B.   Prospective Studies are needed in this field of study

LEARNING OBJECTIVES

1. List and describe four sexual dysfunctions that affect men.
2. List and describe three sexual dysfunctions that affect women.
3. List and describe two sexual dysfunctions that may affect both men and women.
4. List and explain four factors that may cause sexual dysfunctions.
5. Describe the recent revolution in the treatment of sexual dysfunctions and explain why they are not normally disorders of individuals.
6. Differentiate between *victimless* and *nonconsent* types of sexual variations and list several examples of each.
7. Summarize the results of research concerning biological and psychosocial causes of gender identity disorders and evaluate sex reassignment surgery as a solution.
8. Define *paraphilias* and list nine examples recognized in DSM-IV.
9. Define *fetishism*, give several examples, and summarize what is known about its causes.
10. Define *transvestic fetishism* and summarize what is known about its causes.
11. Define *voyeurism*, list two other terms that are synonyms, and summarize what is known about its causes.
12. Define *exhibitionism* and describe types of causes that may underlie the practice.
13. Define *sexual sadism* and describe three sets of causes for this disorder.
14. Define *sexual masochism* and summarize what is known about its causes.
15. Define *pedophilia* and describe four sets of causes for this disorder.
16. Define *incest*, describe five sets of causes for this disorder, and summarize what is known about the psychological effects on its victims.
17. Differentiate between *forcible* and *statutory* rape and describe three sets of motives which may influence the rapist.
18. Summarize what is known about the successful treatment of sexual variants and deviations.

KEY TERMS

sexual dysfunction
premature ejaculation
male orgasmic disorder
female orgasmic disorder
hypoactive sexual desire disorder
sexual aversion disorder
transsexualism
fetishism
voyeurism
sadism
pedophilia
rape
gender dysphoria

male erectile disorder
sexual abuse
female sexual arousal disorder
dyspareunia
vaginismus
gender identity disorder
paraphilias
transvestic fetishism
exhibitionism
masochism
incest
cross-gender identification

FOCUS ON RESEARCH 1

Babinski, S., and Reyes, A. (1994). "Identity Formation in Adolescence: Case Study of Gender Identity Disorder and Treatment Through an Intermediate Care Day Hospital." <u>Psychiatric Quarterly</u>, <u>65</u>, 121-133.

The authors present an extensive case study of a psychiatrically disturbed nineteen year-old male who is a transvestite. The subject was born in Puerto Rico and demonstrated normal developmental milestones. His mother and father separated after his father was imprisoned for drug charges. The subject currently lives with his mother and step-father together with two step-siblings. The subject showed a number of problems during his childhood including language deficits, verbal aggressiveness, suicide attempts, impulsivity, and difficult behavior for his teachers to manage.

He showed signs of cross-dressing for several years, and was obsessed with being a girl. He claimed he had a uterus and would soon begin menstruating. He also was reported a past history of audible hallucinations. The patient required repeated hospitalizations for his suicidal and homicidal intentions.

His childhood history showed a preference for playing with girls and gender type toys. He claimed that he always wanted to be a girl and first dressed as one when he was ten years old. When he is alone he dresses in female attire, elaborate hair styles, applies fingernail polish, and makeup. In his community many individuals call him "she."

The article provides extensive details about his treatment experiences for the numerous problems he was experiencing. The conclusion of the article shows how individuals often do not reach a satisfactory conclusion to their treatment, as he was discharged when he became overage for the treatment program.

Questions for Discussion

1. What are the various factors contributng to identity formation in adolescence?

2. What type of reactions would someone similar to this person receive from peers and family?

3. How can the inadequacies in treatment programs for difficult cases be overcome?

FOCUS ON RESEARCH 2

Kafka, M. (1991). "Successful Antidepressant Treatment of Nonparaphilic Sexual Addictions and Paraphilias in Men." <u>Journal of Clinical Psychiatry</u>, <u>52</u>, 60-65.

The author reports on the treatment of ten men evaluated for paraphilias using the DSM criteria.

The paraphilias are sexual disorders which have intensely arousing fantasies, urges, or behaviors that are not part of the sexual arousal pattern norms. The nonparaphilic sexual addictions are culturally acceptable sexual interests which have increased in frequency to a point which inhibits sustained intimate sexual relationships. Some examples of the nonparaphilic addictions include compulsive masturbation, telephone sex, and repetitive promiscuity.

The author's treatment strategy for his sample of cases is based upon a comorbidity of affective disorder in males with paraphilias. The subjects were evaluated using the Sexual Outlet Inventory, a structured Intake Questionnaire, and the Inventory to Diagnose Depression. The author's ten cases showed sexual addiction or paraphilia in the following forms: excessive masturbation, phone sex, exhibitionism, addiction to pornography, sadism, masochism, transvestic fetishism, voyeurism, and promiscuity. The author provides brief case descriptions of each with past diagnoses. All of the patients exhibited high sexual drive behaviors at some time. The author concluded that they could be classified as exhibiting hypersexuality, and the hypersexuality may be a neurovegetative symptom of depressive disorder.

The cases reported an onset of depressive symptoms early in life and fit the DSM typology of dysthymia. The patients were treated with the antidepressants Fluoxetine and Imipramine. All of the patients, except for one with severe masochism and transvestic fetishism, experienced substantial and sustained improvement in sexual symptoms while taking the antidepressants.

The author does address a number of shortcomings for this study. The small sample size and data collection by a single clinician could have biased the results. The self-report measures may have been inadequate, and supportive psychotherapy received by the patients may have confounded the results. And the antidepressant medications have a potential side effect of diminishing sexual disorder. This article can be useful for class discussion since it presents potential problems in design and methods for the reader.

Questions for Discussion

1. What leads a person with a paraphilia to treatment?
2. What are some of the maladaptive qualties of the sexual addictions?
3. Should phone sex services be limited or banned?

FOCUS ON RESEARCH 3

Safir, M., and Almagor, M. (1991). "Psychopathology Associated with Sexual Dysfunction." Journal of Clinical Psychology, 47, 17-27.

The authors investigated the association between sexual disorders and psychological functioning. They contend that adequate sexual functioning requires a balance between physiological and psychological factors. Since the DSM-III, sexual disorders have been removed from the general category of neuroses and given a separate classification. A number of viewpoints attempt to explain sexual disorders. Family-system theory views the disorders as resulting from faulty interactions in the couple. Inadequate sex education and personal value systems can also inhibit sexual expression. Previous research that attempts to find psychological disorders coexisting with the sexual ones has produced inconclusive outcomes.

This study examined a group of patients at a sex therapy clinic and compared them to a control group without sexual problems. The subjects were administered a variety of measures including the MMPI and the Leif and Ebhart Sexual Performance Evaluation Questionnaire. Four groups of sexual disorders among the clinic sample were identified: sexual desire disorder, erectile disorder, orgasm disorder, and premature ejaculation.

Results on the MMPI showed significant differences on the profiles for the treatment groups. Disorders associated with the earlier phases of the sexual cycle (i.e., appetitive and excitement) had a higher degree of self-reported symptomatology. Thus, males who are suffering from erectile disorder tend to be more depressed, stressed, and anxious than males who suffer from premature ejaculation. This distinction was clearer for males than for the female subjects. The authors speculate that the distinction between stages is less clear for women than it is for men. Premature ejaculation represents a clear sign for the male, while orgasmic problems in women show no such obvious signal.

This study can demonstrate some of the difficulties inherent in sexual dysfunction investigations. Clear definitions for males and females may be difficult to attain when categorizing sexual disorders. The subjective nature of sexual expression may contribute to difficulties in research.

Questions for Discussion

1.   What social factors contribute to sexual disorder?
2.   Why were the sexual disorders removed from the anxiety classification?
3.   Explain how faulty communications between individuals in a sexual relationship can lead to sexual disorders.

FOCUS ON RESEARCH 4

Blanchard, R., and Collins, P. (1993). "Men with Sexual Interest in Transvestites, Transsexuals, and She-Males." The Journal of Nervous and Mental Disease, 181, 570-575.

The authors present an interesting article that can supplement textbook material on gynandromorphophilia. This is the sexual interest in cross-dressing or anatomically feminized men. These individuals remain an obscure group to clinicians and scientists since they seldom request psychiatric or psychological services.

Their interests are primarily noted in selected pornography or personal advertisements for sexual partners. They seek pornography devoted to images of feminized males with either a she-male appearance or a transvestitic type with men dressed as women while exposing their genitals. The former image, that of the she-male, refers to a man who has achieved a female chest contour with breast implants or hormonal medication. Yet they still retain their male genitalia. The she-male pornography emphasizes the simultaneous presence of male primary and female secondary sexual characteristics.

Although few people are aware of this condition, the authors found it to be fairly well known among prostitutes and persons in the pornography industry. The authors studied this phenomenon through the voice mail services devoted to personal advertisements for sexual and romantic partners. They concluded from analysis of the advertisements that gynandromorphophilia constitutes a separate erotic interest different from the familiar cross-dressing population.

Questions for Discussion

1. How familiar is the general population to the variety of possible paraphilias?

2. What are some of the contributing factors in the development of such conditions as described in this study?

3. Should treatment be provided for individuals similar to those described in this article?

READINGS

1. Darling, C., Davidson, J., and Cox, R. (1991). "Female Sexual Response and the Timing of Partner Orgasm." Journal of Sex and Marital Therapy, 17, 3-21.

2. Grubin, D.,and Thornton, D. (1994). "A National Program for the Assessment and Treatment of Sex Offenders in the English Prison System." Criminal Justice and Behavior, 21, 55-71.

3. Hirshkovitz, M., Karacan, I., Howell, J., and Williams, R. (1990). "Nocturnal Penile Tumescence and Marital Status in Men with Erectile Dysfunction." Journal of Sex Education and Therapy, 16, 92-100.

4. Freund, K, and Blanchard, R. (1993). "Erotic Target Location Errors in Male Gender Dysphorics, Paedophiles, and Fetishists." British Journal of Psychiatry, 162, 558-563.

5. Mass, M., and Al-Krenawi, A. (1994). "When a Man Encounters a Woman, Satan is Also Present: Clinical Relationships in Bedouin Society." American Journal of Orthopsychiatry, 64, 357-346.

6. Maybach, K, and Gold, S. (1994). "Hyperfemininity and Attraction to Macho and Non-Macho Men." The Journal of Sex Research, 31, 91-98.

7. McCabe, M. (1994). "The Influence of the Quality of Relationship on Sexual Dysfunction." Australian Journal of Marriage and Family, 15, 2-8.

8. McCarthy, J., and McMillan, S. (1990). "Patient/Partner Satisfaction with Penile Implant Surgery." Journal of Sex Education and Therapy, 16, 25-38.

9.   Meyer-Bahlburg, H. (1994). "Intersexuality and the Diagnosis of Gender identity Disorder." Archives of Sexual Behavior, 23, 21-40.

10.   Roehrich, L., and Kinder, B. (1991). "Alcohol Expectancies and Male Sexuality: Review and Implications for Sex Therapy." Journal of Sex and Marital Therapy, 17, 45-54.

11.   Serlin, R., Malcolm, P., Barbaree, H. (1994). "Psychopathy and Deviant Sexual Arousal in Incarcerated Sexual Offenders." Journal of Interpersonal Violence, 9, 3-11.

12.   Shikai, X. (1990). "Treatment of Impotence in Traditional Chinese Medicine." Journal of Sex Education and Therapy, 16, 198-200.

13.   Weinberg, T. S. (1987). "Sadomasochism in the United States: A Review of Recent Sociological Literature." Journal of Sex Research, 23, 50-69.

14.   Wilson, G., and Wilson, L. (1991). "Treatment Acceptability of Alternative Sex Therapies: A Comparative Analysis." Journal of Sex and Marital Therapy, 17, 35-45.

DISCUSSION AND LECTURE IDEAS

1.   An interesting lecture can involve the use of denial among sex offenders. C. Jackson and B. Thomas-Peter (1994) report on working with sex offenders in treatment groups (Criminal Behavior and Mental Health, 4, 21-32). They found that two factors of denial emerged among the offenders: denial of factors about the offense and denial of responsibility. This class lecture could stimulate discussion concerning how to deal with these forms of denial, and goals of mental health professionals working with sex offenders. The Denial Questionnaire used in this study could also be a classroom demonstration.

2.   Individuals taking medications for a number of medical conditions may experience sexual dysfunction as a side-effect of their treatment. How does this affect the utilization of the medications and how does it influence the psychological adjustment of the patient? R. Rosen and his associates (1994) report on the sexual sequelae of various medications (Archives of Sexual Behavior, 23, 135-152). This article reporting on middle age males could form the foundation of an infomative lecture-discussion on the topic.

3.   Sexual reassignment is often a topic found to be of interest among students. A lecture on this topic can be developed around the article by J. Noble and K. McConkey (1995) who suggested a change of sex among a group of hypnotic suggestible persons (Journal of Consulting and Clinical Psychology, 104, 69-74.). The researchers found that virtuoso participants showed a transient delusion about their sex that was resistant to change or challenge.

4.   Inhibited sexual desire is a fairly recent addition to the psychiatric nomenclature. Little research has been completed on the frequency of hypoactive sexual desire disorders. J. Segraves and S. Segraves (1991) provide some current evidence on the frequency of this disorder

and its comorbidity with other conditions. Questions surrounding the problems of diagnosis and definition of hypoactive sexual desire disorder can be addressed in class and lead to a good discussion (Journal of Sex and Marital Therapy, 17, 55-59).

5.   What are students' attitudes about the sexual dysfunctions reviewed in this chapter? What associations do students have to such terms as frigidity and impotence? What connotations do these terms have? How do students describe persons who experience these sexual dysfunctions? This discussion can examine current student attitudes surrounding sexual performance and expression.

6.   What areas of behaviors should be considered out of the norm? Have students discuss the possibility of society accepting the different paraphilias. There are groups that advocate free sexual expression and the "freedom" of a child to have sexual relations with an older adult. How do students feel about removing sanctions against all forms of sexual activity?

7.   When should a person be advised to seek help for a sexual dysfunction? What would the class members do if a friend or roommate complained of some sexual problem?

8.   H. Heiman and P. LoPeiolo (1988) published a book called Becoming Orgasmic: A Sexual and Personal Growth Program for Women, (New York: Prentice-Hall), which gives the reader a series of interventions aimed at treating sexual dysfunction. This is a self-help book that is sensitive, informative, and very readable. The program described can illustrate for classroom discussion an empirically based intervention strategy for female sexual dysfunction. The manner of presentation helps to dispel some common sexual myths which can promote classroom discussion.

ACTIVITIES AND PROJECTS

1.   Students can investigate the current legal restrictions and laws associated with sexual behavior discussed in this chapter. What laws are broken and what are the legal penalties for the various behaviors? How have the laws changed in recent times? Are state legislatures pressured to pass laws controlling certain actions today?

2.   A panel discussion could be developed concerning how sexual dysfunctions may influence a relationship. Have students take different sides to this issue and explore different dysfunctions. Would the relationship continue depending upon the type of dysfunction? Or would other relationship factors maintain the relationship despite sexual dysfunctions?

3.   Students can be asked to research the question of the existence of female ejaculation during orgasm. This issue has been discussed for many years, and is a popular topic of pornographic stories. Students can review the varied opinions on this topic, and a good classic source for this information is a review by a researcher named P. Belzer (1981, Journal of Sex Research, 11, 1-12).

4.   Have students seek out old books and articles dealing with the topics outlined in

this chapter. Have students share with the class how attitudes have changed over time concerning sexual behavior and life-styles.

5. How would the students respond if a friend told them he or she had a paraphilia? Have different class groups prepare a report on the reactions to these different conditions. How would they react? Would their opinions change about the person?

6. Have students research the incidence of rape by men of other men. Are these rapes reported with the same frequency as rapes of women by men? What factors influence the reporting of male rape? What aftereffects are common in the victims following rape? Reports on this topic can be compared to the information about female rape reported in the text.

7. Have students investigate attempts on campus to have victims report rape. Does the campus have a mechanism to support rape victims? What services are called into action when a rape is reported on campus? Does the campus have a rumor control service that may deal with inaccurate information following a sexual assault?

CHAPTER 12

Schizophrenias and Delusional Disorders

CHAPTER OUTLINE

I. The Schizophrenias
   A. A case study
      1. A history of dementia praecox is given
         a. Kraepelin's work
         b. Bleuler's definition for schizophrenia
      2. The schizophrenias are found in all societies
      3. The case study involves a family of six including parents and quadruplet daughters
         a. Background and early years included fame and publicity
            1) They were treated as two sets of twins
            2) Parents showed sexual preoccupation
         b. Adolescence, young adulthoood, and breakdown
            1) Problems begin to emerge
            2) The age of twenty-four, all had developed schizophrenia
         c. Course and outcome
            1) Their disorders differed markedly
            2) Adjustments vary yet all on continued medication
         d. Interpretive comment
   B. Clinical picture in schizophrenia
      1. Process (chronic) schizophrenia versus reactive (acute) schizophrenia
      2. Negative-symptoms versus positive-symptoms
         a. Doubts about the usefulness of this distinction
         b. Most symptoms fit a bell-shaped curve rather than extremes
      3. Paranoid versus nonparanoid symptom patterns
      4. Disturbance of language and communication
      5. Disturbance of thought content
      6. Disruptions of perception
      7. Inappropriate emotions
      8. Confused sense of self
      9. Disrupted volition is disrupted

        10.   Retreat to inner world
        11.   Disturbed motor behavior
C.   Problems in defining schizophrenic behavior
        1.   Diagnostic criteria is exact and enhances the valdity of diagnosis
                a.   Some problems exist when differentiating
                        schizophrenia from mood disorders
                b.   Some problems revolve around the inability to verify
                        hallucinations
        2.   Radical approaches to defining schizophrenia include the denial of
                its existence
                a.   Behaviors do not prove existence of a disease
                b.   Functioning is definitely negatively affected
D.   Subtypes of schizophrenia
        1.   Undifferentiated type
                a.   "Wastebasket" category
                b.   The breakdown erupts suddenly following some psychic
                        trauma
        2.   Catatonic type
                a.   Pronounced motor symptoms are apparent
                b.   Stupor and excitement phases can be seen
                c.   Imitation of speech and movements can be seen
                d.   Some violent episodes can emerge
        3.   Disorganized type
                a.   This is a pattern of severe disorganizaton
                b.   Hallucinations are common
                c.   Only modest recoveries are found in this type
        4.   Paranoid type
                a.   Delusions of persecution and grandeur are common
                b.   The "paranoid construction" gives the person some sense
                        of purpose and identity
        5.   Other schizophrenic patterns
                a.   Residual type
                b.   Schizoaffective disorder
                c.   Schizophreniform disorder
E.   Causal factors in schizophrenia
        1.   Biological factors in schizophrenia
                a.   Heredity
                        1)   Twin studies
                        2)   Adoption studies
                        3)   Studies of high risk
                b.   Biochemical factors
                        1)   Early studies attempted to identify an endogenous
                                hallucinogen
                        2)   One hypothesis focuses on the neurotransmitter dopamine
                c.   Neurophysiological factors
                        1)   An imbalance in excitatory and inhibitory processes may

occur
2) Inappropriate autonomic arousal may be present
3) The processing of information is abnormal and specific in schizophrenia
4) Genetic or faulty conditioning could produce the abnormal processes

d. Neuroanatomical factors
1) CAT scans and MRI techniques have permitted the study of brains
2) Enlarged ventricles have been found
3) Can the long-term use of antipsychotics cause brain anomalies?

e. Interpreting the biological evidence

2. Psychosocial factors in schizophrenia
a. Pathogenic parent-child and family interactions
1) Schizophrenogenic parents
2) Destructive family interactions
3) Faulty communication

b. Excessive life stress and decompensation
a. Relapses are associated with an expressed emotion (EE) negative communication
b. Prevention of relapse has focused on family communications

3. Sociocultural factors in schizophrenia
1. Differences found in African tribal groups
2. Clinical pictures change as social change and technology influence cultures
3. Social class has been correlated with the incidence of schizophrenia

F. Treatment and outcomes
1. One-fourth recover, 65 percent show varying degrees of continued problems, and 10 percent show permanent disability
2. Treatment should combine biological and psychological forms
a. Long-term social adjustment is not addressed by antipsychotic drugs
b. Meta-analysis shows combination approaches to be most effective

II. Delusional (Paranoid) Disorder
A. The clinical picture in delusional disorder
1. The delusional system usually centers on a single theme
a. Increasing aspects of the environment are included into the system
b. The person is unwilling to accept alternative views
2. Away from delusional system the person appears normal
3. Delusional systems are often built upon some convincing

initial premise
   B.   Causal factors in delusional disorder
      1.   Paranoid processes are separate from schizophrenic ones
         a.   Paranoid disorder is one of conception not perception
         b.   Biological factors are rarely implicated
      2.   Faulty learning and development
         a.   These are aloof, secretive, and stubborn children
         b.   Family atmosphere is one of authoritarianism and suppression
         c.   Mistrust merges into patterns of self-importance
         d.   The person may not be able to deal with aggression and power
      3.   Failure and inferiority
         a.   Failures found in social, occupational, and marital roles
         b.   Superiority masks feelings of inferiority
      4.   Elaboration of defenses and the "pseudo-community"
         a.   The paranoid person becomes a target because of his/her actions
         b.   The person seeks reasons for lack of success, and "paranoid illumination" occurs
         c.   The "pseudo-community" is a group against the person
   C.   Treatment and outcomes
      1.   Early stages respond to individual and group psychotherapy
      2.   Once a system is well established the progress of treatment is difficult

III.   Unresolved Issues About Schizophrenia
   A.   The conceptual boundaries remain shifting and unclear
      1.   Lack of research to justify definitional criteria
      2.   The observational and scientific base of some symptoms is problematic
   B.   The etiology involves myriad factors
      1.   Teamwork between disciplines is needed
      2.   Tunnel vision must be avoided

LEARNING OBJECTIVES

1.   List several general symptoms that characterize the schizophrenias and explain how this label came to be used instead of dementia praecox.
2.   Briefly summarize the case study of the Genain quads and explain why their schizophrenic breakdowns were probably due to both heredity and environment.
3.   Distinguish between *process* and *reactive* schizophrenia, list some near-synonyms for each, and explain what is meant by paranoid and nonparanoid.
4.   Describe nine clinical criteria that are used in the diagnosis of the schizophrenias.

5. Give several reasons for the difficulty in defining schizophrenic behavior and describe some suggested solutions to this dilemma.

6. Describe four types of schizophrenia that have been identified and list three additional schizophrenic patterns that appear in DSM-IV.

7. Summarize the evidence from four types of research on the genetic basis for schizophrenia and explain the conclusions your authors have reached.

8. Explain why researchers believe that some biochemical factors may cause schizophrenia and describe the rise and demise of the dopamine hypothesis.

9. Summarize the results of research on neurological factors that may cause schizophrenia and explain why these findings are difficult to interpret.

10. Summarize the results of research on neuroanatomical factors that may underlie the schizophrenias and explain your authors' evaluation of these conclusions.

11. Evaluate the evidence that early psychic trauma may increase a person's vulnerability to the schizophrenias.

12. Describe five aspects of schizophrenic families that have been studied and explain why pathogenic family interactions cannot be the sole cause of this disorder.

13. Explain why learning a deficient self structure and/or an exaggerated use of ego-defense mechanisms may be contributing causes of the schizophrenias.

14. Evaluate Laing's hypothesis that schizophrenia may be a social role and explain how this may be related to the insanity defense used in some criminal cases.

15. Summarize the results of research concerning the connection between excessive stress and decompensation and explain how expressed emotion (EE) of a schizophrenic's family members may be pathogenic.

16. Summarize the results of research concerning the possibility that some general sociocultural factors may contribute to the development of schizophrenia.

17. Summarize the success of biological and psychosocial interventions in the treatment of the schizophrenias and list six research-supported conclusions about these dysfunctions.

18. List and describe six types of delusional (paranoid) disorders that appear in DSM-IV and explain why formal diagnoses of these kinds of abnormal behavior are rare.

19. Describe the clinical symptoms that characterize delusional (paranoid) disorders and evaluate the popular belief that paranoid individuals are dangerous.

20. Differentiate *paranoia* from *paranoid schizophrenia* and describe three major factors which may be involved in the development of delusional disorders.

21. Explain how behavioral therapy may be used successfully in the early stages of a delusional (paranoid) disorder.

22. Describe several major issues surrounding the schizophrenias and delusional disorders that remain unresolved, and note the authors' thoughts about some possible solutions.

KEY TERMS

(the) schizophrenias
poor premorbid or chronic schizophrenia
good premorbid or acute schizophrenia
positive-symptom schizophrenia
schizophrenia, catatonic type

process schizophrenia
reactive schizphrenia
negative-symptom schizophrenia
schizophrenia, undifferentiated type
schizophrenia, disorganized type

schizophrenia, paranoid type

schizophrenia, residual type

schizoaffective disorder

schizophreniform disorder

dopamine hypothesis

schizophrenogenic (parents)

marital schism

marital skew

double-bind communication

expressed emotion (EE)

paranoia

delusional disorder

shared psychotic disorder

psychosis

delusion

hallucination

FOCUS ON RESEARCH 1

Carpenter, W., and Buchanan, R. (1994). "Medical Progress: Schizophrenia." The New England Journal of Medicine, 330, 681-690.

This article provides an excellent review of the schizophrenic disorder from the medical perspective. The authors review the various characteristics of the disorder and outline the treatment strategies that they consider best suited for it. They consider this disorder to be one of the worst diseases afflicting people. The onset is early in life and is associated with life-long adverse affects for most persons afflicted with it. The costs of the disorder are estimated to be $33 billion in the U. S. taking 2.5 percent of the total health care expenditures.

Schizophrenia manifests itself in a diverse pattern that suggests several disease processes are at work. The major symptoms emphasized by the authors are the bizarre behaviors associated with psychosis and the deficits in mental, emotional, and social functioning. Diagnosis is through the process of exclusion in which other conditions are eliminated as possible causes. They note the need to be sensitive to the different cluster of symptoms since they may relate to different neural substrates and different pathophysiological processes. The course of the disorder can follow various patterns that appear to be influenced by age of onset.

The causes of this disorder are considered to be related to genetic vulnerability, with several phenotypes reflecting this condition. Immune and viral theories including a retrovirus that can alter the genome, viral infections, viral activated immunopathology and secondary materal viral infection also have all been proposed. Psychosocial factors are considered for their role in the onset and course of the disorder. Although identified throughout the world, variations of the disease in cultures may be due to gene pooling and migration.

Pathophysiology of schizophrenia has a number of theories. The dopamine hypothesis is based on the observation that drugs that reduce the firing rates of mesolimbic dopamine neurons have an antipsychotic effect. Drugs that stimulate these neurons increase psychotic symptoms. Although there is a lack of decisive evidence for the hypothesis, it has remained a popular one. A reformulted dopamine hypothesis posits the coexistence of hypodomaminergic activity in the mesocortical system which produces negative symptoms, and hyperdopaminergic activity in the mesolimbic system which results in psychotic sympoms. Other hypotheses have considered the interactions between dopamine and other neurotransmitters. Integrative pathophysiologic hypotheses have attempted to explain schizophrenia syptoms in terms of biochemical abnormalities in specific neural circuits.

Treatment consists of a combination of pharmacotherapy, psychosocial therapies, and rehabilitation of social and occupational functioning. The medications block the postsynaptic dopamine receptors. Clozapine is considered an atypical antipsychotic agent with few undesirable side effects. With medication the focus of treatment has shifted away from custodial care to the family, and community. The role of psychosocial therapies is to assist in medication compliance and to help the client deal with stress.

Questions for Discussion

1.   Are physicians trained sufficiently to treat this disorder effectively?

2.   What problems are possible when psychosocial therapies are integrated with medication as a primary focus?

FOCUS ON RESEARCH 2

Breier, A., Schreiber, J., Dyer, J., and Pickar, D. (1991). "National Institute of Mental Health Longitudinal Study of Chronic Schizophrenia." Archives of General Psychiatry, 48, 239-246.

This longitudinal study of chronic schizophrenics attempted to clarify some of the disagreement about the basic features in the course and the outcome of schizophrenia. Some research indicated poor outcomes for schizophrenics while other studies suggested relatively good recovery. Disagreement about predictors for outcome center around gender, presence of affective syndrome, acute versus insidious onset, schizophrenia subtypes, family history, and premorbid functioning.

This longitudinal study was done at the NIH Clinical Center where patients received extensive assessments and comprehensive follow-up. The study followed fifty-eight schizophrenic patients from 1976 to 1986. A number of assessment instruments were used for data collection. These included the Brief Psychiatric Rating Scale, Levels of Functioning Scale, Scale for the Assessment of Negative Symptoms, Global Assessment Scale, and Wisconsin Card Sort. Interview data was collected from the patients as well as from family members, past therapists, and significant others.

The authors found that their sample had substantial impairment, and levels of symptoms a mean of six years after initial assessment. Only 20 percent had a relatively good overall outcome. Complete recovery was considered to be quite rare. During the course of the disorder, symptom levels do not level off soon after the onset of schizophrenia, but they continue throughout ten or more years. Some negative symptoms were found to increase over time. Once symptoms reach their most severe point, a plateau of extended little change is found. During the follow-up, more than three-quarters of the sample had at least one serious psychotic relapse. Poor outcome was related to the presence of negative symptoms. Treatment designed to reduce negative symptoms

143

may serve to enhance long-term adjustment.

Questions for Discussion

1. These results have what implications for the treatment of schizophrenia in community-based facilities?
2. What factors contribute to long-term adjustment of schizophrenia?
3. How might the attitudes of the public influence treatment for schizophrenia?
4. What would be a graphic presentation of the cause of schizophrenia?

FOCUS ON RESEARCH 3

Mahmood, A., Brennan, A., and Clive, G. (1994). "Delusional Disorder in Tropical Spastic Paraparesis." Irish Journal of Psychological Medicine, 11, 300-312.

Rockwell, E., Krull, A., Dimsdale, J., and Jeste, D. (1994). "Late Onset Psychosis with Somatic Delusions." Psychosomatics, 35, 66-72.

These two articles present some information on delusional disorder that may illustrate the symptoms associated with this disorder in a concise manner to students. The first article describes a case study of a forty-eight year old Afro-Caribbean woman. This woman had a tropical spastic paraparesis. During its course she developed a delusional disorder with vivid audio hallucinations. The tropical paraparesis is a progressive disorder in which the delusional aspects may be a manifestation of the advancement of the disease. The woman was treated with flupenthixol for the delusional symptoms, and experienced complete resolution of them within three months.

The second article presents comparisons of late onset psychosis patients with and without somatic delusions. They authors used MRI reports, and neuropsychological measures in their assessment of the patients. The persons with the somatic delusions were found to have experienced the psychosis longer than those without delusions. Females were found more often in the delusional group than males. The patients with delusional disorder showed lower IQ scores than nondelusional patients, and the former did not comply nor benefit from psychothropic treatment.

Questions for Discussion

1. How do family members or friends respond to the delusional patient?

2. What are some of the difficulties in providing treatment for delusion disorder patients?

READINGS

1. Benes, F, and Turtle, M. (1994). "Myelination of a Key Relay Zone in the Hippocampal Formation in the Human Brain during Childhood and Adolescence, and Adulthood."

Archives of General Psychiatry, <u>51</u>, 477-484.

2. Carone, B., Harrow, M., and Westermeyer, J. (1991). "Posthospital Course and Outcome in Schizophrenia." <u>Archives of General Psychiatry</u>, <u>48</u>, 247-253.

3. Castle, D., Sham, P., and Murray, R. (1994). "The Subtyping of Schizophrenia in Men and Women: A Latent Class Analysis." <u>Psychological Medicine</u>, <u>24</u>, 41-51.

4. Cutler, P. (1994). "Iron Overload and Psychiatric Illness." <u>Canadian Journal of Psychiatry</u>, <u>39</u>, 8-11.

5. DeLisi, L., Hoff, A., and Kushner, M. (1994). "Asymmetries in the Superior Temporal Lobe in Male and Females First Episode Schizophrenic Patients." <u>Schizophrenic Research</u>, <u>12</u>, 19-28.

6. Elkashef, A., Buchanan, R., and Munson, R. (1994). "Basal Ganglia Pathology in Schizophrenia and Tardive Dyskinesia: An MRI Quantitative Study." <u>American Journal of Psychiatry</u>, <u>151</u>, 752-755.

7. Galderisi, S., and Mucci, A. (1994). "Abnormalities of Hemispheric Lateralization in Schizophrenic Patients." <u>New Trends in Experimental and Clinical Psychiatry</u>, <u>10</u>, 25-29.

8. Kety, S., and Wender, P. (1994). "Mental Illness in the Biological and Adoptive Relatives of Schizophrenic Adoptees." <u>Archives of General Psychiatry</u>, <u>51</u>, 442-455.

9. Kinney, D., and Watenaux, K. (1994). "Obstetrical Complicatons and Trail Making Deficits Discriminate Schizophrenics from Unaffected Siblings and Controls. <u>Schizophrenia Research</u>, <u>12</u>, 63-73.

10. Li, T., Yang, W., and Chong, T. (1994). "No Association Between Alleles Or Genotypes at the Dopamine Transporter Gene and Schizophrenia." <u>Psychiatry Research</u>, <u>52</u>, 17-23.

11. Ross, C., and Anderson, G. (1994). "Childhood Abuse and the Positive Symptoms of Schizophrenia." <u>Hospital and Community Psychiatry</u>, <u>45</u>, 489-451.

12. Roy, M., and Crowe, R. (1994). "Validity of the Familial and Sproadic Subtypes of Szhizophrenia." <u>American Journal of Psychiatry</u>, <u>151</u>, 805-814.

13. Seeman, M. (1994). "Schizophrenia: D-Sub-4 Receptor Elevation: What Does It Mean?" <u>Journal of Psychiatry and Neuroscience</u>, <u>19</u>, 171-174.

14. Smith, J., and Birchwood, M. (1990). "Relatives and Patients as Partners in the Management of Schizophrenia: The Development of the Service Model." <u>British Journal of Psychiatry</u>, <u>156</u>, 654-660.

15.   Zipursky, R., and DeMent, S. (1994). "Volumetric MRI Assessment of Temporal Lobe Structures in Schizophrenia." <u>Biological Psychiatry</u>, <u>35</u>, 501-516.

DISCUSSION AND LECTURE IDEAS

1.   An article by Lindstrom and Von Knorring (1994) can be used to develop a lecture on the five-factor model of schizophrenia (<u>Acta Psychiatrica Scandinavica</u>, <u>89</u>, 274-279). Positive, negative, excited, anxious/depressive, and cognitive factors comprise the model. Age of onset was found to be a significant factor in their review of this model among 140 patients.

2.   What is the power of initial subtype diagnosis of schizophrenia to predict various aspects of long term outcomes? A. Deister and M. Marneros (1994) studied this question for 144 patients diagnosed with various subtypes of schizophrenia (<u>Schizophrenia Research</u>, <u>12</u>, 145-157). A classroom discussion can examine the importance of initial diagnosis in the long term prognosis for persons with schizophrenia.

3.   Can it become difficult to judge what is delusional? How should a lover's jealousy or suspiciousness be judged? What about unusual religious beliefs? Is the person who believes in miracles, reincarnation, and faith healing delusional? Astrology has numerous followers, and people become defensive about such beliefs.

4.   Visual hallucinations are common among schizophrenics. How are dreams similar to hallucinations? While asleep, do people react to dreams as though they were real? Have students imagine a life in which the distinction between dreams and the sensory world could not be made. Do vivid dreams "stay" with a person and stimulate thought about the dream experience?

5.   The social stigma associated with the diagnosis of schizophrenia affects the adjustment of individuals following hospitalization. Discuss the reasons for labeling and why it occurs in society. What factors can the class identify that contribute to the negative labeling of mental disorders such as schizophrenia? What are the potential dangers for the schizophrenic patient returning to the community?

6.   Textbooks on abnormal psychology are readily available to the public at libraries. Could a textbook's description of schizophrenia or paranoia unnecessarily frighten a person who may be experiencing some of the symptoms? Information about the poor prognosis for some schizophrenics could be upsetting information for an ex-patient who received the schizophrenic diagnosis. In what other ways could reading such a textbook be detrimental to a person labeled schizophrenic?

7.   The schizophrenogenic mother has long been proposed as a prime causal factor in schizophrenia. Have the class the discuss this early concept and what the appeal was of this proposed causation of schizophrenia? An article by B. Karon and A. Widener (1994) discusses the current thinking on this topic (<u>Psychoanalytic Psychology</u>, <u>11</u>, 47-61).

8.   Early memories have been used by practitioners following various psychodynamic perspectives when treating patients. What differences exist among different mental disorders in terms of the first memories reported by the patients? E. Arnow and D. Harrison (1991, Journal of Personality Assessment, 56, 75-83) investigated the first memories of borderline personality disorder patients and compared them to paranoid schizophrenics' memories. Borderline patients had significantly fewer positively toned early memories than the schizophrenics or a group of patients with anxiety disorders. The anxiety disorder patients appeared to have the early memories most useful for the traditional applications in treatment. Students' early memories may be compared to those described in this article.

ACTIVITIES AND PROJECTS

1.   Students can be assigned the task of identifying the support for the genetic hypothesis for the mental disorders. Genetic links have been examined for numerous disorders and is particular pertinent in the study of schizophrenia. J. Nigg and H. Goldsmith (1994) provide a good initial resource for ideas in contrasting such an assignment (Psychological Bulletin, 115, 346-380).

2.   There are a number of interesting and informative personal accounts of the schizophrenic experience. Assign students the project of locating and reporting on books such as A. Freud's Autobiography of a Schizophrenic Girl and S. Plath's The Bell Jar. These personal reports can present realistic portrayals of mental disorder for the student.

3.   The Social Anhedonia Scale may be a good classroom illustration of one aspect of schizophrenia. Leak (1991, Journal of Personality Assessment, 56, 84-95) reports on the validity of the scale and provides some useful information that can be used to stimulate class discussion. The Social Anhedonia Scale is a forty item true-false measure that can be adapted for classroom illustration purposes. Other measures suggested by the author can be used in conjunction with this scale to further illustrate the symptoms of certain forms of psychopathology.

4.   Some societies develop attitudes and beliefs that may have limited truth in fact. Can a society become paranoid? Did the United States become delusional during the communism scare of the 1950s? Have other delusional beliefs developed in the 1990s? Have students research other examples of delusional beliefs that may influence a country. How is the population's behavior affected? What factors produced a change in attitudes? Are delusional beliefs detrimental to the society's functioning? The recent terrorist bombing in the United States may reinforce some current delusional beliefs held by persons in our society.

5.   Have students research the use of antipsychotic medication for schizophrenia. Does the schizophrenic patient have the right to refuse medication? How can compliance be achieved if medication is indicated for a paranoid type of schizophrenia?

6.   Students may have faulty impressions concerning the diagnosis of different mental illnesses such as schizophrenia. Have students conduct surveys of other students concerning their perception of how schizophrenia may be diagnosed. Students often hear about chemical imbalances as a cause of depression and schizophrenia. Do they believe that medical testing, such

as blooding test can be used in the diagnositic process of schizophrenia?

7.   Students often enjoy taking brief questionnaires that relate to some topic of the course. The Attitudes About Reality Scale (Journal of Personality Assessment, 1989, 53, 353-365) is a forty item measure that samples four conceptual domains. The instrument has been found to be a consistent measure of the influences on a person's perception of reality. An individual's epistemology has a pervasive and important effect on interpersonal consequences. People distort reality in order to fit existing belief structures. This scale can provide the students with some first-hand information on the factors that influence their possible distortion of reality.

CHAPTER 13

Brain Disorders and Other Cognitive Impairments

CHAPTER OUTLINE

I. Brain impairment and adult mental disorder
    A. Adult brain damage and disordered mental functioning
        1. Focal brain lesions are circumscribed areas of abnormal change in the brain with a number of possible consequences
            a. Impairment of memory
            b. Impairment of orientation
            c. Impairment of learning
            d. Impairment of emotional control
            e. Impairment of initiating behavior
            f. Impairment in language
            g. Impairment of propriety
            h. Impairment of visuospatial ability
        2. Neuropsychology/psychopathology interaction
        3. Hardware and software
            a. Computer analogies can be used to portray mental processes
                1) Hardware problems can involve problems with the machine
                2) Software programs can involve "bugs" in the programs
            b. The brain can be viewed as a programmable system of hardware
                1) Loaded information may be lost as in dementia
                2) Functions cannot be achieved because of a breakdown
            c. Software breakdown manifestations reflect life experiences
        4. General clinical features of neuropsychological disorders
            a. Symptoms reflect the underlying brain pathology
            b. The location of the damage is important
        5. Diagnostic issues in neuropsychological disorders
            a. Axis I coding of associated mental symptoms
            b. Axis II coding of disease
    B. Neuropsychological symptom syndromes
        1. Delirium and dementia
            a. Delirium shows a rapid onset in disorganization of mental processes
                1) Acute conditions lasting a week or less

        2)   Caused by many conditions that deplete oxygen to the brain
- b. Dementia is a progressive deterioration in brain functioning
    1) Strokes, disease, injury, and toxic substances can produce the condition
    2) Alzheimer's disease is one dementia
3. The amnestic syndrome
    a. The inability to recall events is the main feature in amnestic syndrome
    b. A retrieval deficit may be present
    c. Alcohol and barbiturate addiction is often a cause
3. Neuropsychological delusional and mood syndromes
    a. Delusional systems are central to organic delusional syndrome
    b. Manic or depressive states can be caused by impairment in cerebral function
    c. Organic anxiety syndrome is a new classification with limited research evidence
4. Neuropsychological personality syndrome
    a. Personality style or traits change following brain injury
    b. Medication can induce a transitory change

C. Neuropsychological disorder with HIV-1 infection
1. Two forms of central nervous system pathology have been identified
    a. Asceptic meningitis
    b. AIDS Dementia Complex (ADC)
        1) The brain shows signs of edema, atrophy, and inflammation
        2) Clinical features include memory loss, psychomotor slowing, and later progression to dementia
2. Persons with AIDS-related complex (ARC) can also experience some cognitive difficulties
3. Prevention of infection is the only certain defensive strategy

D. Dementia of the Alzheimer type (DAT)
1. Clinical picture in dementia of the Alzheimer type (DAT)
    a. Gradual and slow mental deterioration is seen
    b. The person withdraws from active engagement with life
    c. Impairments in many functions progress in severity
    d. Psychopathological symptoms are transitory and inconsistent
        1) Some patients do develop a paranoid orientation
        2) The jealousy delusion can also emerge toward a spouse
    e. Death usually comes from lowered resistance to opportunistic infections
2. Causal factors in DAT
    a. Senile plaques
    b. Neurofibrillary tangles
    c. Granulovacuoler

        d.   Theories of causation
             1)   Acetylcholine depletion
             2)   Amyloid hypothesis
             3)   ApoE
        e.   Early onset type may have genetic component

3. Treatment and outcomes in DAT
   a. No effective treatment exists
   b. Behavioral techniques attempt to control wandering and poor self-care behaviors
   c. Medication is used to help with emotional reactions
   d. The stresses on family caregivers are enormous
   e. Institutionalization is usually required

E. A note on vascular dementia
   1. A similar clinical picture to Alzheimer's exists
   2. Cerebral infarcts are found over brain regions
   3. Cerebral arteriosclerosis can be medically managed to some extent

F. Disorders involving head injury
   1. Clinical picture in disorders with head injuries
      a. The historical American crowbar case from 1868 is described
      b. Three types of injury are distinguished
         1) closed head
         2) penetrating
         3) skull fracture
      c. Retrograde amnesia is common.
      d. Intracerebral hemorrhage can occur with head injury
         1) Petechial hemorrhage
         2) Subdural hematoma
         3) Cerebral edema
      e. Most one-time injuries produce temporary effects
   2. Treatment and outcomes
      a. Prompt medical care is required
      b. The majority suffering mild concussion improve quickly
      c. Severe injury cases have a poor prognosis

II. Mental Retardation
   A. Levels of mental retardation
      1. Mild mental retardation
         a. The largest number of mentally retarded are in this level
         b. Persons in this group are considered educable
         c. Social adjustment is similar to adolescence
      2. Moderate mental retardation
         a. This group of individuals are considered trainable
         b. Most in this group can achieve partial independent living
      3. Severe mental retardation
         a. This group is known as the dependent retarded

        b.   Institutionalization is usually required
    4. Profound mental retardation
        a.   This is the life support retarded
        b.   Physical deformities are common in this group
        c.   This group can usually be diagnosed in infancy
    5. The IQ distribution of scores does not precisely fit a normal curve
        a.   An "intruding factor" inflates the number of low IQ scores
        b.   An extraordinary skill can be shown in the "idiot savant"
B. Brain defects in mental retardation
    1. Genetic-chromosomal factors
        a.   Down syndrome and Fragile X show the clear role of genetics
        b.   Chromosomal defects may influence metabolism which affects the brain
    2. Infections and toxic agents
        a.   A number of infections such as syphilis, measles, and viral encephalitis can cause brain damage
        b.   Lead, alcohol, and Rh factor are toxic agents that cause brain damage
    3. Prematurity and trauma (physical injury)
        a.   Low birth weight and prematurity are risk factors
        b.   Hypoxia can result from a number of factors
    4. Ionizing radiation
        a.   X-rays
        b.   Nuclear power leakages
    5. Malnutrition and other biological factors
        a.   Protein deficiencies
        b.   Brain tumors
C. Organic retardation syndrome
    1. Down syndrome
        a.   Most common condition associated with moderate and severe conditions
        b.   Amniocentesis has reduced the incidence
        c.   Physical features usually are present in this syndrome
        d.   Life expectancy for the Down child has risen dramatically
        e.   Mongolism is an archaic term for the condition
        f.   Most learn self-help skills and acceptable social behaviors
        g.   The greatest intellectual deficits are found in verbal and language skills
        h.   A trisomy of chromosome 21 is characteristic of Down syndrome
        i.   Age of parent is an apparent risk factor
    2. Phenylketonuria (PKU)
        a.   A rare metabolic disorder found in 1 of 20,000 births
        b.   Phenylalanine is not broken down
        c.   Severe to profound retardation is seen in older patients
        d.   Early detection can be achieved through urinalysis

   e. Restriction of diet can prevent mental retardation
  3. Cranial anomalies
   a. Microcephaly is the impaired development of the brain
    1) The majority show little language development
    2) The condition may be caused by infection, irradiation, and possible genetic factors
   b. Hydrocephalus is an accumulation of cerebrospinal fluid causing brain damage
    1) The clinical picture depends upon the extent of neural damage
    2) Surgery is used in treatment
D. Cultural-familial retardation
  1. Mental retardation associated with sensory and social deprivation
  2. Cultural familial retardation involves an inferior quality of interaction
   a. A progressive loss in IQ is found among deprived children
   b. Parents do not stimulate cognitive growth
   c. Mild retardation is the usual result
   d. Identification is during the school years
E. The problem of assessment
  1. Errors in diagnosis can occur from the testing, personal characteristics of the child, and limitations in the tests
  2. The label of retardation can have numerous long-term aversive effects on a child
F. Treatment, outcomes, and prevention
  1. Treatment facilities and methods
   a. Favorable emotional and mental development usually is found in home care
   b. Community-oriented residential care has positives for adolescents
   c. Many state institutions are overcrowded and have limited education programs
   d. It is questionable if the mentally retarded at any level receive adequate services
   e. Public Law 94-142 requires education in the "least restrictive" environment
   f. Group homes or halfway houses began to appear in the 1970s
   g. Operant conditioning is used to teach many skills
    1) Target areas of improvement are identified
    2) Skills are divided into simple components
   h. Mainstreaming can benefit many children with good planning
  2. Frontiers in prevention
   a. Genetic counseling has been expanded
   b. Sociocultural factors that inhibit growth are alleviated
    1) Provide adequate health care
    2) Community-centered facilities provide numerous services
III. Specific Learning Disorders
 A. Clinical picture in learning disorders

1. A disparity between expected and actual academic performance is found
2. Blaming the victim often takes place
   a. The children are seen as troublesome
   b. The child's self-esteem can suffer

B. Causal factors in learning disorders
1. A subtle central nervous system immaturity, defect, or dysfunction is probably present
   a. A defect in the brain's normal laterality has been proposed
   b. Minimal brain dysfunction was a popular term a few years back
2. Psychosocial-based hypotheses have limited empirical support
3. What strategies do good learners use? (Worden's approach)
   a. Memory strategies
   b. Monitoring their peformances
   c. Metastrategy information
   d. Motivational factors

C. Treatment and outcomes
1. Few well-designed outcome studies exist
2. Research has generally focused on reading disorders
3. Long-term follow-up suggests that problems continue into college

IV. Unresolved Issues on Cultural-Familial Retardation
A. Problems in test instruments and schools that reflect an "approved culture"
B. Initiatives at remedies have not attracted national support
C. Controversy engendered by the publicaton of The Bell Curve

LEARNING OBJECTIVES

1. Define *organic mental disorders*, and describe three major conditions that lead one to believe the presence of organic disorders.
2. Give eight possible areas of functioning that may be impaired by organic brain disorders.
3. Describe the analogy the authors make between brain function and computer hardware and software.
4. Describe the general functions attributed to the right and left hemispheres of the brain.
5. Define syndromes and describe four types that are typical of persons with organic brain pathology.
6. Describe the behavioral symptoms associated with AIDS dementia complex (ADC).
7. Define *tumor*, describe some symptoms of tumors, and indicate the nature of treatment.
8. Indicate the incidence of brain damage resulting from head injuries, describe some symptoms that result from damage of various areas of the brain, and summarize what is known about its treatment.
9. Differentiate between senile and presenile dementias, and describe two presenile types.
10. Outline some causal processes that may underlie Alzheimer's disease.
11. Describe the differences and similarities between DAT and MID.
12. Define mental retardation and describe its classification by DSM-IV.
13. List and describe the behavior of four levels of mental retardation, and explain their

distribution in the United States.

14. List five biological conditions that may lead to mental retardation, and describe four clinical types that have been identified.
15. Distinguish between two subtypes of mental retardation that are caused by sociocultural deprivation, summarize what is known about the cultural-familial type, and explain why mental retardation is so difficult to assess.
16. Summarize what is known about educational and therapeutic methods that have been successful in helping mentally retarded individuals.
17. Describe two new frontiers in the prevention of mental retardation, and explain the three-pronged "broad spectrum" approach to providing a more supportive sociocultural setting for children.

KEY TERMS

organic mental disorders
delirium
senile dementias
macrocephaly
organic mood syndrome
AIDS-Dementia Complex (ADC)
presenile dementias
multi-infarct dementia (MID)
specific learning disorders
phenyketonuria (PKU)
cultural-familial retardation

neuropsychological disorders
dementia
Down syndrome
amnestic syndrome
organic personality syndrome
AIDS-Related Complex (ARC)
Dementia of the Alzheimer's type (DAT)
hydrocephalus
mental retardation
microcephaly
mainstreaming

FOCUS ON RESEARCH 1

Seltzer, B, and Buswell, A. (1994). "Psychiatric Symptoms in Alzheimer's Disease: Mental Status Examination Versus Caregiver Report." The Gerontologist, 34, 103-109.

The authors state that the symptoms of dementia of the Alzheimer type (DAT) have both a theoreticl and practical significance. The emotional changes as well as the behavioral ones permit the opportunity to correlate symptoms with brain anatomy and pathology. Currently there is a disagreement in the professional literature concerning the prevalence of a number of symptoms in DAT patients. For example, hallucinations are reported to have frequency ranging from 3 percent to 49 percent.

The authors consider some of the discrepancies to be due to the method of obtaining the clincial data. The use of collateral sources for information may result in various periods of observations being used with different lengths and intensity. In this study, the researchers completed an investigation of behavioral and emotional symptoms using mental status testing by a single individual. Additionally, caregivers provided checklist information about the patient with DAT.

The study examined 222 males and 6 females with a formal diagnosis of DAT. All the patients received a complete mental state examination by a physician. The caregiver assessment used the Alzheimer's Disease Psychiatric Symptom Checklist.

The results revealed a considerable difference between formal examination and caregiver questionnaire in determining the prevalence of psychiatric sypmtoms. Hallucinations, depression, lack of insight, anxiety, disinhibition, and overactivity were all reported to a significantly less degree by the examining physician than by the caregivers. Agreement was greatest on the assessment of suspiciousness, irritability, argumentation, and belligerence.

Explaining the differences, the authors point to the fact that caregivers observe symptoms over much longer periods of time than physicians. Also, patients may be more guarded with physicians than with a familar caregiver, or the testing situation may be affected by the anxiety it may provoke in the patients. The authors also suggest that caregivers may be confusing hallucinations with "misidentifications" syndromes which are common in DAT. Further, the lay definitions of depression and anxiety may be different than the professinal ones, and the stresses coming from caregiving may produce negative assessments of the DAT patient.

The authors make a call for improved techniques in assessment as a way to narrow the gap between clinical and nonprofessional caregivers in their descriptions of DAT patients. This has an importance for both research and treatment.

Questions for Discisson

1. What are the implication for treatment of the gap between caregiver and professional assessments of DAT patients?

2. What are some methods that can be used to provide reliable assessment of symptoms?

3. What are some of the stresses associated with providing care for DAT patients?

FOCUS ON RESEARCH 2

Matson, J., and Gardner, W. (1991). "Behavioral Learning Theory and Current Applications to Severe Behavior Problems in Persons with Mental Retardation." Clinical Psychology Review, 11, 175-188.

The behavioral treatment strategies based on operant conditioning have been, and continue to be, the dominant methods when dealing with mentally retarded children and adults. The success of behavioral therapy in this population has contributed to its continued use, despite some criticisms and alternative treatments being identified. This article provides a good review of the effectiveness of behavioral treatments for severe problems.

Self-injurious behavior has been investigated by a number of clinicians. The behavior occurs in one typography and is repetitive and resistant to change. One viewpoint suggests that the behavior reflects or communicates a purpose for the individual. Thus, the self-injurious person may be in a state of social deprivation, or the person may be in a state of excessive stimulus conditions. The clinician determines the function of the behavior, and the teacher determines alternative, socially appropriate means of expressing the personal states of deprivation or aversive arousal. Although the behavioral methods have met success, a residual group of individuals have remained unresponsive to these therapeutic approaches. Current operant learning concepts are inadequate for the residual group. A promising direction for this group has been operant behavioral pharmacology, with applied behavior analysis methodology, employed to analyze the effects of pharmacological agents.

The authors present two frequent problems for the behavior therapist. The first is the lack of generalization across stimulus conditions and durability of change across time. They suggest that many therapists use a "train and hope" strategy when dealing with the mentally retarded person. Schedules of reinforcement and stimulus control have been met with some success, but systematic research is needed in this area.

The second problem involves the use of punishment. Previous research has employed a wide range of aversive stimuli including restraint, shock, slaps, lemon juice, facial screening, verbal reprimands, and brief disruption. Severity of the treated behavior, age, and cognitive functioning of the person are all related to the effectiveness of the punishment methods. Attempts to pass legislation to ban various punishment procedures have been made in numerous locations. The authors call for further study in this area. They believe that theoretical developments have not kept pace with the applications of behavior principles initially identified in the animal laboratory.

Questions for Discussion

1. Should aversive or harmful stimuli ever be used in the treatment of mental retardation?
2. Should the mentally retarded person be able to "consent" to a therapy method?
3. What abuses in the care of mentally retarded persons may be promoted in the name of treatment?

FOCUS ON RESEARCH 3

Schalock, R., Stark, J., Snell, M., Coulter, D., and Spitalnik, D. (1994). "The Changing Conception of Mental Retardation: Implications for the Field." Mental Retardation, 32, 181-193.

This article discusses the numerous changes in terminology, IQ cut-off levels, and the role of adaptive behavior in the diagnosis of mental retardation that have taken place over the past four decades. An important paradigm shift has taken place in which mental retardation is not seen as an absolute trait expressed solely by the person, but as an expression of the functional impact of the interaction between a person with limited intellectual skills and the environment.

This shift required the change in thinking toward categories based upon more than one aspect of the person. Secondly, the consideration of actual functioning requires the clarification of adaptive skills that are needed for coping with the environment. Additionally this shift has influenced the delivery of services to the mentally retarded. The focus is toward the strengths of the individual, normalized, or typical environments, integrated services, and the empowerment of those serviced.

The new emphasis advocates the use of professinal/clinical judgments in making decisions. The use of interdisciplinary teams is needed to process and integrate the multidimensional assessment. The team process requires certified personnel who can make the appropriate clinical judgments. These judgments are considered critical in today's multicultural world. Sensitivity to cultural and linguistic variations requires multifactorial assessment.

Previous services to the mentally retarded was based upon a level of deficit model that segregated the individuals. The new focus encourages the movement away from traditional uses of such terms as educable and trainable. These terms have the power to conjure up stereotypic images of the retarded. The inclusion of students with mental retardation in the regular classroom and the merger of general and special education is encouraged.

Adults with mental retardation recieve systems of care that are directed toward their demonstrated needed supports. An increased array and variety of service delivery mechanisms are needed. The service delivery system is seen to move away from a maintenance orientation to one that emphasizes the linking of planning, eligibilty determination, and service provision to the person's intellectual and adaptive skills level.

Questions for Discussion

1. What are the potential negative outcomes of separating children in special education classes?

2. What professionals are needed on the multidisciplinary assessment teams mentioned by the authors?

3. What is the primary goal of this paradigms shift in viewing and treating mental retardation?

READINGS

1. Bondi, M., Monschk, A., and Butters, N. (1994). "Preclinical Cognitive Markers of Dementia of the Alzheimer Type." Neuropsychology, 8, 374-384.

2. Calne, D., and Zigmond, M. (1991). "Compensatory Mechanisms in Degenerative Neurologic Diseases: Insights from Parkinsonism." Archives of Neurology, 48, 361-364.

3. Carpentieri, S., and Morgan, S. (1994). "A Comparison of Patterns of Cognitive Functioning of Autistic and Nonautistic Retarded Children on the Stanford-Binet." Journal of Autism and Developmetal Disorders, 24, 215-223.

4. Dollear, T., Gorelick, P., and Dollear, W. (1994). "Comparison of Dementia Criteria:

Sensitivity and Specificity Testing Among African American Patients." Neuroepidemiology, 13, 59-63,

5. Dunkin, J, Leuchter, A., and Cook, I. (1994). "Reduced EEG Coherence in Dementia: State or Trait Marker?" Biological Psychiatry, 35, 870-879.

6. Doraiswamy, P., Shah, S., and Krishnan, R. (1991). "Magnetic Resonance Evaluation of the Midbrain in Parkinson's Disease." Archives of Neurology, 48, 360-361.

7. Hodapp, R., and Dykens, E. (1994). "Mental Retardation's Two Cultures of Behavioral Research." American Journal of Mental Retardation, 98, 675-687.

8. Karsh, K, and Dahlquist, C. (1994). "A Comparison of Static and Dynamic Presentation Procedures on Discrimination Learning of Individuals with Severe or Moderate Mental Retardation." Research in Developmental Disabilities, 15, 167-186.

9. Liberty, K, and Fitzpatrick, T. (1994). "Effects of Models and Demonstrations of Personal Narratives on the Use of Lexical Ties by Writers with Mental Retardation." Journal of Behavioral Education, 4, 7-20.

10. Mayeux, R., Sano, M., Chen, J., and Stern, Y. (1991). "Risk of Dementia in First-Degree Relatives of Patients with Alzheimer's Disease." Archives of Neurology, 48, 269-273.

11. McCormick, W., Kukull, W., and Bowen, J. (1994). "Symptom Patterns and Comorbidity in the Early Stages of Alzheimer's Disease." Journal of the American Geriatrics Society, 42, 517-522.

12. Reiss, S. (1994). "Issues in Defining Mental Retardation." American Journal of Mental Retardation, 99, 1-7.

13. Tierney, M., Alvaro, N, and Fisher, R. (1994). "Use of the Rey Auditory Verbal Learning Test in Differentiating Normal Aging From Alzheimer's and Parkinson's Dementia." Psychological Assessment, 6, 129-134.

14. Webster, M, Fancis, P., Procter, A., and Tratmann, G. (1994). "Postmortem Brains Reveal Similar But not Identical Amyloid Precursor Protein Immunoreactivity in Alzheimer Compared with Other Dementias." Brain Research, 644, 347-351.

15. Whitman, C. (1994). "Residential Care for Adults with Mental Retardation." Adult Residential Care Journal, 8, 16-26.

DISCUSSION AND LECTURE IDEAS

1.   An interesting lecture on the use of exercise to encourage social interaction among preschoolers with mental retardation can be developed from a research article by T. Yamanaka

(1994) and his associates (<u>Perceptual and Motor Skills</u>, <u>78</u>, 5751-578). Running exercises were used by the researchers in a preschool setting.

2.	The diagnosis and treatment recommendations for persons with mental retardation are increasingly made by interdisciplinary teams of professionals. Students may readily see the advantages of this procedure, but what are the possible shortcomings? Siperstein and his colleagues (1994) suggests a number of problems in consensus building on such teams (<u>American Journal on Mental Retardation</u>, <u>98</u>, 519-526).

3.	In addition to the cognitive impairments usually described in Alzheimer's disease, other changes are found in sensory perception. Serly, Larson, and Kalkstein (1991) studied the course of olfactory deficits in a population of Alzheimer's disease patients (<u>American Journal of Psychiatry</u>, <u>148</u>, 357-360). Significant deficits in olfactory perception progressed as the dementia became extensive. The authors call into question some current attempts to utilize olfaction as an early screening method to identify Alzheimer's disease.

4.	The role of inheritance in Alzheimer's disease is one issue students usually wish to discuss in class. An excellent resource on these findings can be found in a report by Kumar and his colleagues (1991). The article provides extensive review of the assessment methods employed by the investigators, and provides examples of the position emission tomographic scans (<u>Archives of Neurology</u>, <u>48</u>, 160-168). The authors conclude that environmental factors may be involved in the development of Alzheimer's disease.

5.	What is the impact of dementia on daily functioning? J. Teunisse, M. Derix, and G. Van Crevel, (1991) report on an assessment project being completed in the Netherlands on this topic (<u>Archives of Neurology</u>, <u>48</u>, 274-278). They examined areas of functioning that are often overlooked in other assessment methods. Disability in daily living activities, behavioral disturbances, and the burdens experienced by the caregiver were three of the main areas examined by the investigators. They concluded that the severity of dementia cannot be assessed from cognitive impairment alone.

6.	Students can be encouraged to share any personal experiences they have had with relatives who demonstrated such disorders as Alzheimer's disease. How did the family deal with the disorientation and memory impairment of the older person? What major problems developed in the family when the disorder was obvious? Was institutionalized care called for? How did that affect the family?

7.	Stroke has a number of debilitating effects on its victims. The material in the chapter focuses on the mental impairments that may result. Further information on the after effects of stroke in the area of emotional responses can be obtained from the work of Stern and Backman (1991). They show how depressive symptoms following stroke can depend upon the location of the resulting lesion (<u>American Journal of Psychiatry</u>, <u>148</u>, 351-336). This report nicely supplements the textbook's material.

ACTIVITIES AND PROJECTS

1.   Students can be shown the Mini-Mental Status Examination which was developed by Evelyn Lee Teng and her associates (1987). This instrument is commonly used in the assessment of dementia. The examination can be demonstrated in class as a way to review the various impairments suffered by an Alzheimer's disease victim (Journal of Consulting and Clinical Psychology, 55, 96-100).

2.   Try to arrange a class trip to a nursing home that cares for persons with organic brain syndrome. (Or students could serve as volunteers in order to interact with the residents.) What are the major problems that members of the nursing home staff have in caring for persons with such conditions as Alzheimer's disease?

3.   The assessment of dementia can be completed using the Dementia Rating Scale. This instrument provides information on five areas of ability that show deterioration in dementia. Scores for capacity in attention, initiation/ perseveration, construction, conceptualization, and memory can be obtained. The scale can easily be adapted for classroom demonstration. It provides a good illustration of the assessment process for the various dementias. The scale is available from: Psychological Assessment Resources, Inc., P.O. Box 998, Odessa, FL 33556.

4.   There are methods of estimating risks for Pick's disease and Alzheimer's disease from known familial situations. Heston and White (1991) in their book, The Vanishing Mind, (San Francisco: Freeman Publishers), provide the necessary table and formula to estimate risk. This information can be used to develop a class project or demonstration that centers on the importance of familial characteristics in disease processes.

5.   The Wechsler Adult Intellience Scales-Revised (WAIS-R) can provide illustrations of how various impairments can be assessed when trying to identify the symptoms associated with dementia. In dementia, the most defects are seen in the subtests assessing memory and abstract reasoning. At what point would a progressive dementia show deficits on all of the WAIS-R subtests? The WAIS-R can be used in class to illustrate the potential declines in cognitive performance among dementia patients.

CHAPTER 14

Behavior Disorders of Childhood and Adolescence

CHAPTER OUTLINE

I. Maladaptive Behavior in Different Life Periods
   A. Varying clinical pictures
      1. Childhood disorders differ from those in other life periods
      2. Some emotional disturbances in childhood are short-lived
   B. Special vulnerabilities of younger children
      1. Children have a limited capacity to understand problems
      2. Children are dependent on others for help

II. The Classification of Childhood and Adolescent Disorders
   A. Historically, childhood disorders have not been clearly described
      1. Inadequacies stemmed from using adult models of pathology
      2. The developmental level of a child was ignored
      3. The influences of the environment were not discussed
   B. The DSM-IV is a categorical strategy of diagnosis that overcomes many early deficits in diagnosis
      1. This model is based upon the disease model of psychopathology
      2. The dimensional approach is a seldom used alternative method of diagnosis

III. Disorders of Childhood
   A. Attention-deficit hyperactivity disorder
      1. The clinical picture in attention-deficit hyperactivity disorder
         a. Difficulty in sustaining attention is a central feature
         b. Aggression is often confused with this disorder
      2. Causal factors in attention-deficit hyperactivity disorder
         a. Dietary factors have been proposed
         b. No clearly established psychological factors have been identified
      3. Treatment and outcomes
         a. Cerebral stimulants are widely used in treatment
         b. Behavior techniques using programmed learning have been successful
         c. Long-term outcome may include the development of other

psychological problems

B. Conduct disorders
   1. The clinical picture in conduct disorders
      a. A repetitive violation of rules is a central feature
      b. Three subtypes are identified by the DSM-IV
   2. Causal factors in conduct disorders
      a. The family setting is marked by ineffective parenting
      b. Hostility is a central variable
   3. Treatment and outcomes
      a. Treatment is often ineffective
      b. Cohesive family model often required for treatment
      c. Early aggressiveness is related to adult criminality
      d. Behavior techniques emphasizing control are effective

C. Delinquent behavior
   1. The incidence and severity of delinquent acts
      a. Delinquency is not fully reported
      b. Delinquency is a legal term
   2. Causal factors in delinquency
      a. Personal pathology
         1) Genetic determinants
         2) Brain damage and mental retardation
         3) Psychological factors
         4) Antisocial traits
         5) Drug abuse
      b. Pathogenic family patterns
         1) Broken homes
         2) Personal rejection and family discipline
         3) Antisocial parental models
         4) Limited parental relationships outside the family
      c. General sociocultural factors
         1) Alienation and rebellion
         2) The social rejects
         3) Delinquent gang cultures
   3. Dealing with delinquency
      a. Behavior techniques have shown promise
      b. Counseling parents is a vital concern
      c. Institutionalization is questionable for status offenders

D. Anxiety disorders of childhood and adolescence
   1. Separation anxiety disorder
      a. Characterized by excessive fears
      b. Clear stressors are usually identified
   2. Overanxious disorder
      a. Excessive generalized worries are at the core
      b. Somatic complaints are often found
   3. Causal factors in anxiety disorders
      a. Unusual constitutional sensitivity may be present

        b.   Feelings of inadequacy may be due to trauma
        c.   Modeling of anxious parents
        d.   A detached parent may instill insecurity
    4.   Treatment and outcomes
        a.   Behavior techniques are used in group settings
        b.   Instruction for parents is often needed
E.   Childhood depression
    1.   Clinical picture in childhood depression
        a.   The depressive symptoms include withdrawal, crying, and
                physical complaints
        b.   The depressive disorder increases in incidence over the age span
        c.   Adult criteria for depression is used in diagnosis
    2.   Causal factors in childhood depression
        a.   Biological factors
        b.   Learning factors
    3.   Treatment and outcomes
        a.   Supportive environments are needed
        b.   Suicide appraisal is appropriate for many cases
F.   Other symptom disorders
    1.   Functional enuresis
        a.   Primary versus secondary functional enuresis
        b.   Causes can include faulty learning, immaturity, or disturbed
                family relationships
        c.   Conditioning procedures are used in treatment
    2.   Functional encopresis
        a.   Medical and psychological strategies are needed in treatment
        b.   Encopretics are usually males
    3.   Sleepwalking (somnambulism)
        a.   Children do not recall the sleepwalking episodes
        b.   Risks for injuries are real concerns
        c.   Sleepwalking appears related to anxiety
    4.   Tics
        a.   The term is used to describe a large range of behaviors
        b.   Tourette's syndrome involves multiple motor and vocal patterns

IV.   Pervasive Developmental Disorder: Autism
    A.   The Clinical Picture in Autistic disorder
        1.   Absence or restricted language
        2.   Aversion to auditory stimuli
        3.   Self-stimulation
        4.   Relationship deficits
        5.   Repetitive behaviors
        6.   Autistic savants
    B.   Causal factors in autism
    C.   Treatments and outcomes

V. Planning Better Programs to Help Children and Youth
    A. Special factors associated with treatment for children
        1. The child's inability to seek assistance
        2. Double deprivation of children from pathogenic homes
        3. The need for treatment of the parents as well as the child
        4. The possibility of using parents as change agents
        5. The problem of placing the child outside of the family
        6. The importance of intervening early before the problems become acute
    B. Child abuse
        1. The number of reported cases continues to rise
        2. Realization of the serious nature of abuse arose in the 1960s
        3. Abused children may show impaired cognitive ability
        4. Long-term consequences are commonplace
        5. Causal factors are still unclear
        6. Programs have evolved to prevent child abuse
    C. Causal factors in chld abuse
    D. Prevention of child abuse
    E. Child advocacy programs
        1. Advocacy attempts to secure services for children in need
        2. Confusion continues to hamper various advocacy groups

VI. Unresolved Issues on Parent Pathology and Childhood Disorders
    A. Parents of disturbed children showing psychological problems had higher rates than parents of normal children.
        1. Do parents transmit their disturbances?
        2. The actual mode of transmission is unclear.
    B. Children with multiple-risk factors have worse outcomes than those with low-risk factors.

LEARNING OBJECTIVES

1. List several ways in which childhood disorders are different from those of other ages.
2. List and explains several special vulnerabilities of childhood.
3. Explain three reasons why early childhood diagnostic systems were inadequate, and describe two kinds of systems that have been used.
4. List three goals that guided the revision of DSM-IV for childhood disorders, and explain the changes that were made to reach these objectives.
5. Explain the structure of the Child Behavior Checklist (CBCL) developed by Achenbach and his colleagues.
6. Explain three ways in which categorical and dimensional approaches to diagnosing childhood disorders differ.
7. Define *hyperactivity*, and describe its clinical picture.
8. List several of the multiple causes of hyperactivity, and summarize what is known about its treatment.
9. Define *conduct disorders*, and describe their clinical picture including the three subtypes

noted by DSM-IV.
10. Describe the family patterns that contribute to childhood conduct disorders, and summarize what is known about their treatment.
11. Define *delinquency*, describe some of the forms it takes, and explain several key variables that may be involved in the development of delinquent behavior.
12. Describe and evaluate several systems that have been used to deal with delinquency.
13. List several general characteristics of anxiety disorders in childhood and adolescence, and describe two subclassifications noted by DSM-IV.
14. Explain four causal factors that have been emphasized in explanations of childhood anxiety disorders, and summarize what is known about their treatment.
15. Discuss the symptoms associated with childhood depression and their relationship to adult depression.
16. Summarize what is known about *functional enuresis, functional encopresis, sleepwalking,* and *tics* as they occur in children and adolescents.
17. List and explain six special factors that must be considered in relation to treatment for children.
18. Define *advocacy* and evaluate the success of several governmental agencies and private groups that have tried to provide this function for children.
19. Describe the current controversy over whether childhood depression should be considered a separate clinical syndrome.
20. Discuss the evidence regarding the transmission of psychopathology from parents to children.

KEY TERMS

developmental psychopathology
hyperactivity
juvenile delinquency
overanxious disorder
encopresis
tics
echolalia

attention-deficit hyperactivity disorder (ADHD)
conduct disorders
separation anxiety disorder
enuresis
sleepwalking disorder
Tourette's syndrome
Autism

FOCUS ON RESEARCH 1

Ferguson, D., Horwood, L., and Lynskey, M. (1995). "The Stability of Disruptive Childhood Behaviors." Journal of Abnormal Child Psychology, 23, 379-396.

Researchers have shown a long interest in determining the stability and continuity of deviant childhood behavior. With such information the natural history of some conditions like conduct disorders or oppositional defiant behavior could be identified. Previous research suggests that childhood behavior problems are frequently persistent and endure over time. Antisocial behavior has been found to be one of the more enduring of the childhood behavior disorders.

The authors suggest that previous research showing stability may have included some measurement errors. If these errors were corrected and an appropriate range of indicators measurements were employed, then a true picture of the nature of stability could be obtained.

This article reports on a longitudinal analysis of the stability of conduct disorder behaviors in a New Zealand sample. The children were observed from the ages of seven to fifteen years. The results of these observations were corrected for possible errors of measurement. They found a much smaller percentage of children who showed improvement of conduct disorders than has been reported previously in the literature.

Reasons for the errors in measurement came from the use of fallible report data with poor reliability. The reliability may be adequate for single observations, but with multiple reports in the course of a longitudinal study the errors emerge. Also, the range of measurement techniques is often limited in previous studies which may not assess the conduct disorders as their symptoms change. This study attempted to deal with the reliability issue and included sufficient measurement techniques to assess conduct disorders in all their manifestations.

Questions for Discussion

1. What are the possible sources for reliability errors?

2. How can the symptoms in conduct disorders change over time?

3. What are the implications of the findings of enduring patterns of conduct disorders?

FOCUS ON RESEARCH 2

Osterling, J, and Dawson, G. (1994). "Early Recognition of Children with Autism: A Study of First Birthday Home Videotapes." Journal of Autism and Developmental Disorders, 24, 247-257.

Previous research has shown that autism is usually diagnosed around the age of four years, although parents of the child report that they suspected problems around one year of age. Because of this late diagnosis, professionals often do not see the early developmental aspects of the condition. Usual reports of the early behavior of these children come from parental retrospective reports. These reports are subject to distortion and may be clouded by the events of the intervening years.

These authors suggest that one method that can be used to attain objective measurement of the early developmental period of autism is through the examination of home movies taken before the child was formally diagnosed. The purpose of this study was to document with the use of home videotapes the early behavior displayed by infants later diagnosed with autism.

The authors compared the early videotapes of a group of children with autism to those of normally developing children. Videotapes of birthday parties for the two groups were coded and judged on a variety of dimensions related to autism and developmental issues.

There results showed that autism can be differentiated from the normally developing child by age one year. Differences were obtained in the three general areas of social behavior, joint attention, and certain specific autistic actions. How often the child looked at others was the single best predictor of a child's later diagnosis. Showing, pointing, and failing to orient oneself in response to name were common behaviors. The authors suggest the importance of the development of screening instruments that can be used in the first year to identify autism.

Questions for Discussion

1.   What would be the value of early detection of autism?

2.   How do parents respond to the behaviors found to be indicative of later diagnosis of autism?

FOCUS ON RESEARCH 3

Fischer, M. (1990). "Parenting Stress and the Child With Attention Deficit Hyperactivity Disorder." Journal of Clinical Child Psychology, 19, 337-346.

This is a good review of the research dealing with the various stresses faced by parents of children with attention deficit hyperactivity disorder (ADHD). Four categories of research are identified by the author. The first categorization of research deals with the stress reported by parents of ADHD children. This group of studies has a focus on the mother. The parenting Stress Index has been used by a number of investigators. Mothers have been found to report stress from their child's distractibility, feelings of depression, self-blame, social isolation, and incompetence in parenting skills. These stresses were more pronounced when the child was younger than over eight years of age. Other events outside of direct child-parent interactions also contributed to the parent's stress. These included the ADHD child's interactions with siblings and the attempts by siblings to isolate the hyperactive child. Recent studies suggest that the stresses are similar for parents of either ADHD boys or girls.

The second line of research reviewed by the author deals with parental psychopathology. The existence of maternal psychopathology has been reported by a number of researchers. Depression was a common disorder found in parents, and this condition was believed to heighten the perception of maladjustment in the ADHD child. Alcoholism and hyperactivity in the parents when they were children were also found at an elevated prevalence rate. This has led a number of investigators to address the possible genetic transmission of hyperactivity. Currently, the research record does not clearly show a genetic cause of ADHD.

The third category of research deals with parental marital discord. Longitudinal studies have shown a causal relationship between a child's characteristics and marital conflict. Impulsivity, excessive energy, and aggression were some of the precursors found in ADHD children that led to family discord. The final area examined by the investigator was the quantity and quality of interactions between parent and ADHD child.

The ADHD child's interactions with parents typically show a lack of compliance toward parental requests. Off-task behavior frequently takes place, and excessive demands for attention are found. Children in the four to five year range were found to produce the highest incidence of conflicts during interactions with parents. Parents of ADHD children appear to develop a pattern of reprimand, command, and unresponsiveness toward the child.

The author concludes her review with a number of recommendations for future research endeavors. There is a need to expand the research to include fathers of ADHD chidren, since mothers have been the primary focus to date. Other research efforts need to compare parenting stresses found in other clinical groups to determine the possible unique stressors associated with ADHD children.

Questions for Discussion

1. Describe some of the daily hassles parents may encounter with their ADHD child.
2. Should medication influence the level of stress in an ADHD child's family?
3. What behaviors cause parents the most stress? Why?

READINGS

1. Douglas, V., and Parry, P. (1994). "Effects of Reward and Nonreward on Frustration and Attention in Attention-Deficit Disorder." Journal of Abnormal Child Psychology, 22, 281-302.

2. Harkmimoto, T., Tyama, M. and Kuroda, Y. (1995). "Development of the Brainstem and Cerebellum in Autistic Patients." Journal of Autism and Developmental Disorders, 25, 1-18.

3. Lattimore, P., Visher, C., and Linster, R. (1995). "Predicting Rearrest for Violence Among Serious Youthful Offenders." Journal of Research in Crime and Delinquency, 32, 54-83.

4. Menard, S. (1995). "A Developmental Test of the Mertonian Anomie Theory." Journal of Research in Crime and Delinquency, 32, 136-174.

5. Rutter, M. (1994). "Family Discord and Conduct Disorder: Cause, Consequence, or Correlate?" Journal of Family Psychology, 8, 170-186.

6. Schatz, J., and Hamdam-Allen, G. (1995). "Effects of Age and IQ on Adaptive Behavior Domain for Chidren With Autism." Journal of Autism and Developmental Disorders, 25, 51-60.

7. Slomkouski, C., Klein, R., and Mannizza, S. (1995). "Is Self-Esteem an Important

Outcome in Hyperactive Children?" <u>Journal of Abnormal Child Psychology</u>, <u>23</u>, 303-316.

8.   Slylvester, C, and Kruesi, M. (1994). "Child and Adolescent Psychopharmacotherapy: Progress and Pitfalls." <u>Psychiatric Annals</u>, <u>24</u>, 83-90.

9.   Tolan, P.H., and Thomas, P. (1995). "The Implications of Age of Onset for Delinquency: Longitudinal Data." <u>Journal of Abnormal Child Psychology</u>, <u>23</u>, 157-182.

10. Varey, M., Daleiden, E., and Brown, L. "Biased Attention in Childhood Anxiety Disorders." <u>Journal of Abnormal Child Psychology</u>, <u>23</u>, 267-277.

11. Webster, S. (1994). "Advancing Videotape Parent Training: A Comparison Study." <u>Journal of Consulting and Clinical Psychology</u>, <u>62</u>, 583-593.

12. Wilens, T., Biederman, J., and Spencer, T. (1994). "Clonidine for Sleep Disturbances Associated with Attention-Deficit Disorder." <u>Journal of the American Academy of Child and Adolescent Psychiatry</u>, <u>33</u>, 424-426.

LECTURE AND DISCUSSION IDEAS

1.   Locus of control can be easily measured in a classroom demonstration. A research article by B. Yates, H. Lewis, and G. Wells (1994) examined the connection of this construct to severly disturbed adolescents (<u>Journal of Youth and Adolescence</u>, <u>23</u>, 289-314). A classroom discussion can examine what characteristics of locus of control relate to mental disorder in adolescents, and how this may be a useful measure for considering future implications for the adolescent with a mental disorder.

2.   Because schools play a major role in the experience of children, their role in contributing to the mental health needs of children is of central importance. Knitzer, Steinberg, and Fleisch (1991) review the various ways that schools can expand their role in enhancing self-esteem and build a sense of competence in children. These authors provide an excellent overview of the legal and administrative issues in implementing programs designed to enhance mental health in school-age children. They also provide a number of implications for the clinician who serves children with behavioral and emotional problems (<u>Journal of Clinical Child Psychology</u>, <u>20</u>, 102-111).

3.   An interesting lecture to supplement the textbook's material on attention deficit disorder can be developed from an article by P. Dahl, D. Pelham, and E. Wierson (1991). They explored the role of sleep disturbance in contributing to the symptomatology of attention deficit disorder. They provide a case study that is a good illustration of symptoms and the methods used to treat sleep disturbance. Chronotherapy facilitated a clinically significant improvement in the symptoms of the case study (<u>Journal of Pediatric Psychology</u>, <u>16</u>, 229-239).

4.   The class can discuss what they view as symptoms of psychological disorder in

children. Do the students evaluate hyperactivity as a major problem? Discuss how problems may change depending on who is making the evaluation--for example, teacher vs. parent.

5.   What opinions does the class have concerning divorce and marital discord in the emotional development of the child? Once divorce takes place, should children have a voice in determining which parent he or she will live with? Should a couple stay together for the benefit of the children? A number of recent legal cases can be used for resources.

6.   Children are usually involuntary patients when they are brought to a psychologist or psychiatrist for treatment. What are the ethical implications of "forcing" a child to receive treatment? What special problems might this produce for the therapist?

7.   An interesting lecture-discussion can involve the review of a case report on a person who has an autistic child and managed to overcome many problems when he reached adulthood. James Bemporand (1979, Journal of Autism and Developmental Disorders, 9, 179-198) presents this case report.

8.   What long-term problems may evolve from an early dependency on medication to control such behavior as hyperactivity? Does the child begin to feel that the use of a drug is necessary for his or her healthy functioning? Peers may also have negative reactions to a child who "needs" a drug every day.

ACTIVITIES AND PROJECTS

1.   Students can be assigned the task of trying to identify the possible personality patterns and coping styles found among children with attention-deficit hyperactivity disorder. These patterns could be presented and discussed to demonstrate the problems many parents and teachers have when trying to deal with attention deficit disorder in children. The research by Lufi and Parish-Plass (1995) is a good starting point for student investigation into this issue (Journal of Clinical Psychology, 51, 94-99). Discussion with the class, can focus on the possible intervention strategies that can be used in the home and school to assist children with these characteristics.

2.   What agencies are available for the child? Students can be assigned the task of investigating the types of services rendered by the different human service agencies around the community. What facilities treat children exclusively? What are the qualifications of the agencies' staff? Have staff members received special training?

3.   What advocacy groups or programs are represented in the community? Have students investigate current issues that advocacy groups are pursuing. An article that presents good background information is one by J. Bernier and D. Siegel (1994) who describe the importance of family and community in attention-deficit disorder management (Families in Society: The Journal of Contemporary Human Services, 40, 142-150).

4.   Students may gain valuable firsthand experience with childhood problems through

volunteer work. Students may become involved with such programs as Big Sister/Big Brother.

5.	Assign the class the project of observing children of different ages at play. Have the students categorize problem behaviors they might observe. Common categories include hostility, hyperactivity, distractibility, anxiousness, shyness. What common problems were observed the most frequently? What behaviors typically disappear as children become older? Which behaviors appear to be the most long-lasting? How do other children react to those peers who evidence "problem" behaviors?

6.	Are the portrayals of children on television good models for youngsters? Have students review some current programs and describe the children in the shows. Are children on television exhibiting prosocial and desirable characteristics? What are the most common traits shown? What characteristics are least likely to be part of the child's behavioral repertoire?

7.	Students can examine the bell and pad that are commonly used for treating enuresis in children. This device is sold through most major catalog services and in many department stores. The instrument can be purchased for classroom demonstrations.

CHAPTER 15

Clinical Assessment

CHAPTER OUTLINE

I. The Information Sought in Assessment
   A. The problem must be identified
      1. Formal diagnoses are needed for insurance purposes
      2. Planning for treatment follows from diagnosis
      3. It is essential for administrative purposes
   B. The diagnostic process involves gathering a range of information about the person
      1. Descriptions of long-term personality characteristics are included
      2. The social context of the individual is described
      3. A dynamic formulation is produced by the clinician
         a. Hypotheses about future behavior are derived
         b. Decisions about treatment are made with consent of the client

II. Varing Types of Assessment Data
   A. Coordination of physical, psychological, and environmental procedures is needed in assessment
   B. Assessment procedures are influenced by a clinician's orientation
      1. Psychiatrists are biologically-oriented practitioners
      2. Psychoanalytically-oriented clinicians use unstructured assessment methods
      3. Behaviorally-oriented clinicians determine the reinforcers for behaviors

III. Importance of Rapport Between the Clinician and the Client
   A. Assurances of confidentiality
   B. Motivation of client for being assessed

IV. Assessment of the Physical Organism
   A. The general physical examinaton
      1. A medical history is obtained
      2. This medical exam is needed when dealing with potential psychogenically induced disorders
   B. The neurological examination
      1. Electroencephalogram (EEG) assesses the brain wave patterns

2. Computerized axial tomography (CAT-scan) can reveal diseased parts of the brain
3. Positron emission tomography (PET scan) appraises how an organ is functioning
4. Nuclear magnetic resonance imaging (MRI) allows visualization of the internal organs

C. The neuropsychological examination
  1. Measurement of alteration in behavioral or psychological functioning involves neuropsychological assessment
  2. Test batteries used yield standardized test scores
    a. The Halstead-Reitan is one battery used by clinicians
    b. The Luria-Nebraska battery is another alternative

V. Psychosocial Assessment
  A. Assessment interviews
    1. Information is obtained in a face-to-face interaction
    2. Structured formats have been developed to guide questions
      a. Reliability increases with structured interviews
      b. All interviews need specific goals
    3. Rating scales can increase interview reliability
    4. Computer programs provide branching subroutines to guide interviews
  B. The clinical observation of behavior
    1. Direct observation should occur ideally in the natural environment
      a. Self-observations and objective reporting of behavior are often used in the natural environment
      b. The client can be an excellent source of information
    2. Rating scales help to organize observations
      a. The Brief Psychiatric Ratings Scale (BPRS) is widely used to record observations
      b. Comparisons to other client's symptoms can be made
    3. Trained observers provide data for clinical management
    4. Children's behavior is often rated by parents and/or teachers
  C. Psychological tests
    1. Tests are standardized procedures to sample behavior
    2. The competence of the tester is a crucial factor in reliability
    3. Intelligence tests
      a. Wechsler Intelligence Scale for Children-Revised (WISC-R)
      b. Wechsler Adult Intelligence Scales-Revised (WAIS-R)
    4. Projective tests
      a. Rorschach
      b. Thematic Apperception Test
      c. Sentence completion test
    5. Objective tests
      a. Minnesota Multiphasic Personality Inventory (MMPI)
      b. The MMPI-2 has recently been developed
    6. Computer interpretation of objective personality tests

176

D. Psychological assessment in forensic or legal cases
    1. Standardized tests are being used
    2. Limitations exist for these tests
E. The use of psychological tests in personnel screening
    1. Psychological screening for emotional problems
        a. "Screening in" versus "screening out" job candidates
        b. Selection of the appropriate test instrument is critical
    2. Issues in personality test job screening
        a. How much weight should a test be given?
        b. Is testing an invasion of privacy?
        c. Is the testing fair to all?
F. A psychological case study: Esteban
    1. Interviews and behavior observations
    2. Family history
    3. Intelligence testing
    4. Personality testing
    5. Summary of the psychological assessment
    6. A follow-up note

VI. Integration of Assessment Data
A. Data must be integrated into a working model for treatment
    1. The data is evaluated during staff conferences
    2. A tentative diagnosis results from the integration of data
B. Feedback data provides a measure of treatment effectiveness
    1. Decisions can have profound effects on the individual
    2. An accurate diagnosis and treatment plan needs to be developed

VI. Unresolved Issues on the Use of Computerized Assessment
A. Critics of computer-based diagnosis cite the lack of supporting research
    1. Weak software programs exist
    2. Computerized tests should be viewed as tools in the diagnostic process
B. Many clinicians remain uninvolved with computerized diagnosis
    1. Some practitioners do not have time to become familiar with them
    2. Many practitioners limit their practice to treatment
    3. Some clinicians view computerized assessment as impersonal
    4. Some clinicians see the computerized assessment as a professional threat

LEARNING OBJECTIVES

1. Explain the difference between diagnosis and clinical assessment, and list several components that must be integrated into the dynamic formulation.
2. Describe several medical and neuropsychological procedures that can be used for the physical evaluation of clients, and explain why each type of data is gathered.
3. Describe the characteristics of a good assessment interview, and list some advantages and disadvantages of the interview method.

4. Describe several techniques and instruments that are used to make clinical observations of client behavior.
5. Explain the kind of data gathered by psychological tests, and list two types that are commonly used.
6. List and describe several intelligence tests used by clinicians, and explain how this information can be used in assessment.
7. Explain the assumptions behind the use of projective tests, and describe the use of the Rorschach Test and the Thematic Apperception Test (TAT) in clinical assessment.
8. Define *objective tests* and describe the Minnesota Multiphasic Personality Inventory (MMPI) and its uses in clinical assessment.
9. Describe the changes made on the new MMPI-2, and discuss the benefits and effects the changes will have.
10. Explain what is meant by the actuarial approach used to interpret the MMPI, and describe three methods of obtaining computer-based interpretation.
11. Cite some general objectives of personnel screening, and describe the use of some psychological tests to accomplish these goals.
12. List and explain three questions which must be addressed before implementing a psychological assessment program for preemployment screening.
13. Summarize the psychological case study of Esteban, noting the various types of clinical assessment that were used to build the dynamic formulation.
14. Explain the functions of a staff conference in integrating the assessment data and making decisions abut the client.
15. Describe the controversy over computerized psychological assessment including the debate over Matarazzo's criticisms.
16. Describe three possible reasons for the underutilization of computer-based assessment procedures.

KEY TERMS

dynamic formulation
dysrythmias
positron emission tomography (PET scan)
neuropsychological assessment
rating scales
projective tests
Thematic Apperception Test (TAT)
objective tests
factor analysis

electroencephalogram (EEG)
computerized axial tomography (CAT scan)
nuclear magnetic resonance imaging (MRI)
self-monitoring
role playing
Rorschach Test
sentence completion test
Minnesota Multiphasic Personality Inventory
actuarial procedures

FOCUS ON RESEARCH 1

Sloan, P., Arsenault, L, Hilsenroth, M., and Handler, L. (1995). "Rorschach Measures of

Posttraumatic Stress in Persian Gulf War Veterans." <u>Journal of Personality Assessment</u>, <u>64</u>, 397-414.

Veterans of the Gulf War were administered both the Rorschach and the MMPI-2. These subjects were reporting symptoms after their experience in the war that could be associated with posttraumatic stress PTS. They were Marine reservists who had been called to active duty during the Persian Gulf War. The authors stated that the Gulf War returnees provided a rare opportunity to study acute psychological sequelae of war stresses.

Usually research has focused on veterans some years after their war experiences and after symptoms had fully developed. They found the average time after the war experience for the studies they reviewed to be five years. The importance of an early intervention is related to the eventual readjustment patterns of PTS veterans. Thus this study provided important information toward the goal of early intervention.

This study was considered by the authors to be valuable for the additional reasons that: 1.) it could serve as an aid to clinicians trying to understand the nature of acute combat stress; 2.) provide information on veterans suffering from PTS to be compared to normative PTSD samples; and 3.) to help establish debriefing procedures for veterans.

The Rorschach was found to be effective in detecting acute PTS. These veterans showed that their capacity to direct and control their behavior was seriously in question. The MMPI-2 established its usefulness in detecting PTS related problems. Further, this study provided the first direct data linking the MMPI-2 to Rorschach responses in the area of PTS. They concluded that both instruments are effective in the identification of PTS. In addition to these measures, the authors administered the Combat Content Scale, which assessed the various aspect of the veteran's experiences in the war zone. They found that noncombat experiences had distinct psychological effects on participants in the Persian Gulf War.

The authors concluded that it is important to immediately assess returning veterans from war zones for signs of PTS. Early interventions could then be implemented for those in need.

Questions for Discussion

1. What is the usefulness of having additional tests for the identification of PTS? The tests in this study are much different in design. Discuss the value of each.
2. What are some of the possible unique sources of stress in the Persian Gulf War experience?
3. What types of experiences relate to the war zone experience?

FOCUS ON RESERCH 2

Schork, E., Eckert, E., and Halmi, K. (1994). "The Relationship Between Psychopathology, Eating Disorder Diagnosis, and Clincial Outcome at the 10 Year Follow-up in Anxorexia Nervosa." <u>Comprehensive Psychiatry</u>, <u>35</u>, 1113-123.

This study is a good example of the use of objective personality measurement techniques in determining long term outcomes among persons with anorexia nervosa. The authors report on the ten year follow-up of seventy-six anorectic women. The original study that the women participated in compared the efficacy of behavior therapy and cyproheptadine in a thirty-five day hospital program. They had been diagnoses with anorexia nervosa at the time of the original study. At that time they completed the MMPI and the Categories of General Outcome. This latter measure has been used frequently in outcome studies with anorectics.

Traditionally two methodological approaches have been used in the study of eating disorders, the structured interview and standardized psychometric assessment instrument. This present study is considered by the authors to be an unusual opportunity to assess psychopathology in a group of diagnosed anorectic clients with various outcomes.

They found a substantial and orderly interrelationship at the ten year follow-up between degree of general psychopathology and severity of eating disorder symptomatology. This conclusion was seen in the converging lines of evidence obtained in the MMPI profiles and correlations between MMPI clinical scale elevations and levels of eating disorder outcomes.

Those individuals who had recovered from anorexia nervosa and had no other eating disorder showed little or no psychopathology on the MMPI. But persons who were still anorectic usually showed levels of serious psychopathology. The scale elevations were noted on the Hs, D, Hy, Pd, Pa, Pt, and Sc scale scores of the MMPI. The scores were indicative of persons with somatization, body preoccupation, immaturity, depression, anxious dysphoria, impulsivity, suspiciousness, obsessive-compulsive thinking, social alienation, and idiosyncratic thinking.

The absence of psychopathology indicators in the recovered group puts in question the assumption that the anorexic nervosa disorder occurs in the context of other psychiatric illnesses. This study found that those who did not recover showed significantly higher levels of psychopathology than the group with most favorable outcomes. These researchers found that dysphoric mood, obsessive-compulsive thinking and behavior, and negative self-attributions (MMPI scales, D and Pt) were most strongly associated with persistant eating disorders.

Questions for Discussion

1. What are some of the shortcomings of using the MMPI for outcome research? What are the strengths?

2. The authors suggest the need to include bulimia when studying anorexia nervosa. What would be the reasons for this?

3. What are some of the long term consequences of experiencing an eating disorder?

4. What other personality measures could be used for long term follow-up of eating disorders?

FOCUS ON RESEARCH 3

Meeks, S. (1990). "Age Bias in the Diagnostic Decision-Making Behavior of Clinicians." Professional Psychology: Research and Practice, 21, 279-184.

The field of gerontology has dramatically grown over the last three decades. This has stimulated the interest in how stereotypes about aging may influence the quality of care received by the elderly population. This article provides information on how attitudes toward the older adult can influence the categorization of mental disorders.

Previous research has shown that psychologists often view older persons as rigid, poor learners, poor candidates for psychological interventions, and lacking in energy. How these attitudes might influence the behavior of professionals during the diagnostic process was a concern of this study. A group of psychologists was recruited through membership in a state psychological association to serve as subjects. These professionals and a group of graduate students in a clinical training program provided judgments of diagnosis and prognosis for ninety-six case vignettes designed by the researcher. The vignettes were constructed to vary age, mood, somatic symptoms, cognitive deficits, and prior diagnosis.

Results revealed that the age of the patient was significantly related to the diagnosis of depression. Depression was given as a diagnosis most often for middle-aged cases. Physical disorders increased into old age and prognosis declined. This pessimism with regard to prognosis of elderly persons suggests that practitioners believe psychological interventions are not effective for this group. The researchers also found that prior diagnosis greatly influenced current decisions about the cases. This reliance on prior diagnoses provided in the vignettes was particularly detrimental to the older adult cases.

Some limitations of this study include the analog nature of it. The quantity of the vignettes and the demand of making diagnostic decisions without personal interaction limit the scope of the researcher's conclusions. But the diagnostic process is a rule-driven endeavor guided by criteria in the DSM-III-R. Some of these criteria appear to have been altered by attitudinal factors. The bias held by clinicians toward the elderly could manifest itself into few efforts to treat functional disorders in the elderly population.

Questions for Discussion

1.   What are some of the misconceptions held by the public concerning the elderly population?

2.   What type of training could be used to overcome age-bias attitudes?

3.   What other disorders besides depression are attributed to the elderly population?

4.   What improvements could be made in this study's research methods?

READINGS

1. Bergen, A., and Mosley, J. (1994). "Attention and Attentional Shift Efficiency in Individuals With and Without Mental Retardation." <u>American Journal of Mental Retardation</u>, <u>98</u>, 732-743.

2. Bidaut, R., Bradford, S., and Smith, E. (1994). "Prevalence of Mental Illnesses in Adult Offspring of Alchoholic Mothers." <u>Drug and Alcohol Dependence</u>, <u>35</u>, 81-90.

3. Cutler, P. (1994). "Iron Overload and Psychiatric Illness." <u>Canadian Journal of Psychiatry</u>, <u>39</u>, 8-11.

4. Day, D., Pal, A., and Goldberg, K. (1994). "Assessing the Post-Residential Functioning of Latency Aged Conduct Disordered Children." <u>Residential Treatment for Children and Youth</u>, <u>11</u>, 45-61.

5. Dunlap, G., Robbins, F., and Darrow, M. (1994). "Parent's Reports of Their Children's Challenging Behaviors." <u>Mental Retardatiopn</u>, <u>32</u>, 206-212.

6. Ernst, M., Godfrey, K., Silva, R., and Pouget, E. (1994). "A New Pictorial Instrument for Child and Adolsecent Psychiatry." <u>Psychiatric Research</u>, <u>51</u>, 87-104.

7. Meyer, B., and Heino, F. (1994). "Intersexuality and the Diagnosis of Gender Identity Disorder." <u>Archives of Sexual Behavior</u>, <u>23</u>, 21-40.

8. Post, R .D. (1986). "MMPI Predictors of Mania Among Psychiatric Patients." <u>Journal of Personality Assessment</u>, <u>50</u>, 218-256.

9. Reynolds, C. (1985). "Clinical Measurement Issues in Learning Disabilities." <u>Journal of Special Education</u>, <u>18</u>, 451-475.

10. Rush, A., and Weissenburger, J. (1994). "Melancholic Symptom Features and DSM-IV." <u>American Journal of Psychiatry</u>, <u>151</u>, 489-498.

11. Schreiter-Gasser, U., and Ziegler, P. (1994). "Quantitative EEG Analysis in Early Onset Alzheimer's Disease: Correlations with Severity, Clinical Characteristics, Visual EEG and CCT." <u>Electroencephalography and Clinical Neurophysiology</u>, <u>90</u>, 267-272.

12. Seidman, L, Yurgelun, T., and Kremen, W. (1994). "Relationship of Prefrontal and Temporal Lobe MRI Measures to Neuropsychological Performance in Chronic Schizophrenia." <u>Biological Psychiatry</u>, <u>35</u>, 235-246.

13. Strakowski, S. (1994). "Diagnostic Validity of Schizophreniform Disorder." <u>American Journal of Psychiatry</u>, <u>151</u>, 815-824.

14.	Toro, J., Salamero, M., and Martinez, E. (1994). "Assessment of Sociocultural Influences on the Aesthetic Body Shape Model in Anorexia Nervosa." Acta Psychiatrica Scandinavica, 89, 147-151.

15.	Young, M., Fogg, L., and Fawcett, J. (1994). "Interactions of Risk Factors in Predicting Suicide." American Journal of Psychiatry, 151, 434-435.

DISCUSSION AND LECTURE IDEAS

1.	What effect does a significant turning point have on a person's life? Are there important life events that influence the perception of a person's mental health? A classroom discussion can result from a simple assessment of students reports of turning points in their lives. Ask students to identify on a time line some events they believe to be turning points in their lives when goals or personal direction in life were changed. Then ask them for comments of how the events changed their lives. Events could be grouped along a dimension of how positive or negative the event was in their lives. A discussion can be directed toward having students identify the usefulness of this type of assessment for mental health concerns.

2.	When presenting the information on projective and objective assessment to the class, an article by Hilsenroth and Handler (1995) may stimulate classroom discussion (Journal of Personality Assessment, 64, 243-257). This article reports on the viewpoints of students who were learning to use the Rorschach. What factors need to be known to make valid assessments using such an instrument can be discussed. Students interested in graduate study may be particularly interested in this study and could be assigned the task of reporting on the article for the class. A classroom discussion could examine differences in learning projective testing versus objective assessment techniques. Would a student need to learn both methodologies?

3.	An interesting class lecture can be developed using the article by J. Meloy and L. Kenney (1994) which reports on a Rorschach investigation of incarcerated sexual homicide perpetrators (Journal of Personality Assessment, 62, 58-67). They compared the Rorschach for the inmates to nonsexually offending but violent psychopaths. They identified distinctive patterns for the sexual homicide offenders.

4.	How do students feel about the use of intelligence tests? Do they feel that scores on such tests are valid indicators of ability? What experiences have the students had with intellience tests? How many students know their IQ score? How was it obtained? Were any decisions concerning education dictated by their IQ scores? Should "gifted" students identified via IQ tests be given special activities and study assignments during their schooling?

5.	What is the probability that a person could "fake" assessment data? Can people make themselves look good or bad during a clinical assesment? What procedures, if any, can be used to detect fraudulent answers on assessment instruments? Could a person secure information about assessment instruments from libraries and learn how to answer assessment questions to portray himself or herself in a certain fashion? Could this method be used by a criminal to substantiate an insanity defense in court?

6.   Some therapists see litle value in completing an extensive assessment of a patient. The assessment could serve to dispose a therapist to view the patient in a predetermined fashion. What are the pros and cons of conducting full-scale clinical assessments? Are the time, cost, and effort of a complete assessment warranted by the value of the data obtained? Student groups can be established to present different points of view on the topic.

7.   The "problem patient" can be the basis of an interesting lecture topic. Persons who show vague and shifting symptoms, yet have chronic complaints, can often tax the professional's patience. Students should be able to identify some symptoms that would cause problems for a therapist. Discuss how assessment instruments could be useful for the clinician faced with a "problem patient" who presents vague or shifting symptoms to the therapist during therapy sessions.

ACTIVITIES AND PROJECTS

1.   How important is information from family members when assessing children? What pattern of family participation in assessment conferences is most beneficial for gaining significant information about the child? Discuss the problems in using reports from parents and teachers when diagnosing problems in a child's behavior or emotional responses.

2.   Students can construct their own projective test instrument by creating some inkblot stimuli. Using food color and white sheets of paper, the students can make some of their own stimulus designs. Have the students "administer" their designs to other students. Are certain responses common to certain designs? A discussion of how such tests as the Rorschach are used and validated can evolve from this project.

3.   Conduct a "clinical interview" with one or more volunteers in class. Demonstrate the use of open-ended questions to secure information from a patient. Illustrate the different topical areas often covered during the clinical interview.

4.   Many of the different assessment instruments can be presented to the class for illustration purposes. Students enjoy completing a Draw-a-Person task. The basic projective aspects of such a test can then be discussed with the class. J. Scribner and C. Handler (1987, Journal of Personality Assessment, 51, 112-122) discuss how the interpreter of a projective test can be influenced by his or her own personality.

5.   The use of self-monitoring can be experienced by the students. Students can be asked to self-monitor some self-selected behavior for a few days. The type of behaviors monitored can include smoking, study time, television watching, or drinking. Have the students attempt to keep careful records of the activity and then discuss their experiences during class. What was it like to monitor a behavior? Did the monitoring have any effect on the behavior? What are the clinical implications of the records? How faithful were they in monitoring their behaviors?

6.   Students can examine the limitations of the clinical interview. Assign certain students the role of interviewee. Give these students a brief biography of a role to play. The

students serving as interviewers are required to conduct brief 5-10 minute sessions with the role players. After the interviewers have had the opportunity to complete their sessions independently of each other, the interviewers' notes can be compared. During class, discussion can focus on how the different interviewers obtained similar information. Who were the most effective interviewers? What techniques did they use?

7. The students can be exposed to clinical assessment using objective tests through the administration of a behavior scale to the class. The Pleasure Scale (1983, Archives of General Psychiatry, 40, 79-84) is a good instrument because it does not imply any psychopathology. The students' ratings for the scale can be compared in class.

CHAPTER 16

Biologically Based Therapies

CHAPTER OUTLINE

I. Early Attempts at Biological Intervention
    A. Coma and convulsive therapies
        1. Insulin coma therapy
            a. Introduced in 1932, it is rarely used today
            b. Insulin is introduced until a person goes into shock
            c. Patients showing improvement were those responding well to other therapy forms
        2. Electroconvulsive therapy (ECT)
            a. Bilateral and unilateral are two types of ECT
            b. Cerletti and Bini developed the procedure
            c. ECT still engenders controversy
            d. The National Institute of Mental Health sponsored an evaluation of ECT's safety
                1) They found it effective for some depression
                2) Modern procedures prevent many medical problems
    B. Psychosurgery
        1. Prefrontal lobotomy was developed by Moniz
            a. Tens of thousands of patients received the procedures from 1935 to 1955
            b. Current practice is more circumspect than years ago
            c. Continued concern about the procedures exist today
        2. Elliot Valenstein published a recent book highly critical of psychosurgery techniques
            a. Professional rivalry is involved in its use
            b. Informed consent may be meaningless

II. The Emergence of Pharmacological Methods of Treatment
    A. Types of drugs used in therapy
        1. Antipsychotic drugs
            a. The major tranquilizers alleviate the psychotic symptoms
            b. Their use has greatly altered the enviroment of mental hospitals
            c. The development of the drugs began with reserpine
            d. The first phenothiazine was chlorpromazine

        e.   The drugs have troublesome side effects
            1)   Tardive dyskinesia
            2)   "Target dosing" attempts to minimize side effects

2.   Antidepressant drugs
    a.   Monoamine oxidase inhibitors and tricyclics
    b.   A second generation of drugs (Prozac) has appeared
    c.   Pharmacological treatment often produces dramatic results
    d.   Research has compared drug treatment with other therapy forms

3.   Antianxiety drugs
    a.   These are widely prescribed by physicians
    b.   Meprobamate drugs produce muscular relaxation
    c.   Benzodiazepines are used as sleeping pills, and diminish generalized fear
    d.   The potential for abuse is significant

4.   Lithium for the bipolar mood disorders
    a.   Lithium is 70-80 percent effective in resolving manic states
    b.   Long-term use must be monitored for complications
    c.   The reasons for its effectiveness are unknown
    d.   Carbamazepine (Tegretal) is a recent drug used for bipolar disorder

B.   Drug therapy for children
    1.   Various medications have been used effectively with children
        a.   Dosage must be carefully maintained
        b.   Paradoxical effects sometimes are found
    2.   Stimulants are used to treat hyperactivity

C.   A biopsychological perspective on pharmacological therapy
    1.   Drug therapy has helped prevent hospitalization for many patients
    2.   Drugs do not cure disorders, and other treatment is needed
        a.   Integrative approaches are expanding
        b.   Optimistic research findings are obtained from combined drug and psychological treatments

III.   Unresolved Issues: Has Pharmacology Opened the Door to Personality Change?
    A.   Reuptake inhibitors are being commonly proscribed
        1.   Help the person "feel better"
        2.   Use for a number of vague complaints
    B.   Controversy in popular press concerning Prozac
    C.   Entering era of "cosmetic psychopharmacology"

LEARNING OBJECTIVES

1.   Briefly summarize the early history of attempts at biological intervention, and explain why medical treatment for physical diseases is far more advanced than medical treatment for behavior disorders.

2.   Describe the use of insulin coma therapy, and explain why it has largely disappeared.

3.   Describe the discovery and use of electroconvulsive therapy (ECT) and its positive and

negative effects on the patient.

4. Explain the controversy about using ECT and the reasons for its continued use.
5. Describe prefrontal lobotomy and its effects on the patient.
6. Compare the psychosurgery of today with its earlier forerunners, and describe the current debate over "brain-disabling' therapies.
7. List four types of chemical agents now commonly used in therapy for mental disorders.
8. List several antipsychotic compunds, and describe their effects and side effects in the treatment of behavior disorders.
9. List several antidepressant compounds, and describe their effects and side effects in the treatment of mental disorders.
10. List several antianxiety compounds, and describe their effects and side effects in the treatment of maladaptive behavior.
11. Describe the use of lithium in the treatment of bipolar mood disorders, and list its effects and side effects.
12. List some of the drugs that have been used in treating maladaptive behavior in children, and explain a danger of using drug therapy for hyperactive youngsters.
13. List some of the overall advantages and disadvantages of using pharmacological therapy for treating behavior disorders.
14. Describe megavitamin therapy, and summarize the conclusions of the American Psychiatric Association Task Force formed to evaluate it.
15. Describe hemodialysis therapy, and evaluate its results in treating schizophrenic patients.

KEY TERMS

insulin coma therapy
psychosurgery
pharmacology
tardive dyskinesia
antianxiety drugs

electroconvulsive therapy (ECT)
prefrontal lobotomy
antipsychotic drugs
antidepressant drugs

FOCUS ON RESEARCH 1

Everman, D., and Stoudemire, A. (1994). "Bipolar Disorder Associated with Klinefelter's Syndrome and Other Chromosomal Abnormalities." Psychosomatics, 35, 35-40.

There have been numerous reports in the literature concerning a possible connection between chromosomal abnormalities and bipolar illness, but no consistent relationship has been established. This article describes an attempt to examine this connection through the use of a case study. The patient has Klinefelter's syndrome which is defined by the 47XXY karyotype. The patient is a 38 year old male with mild mental retardation who was diagnosed with bipolar disorder. He was admitted for hospitalization during acute manic episode. Following his first manic episode at age thirty-three, lithium was used for management. Later he experienced cyclical manic attacks which required six hospitalizations. During these episodes he showed agitation, grandiosity, and delusional thinking. Multiple medications were selected for treatment during the previous hospitalizations including lithium, carbamazepine, clonazepam, perphenazine and valproic acid.

During his most recent hospitalization he exhibited agitation, disorientation, rapid unintelligible speech, labile affect, flight of ideas, and suicidal ideation. Because of the inability for medication to manage his manic mood, a trial of ECT was undertaken. He received a course of eight brief-pulse ECT treatments administered three times a week. The stimulus was applied through unilateral electrodes placed over the temporal and parietal lobes on the right hemisphere.

Clinical improvement was seen after the first three ECT treatments. During the course of the treatment, his mania continued to resolve. At the conclusion of ECT, he demonstrated a consistently calm demeanor with appropriate affect. At discharge, he maintained the demeanor on loxapine and sodium valproate. Follow-up showed that he remained in a stable condition.

Questions for Discussion

1.   What are some of the signs of Klinefelter's Syndrome?

2.   What are some of the problems associated with multiple medication use in treatment?

3.   Should persons with mental retardation receive ECT treatment for mental disorders?

FOCUS ON RESEARCH 2

Evans, M. (1991). "The Deep Structures of Psychology and Prescribing: More than a Supeficial Look." Journal of Clinical Psychology, 52, 9-11.

D'Afflitti, J. (1991). "Profoundly Different Professions: Commentary on Prescribing Privileges for Psychologists." Journal of Clinical Psychiatry, 52, 11-14.

One of the continuing controversies in the fields of clinical psychology and psychiatry centers on prescribing privileges for the former. Psychologists have advocated an expanded role of the clinician to treat psychological disorders through psychoactive medications. These two articles provide insights into the nature of the controversy and the long-standing feud between psychology and psychiatry.

The psychiatric community considers the use of psychoactive medications to be an essential aspect of their profession. The biological studies in medical training are considered more extensive and not at all comparable to those received by doctoral-level psychologists. The psychiatric profession notes that a patient placed on medication needs the supervision and understanding only a medically trained professional can provide. The reactions and interactions to medications would overwhelm the inadequately trained psychologist. Addtionally, legal issues would be extensive for the psychologist. When medication is prescribed, the patient receives various physical checks that cannot be provided by psychologists. This would present the psychologist with numerous medical and legal risks that he/she is not prepared for in training. Rather than sanctioning prescribing privileges for psychologists, some form of combined M.D.-Ph.D. training could be instituted.

Psychologists counter that they seek only limited prescribing privileges for an array of medications that they are familiar with from training. There have been psychologists in the Indian Health Service who have prescribed medication legally for years. Research has shown that they make fewer inappropriate prescriptions than their physician counterparts. Also, the psychological community should be able to provide services at a cheaper rate than psychiatrists. Although this controversy is far from settled, psychologists believe they have made advances in this fight.

Questions for Discussion

1. What factors would influence the decision to seek medication from a psychologist rather than a medical health professional?
2. Are nurses allowed to prescribe psychoactive medications? Should they be given this priviledge?
3. In what circumstances would a psychologist be better able to treat a person in need of psychoactive medication?
4. What financial issues are involved in this controversy?

READINGS

1. Beale, I, and McDowel, J. (1994). "Effects of Methylphenidate on Attention in Children with Moderate Mental Retardation." Journal of Developmental and Physical Disabilities, 6, 137-148.

2. Black, S. (1994). "Naltrexone in Infantile Autism." Journal of Autism and Developmental Disorders, 24, 236-238.

3. Cassano, G., and Cristina, T. (1994). "Adverse Effects Associated with the Short Term Treatment of Panic Disorder with Imipramine, Alprozolam or Placebo." European Neuropsychopharnacology, 4 47-53.

4. Chapman, N. (1994). "Safety of Clonidine and Nortriptyline." Journal of the American Academy of Child and Adolescent Psychiatry, 33, 142-143.

5. DeMaio, D., Buffa, G., and Laviani, M. (1994). "Lithium Ration, Phospholipids and the Incidence of Side Effects." Progress in Neuro-Psychopharmacology, 18, 285-293.

6. Feet, P., and Gotestam, K. (1994). "Increased Antipanic Efficacy in Combined Treatment with Clomipramine and Dixyrazine." Acta Psychiatrica Scandinavica, 89, 230-234.

7. Gupta, B., and Behere, P. (1994). "Selective Serotonin Reuptake Inhibitors for the Elderly." International Journal of Geriatric Psychiatry, 9, 243-244.

8. Harqaue-Nizamie, S., and Chatterjee, S. (1994). "Transient Release Reflexes in Affective Psychoses." Biological Psychiatry, 35, 217-219.

9.   Judd, F., and Burrows, G. (1994). "Serotonergic Function in Panic Disorder: Endocrine Response to D-fenfluramine." <u>Progress in Neuro-Psychopharmacology and Biological Psychiatry</u>, <u>18</u>, 329-337.

10.   Kafka, M. (1991). "Successful Antidepressant Treatment of Nonparaphilic Sexual Addictions and Paraphilias in Men." <u>Journal of Clinical Psychiatry</u>, <u>52</u>, 60-65.

11.   Lepola, U., and Pentinen, J. (1994). "The Effects of Citalopram in Panic Disorder and Agoraphobia: A Pilot Study." <u>Nordic Journal of Psychiatry</u>, <u>48</u>, 13-17.

12.   Mirza, K, and Dinan, T. (1994). "Recent Advances in Paediatric Psychopharmacology: A Brief Review." <u>Human Psychopharmacology Clinical and Experimental</u>, <u>9</u>, 13-24.

13.   Solyom. L. (1994). "Controlling Panic Attacks with Fenfluramine." <u>American Journal of Psyhiatry</u>, <u>151</u>, 621-622.

14.   Sylvester, C, and Kruesi, M. (1994). "Child and Adolescent Psychopharmacotheapy: Progress and Pitfall." <u>Psychiatric Annals</u>, <u>24</u>, 83-90.

15.   Vita, A., Giobbio, G., and Garbarini, M. (1994). "Cerebral X-Ray Absorption Density in Schizophrenia." <u>New Trends in Experimental and Clinical Psychiatry</u>, <u>10</u>, 15-20.

16.   Willens, T., Biederman, J., and Spencer, T. (1994). "Clonidine for Sleep Disturbances Associted with Attention Deficit Hyperactivity Disorder." <u>Journal of the American Academy of Child and Adolescent Psychiatry</u>, <u>33</u>, 424-426.

DISCUSSION AND LECTURE IDEAS

1.   Does the ethnic background of an individual affect the medication levels prescribed for different mental disorders? The importance of understanding the sociocultural characteristics of the patient before administering chemotherapy may be necessary. Mental health professionals may have perceptions about different ethinic groups in terms of appropriate medication levels or type of biological treatments acceptable for an ethinic group.

2.   How is treatment of mental disorder influenced by a family history of different disorders? When family members have taken various medications for different mental disorders, can this influence the perceptions of family members concerning what is appropriate treatment? A study by F. McMahon (1994) and his associates examined this issue for eighty-two families with a history of Bipolar I, Bipolar II and unipolar disorders (<u>American Journal of Psychiatry</u>, <u>151</u>, 210-215). Their findings discuss the influence of family members on medication and gender differences.

3. ECT is still a widely used procedure, and has enjoyed something of a resurgence in

some areas of the country. What are the opinions of the students regarding its use? Are safeguards needed for its continuing use? Should some individuals be always excluded from experiencing this form of treatment? Students can debate the pros and cons of this form of treatment.

4.   Tardive dyskinesis is often a concern in psychopharmacotherapy. Discuss the advantages versus the disadvantages of medications that have a potential of serious side effects. Should the potential side effects be understood by a patient before treatment begins?

5.   Should an entire family be treated with medication when one member shows psychological problems? Could medication reduce or eliminate problems in the family that may be producing problem behavior in different family members? Would it be possible to require treatment of an entire family for mental disorder from a public health standpoint?

6.   How would students feel if they had to take medication every day of their life in order to control some psychological problem? Would there be a problem of compliance? What might cause a person to "forget" to take his or her medication? How might other people react to a person who needs continuous medication?

ACTIVITIES AND PROJECTS

1.   The abuses of psychosurgery have been documented in recent publications. Have students do further research into the methods of psychosurgery that were frequently used. Students can also address the issue of whether psychosurgery should be permitted. What if someone requests it? What conditions should be present before this approach is considered?

2.   Student teams can be assigned the task of discovering the potential side effects of different categories of drugs. When are the benefits of a drug outweighed by the positive side effects? How are side effects usually handled? Are patients completely informed of the potential side effects before they are administered a drug?

3.   People have a tendency to self-medicate. What drugs and dietary supplements are widely used by people? Have students examine their own tendencies toward self-medication. List examples of students' attempts to "cure" themselves. Can individuals being treated with psychoacitve medications inhibit the effectiveness of the drugs with their own self-medications or supplements?

4.   The vitamin industry has been threatened with regulation for a number of years. Should vitamins be restricted? Have students gather literature concerning the claims made for the effects of vitamins. Have students compare the beneficial aspects of the different vitamins that are promoted with the claims that are made. Are the claims justified by research? Students may be assigned to collect examples of the variety of vitamins and mineral supplements that are suggested for various disorders. Have students collect literature on this subject which is supplied by the manufacturers of such products.

5.   Should children be subjected to such biological interventions as drugs and ACT?

Have students investigate further the use of drugs and ECT with children. What conditions or disorders are most likely to receive physical intervention? Would children elect many of the biological treatments suggested for them?

6.   Medication for school age children has become increasingly common place. What are the attitudes about taking these medications for such conditions as attention deficit hyperactivity disorder among children themselves? Assign students the task of conducting a survey of school age children about this issue. Have them check for any age or gender differences in the attitudes they find.

CHAPTER 17

Psychologically Based Therapies

CHAPTER OUTLINE

I. An Overview of Psychological Treatment
    A. Who receives psychotherapy?
        1. Reluctant clients are often referred by many sources
        2. Chronic unhappiness often motivates entry into therapy
        3. Some people seek to realize their potentials
        4. Therapy has been useful for persons with chronic problems
        5. No "typical" client exists
    B. Who provides psychotherapeutic services?
        1. Many different professionals deal with troubled persons including physicians and clergy
        2. Clinical psychologists, psychiatrists, and psychiatric social workers are most often found treating mental disorders
            a. The team approach is frequently employed
            b. Therapy is often provided in community facilities
    C. The therapeutic relationship
        1. Motivation to change is the most crucial factor for success
        2. Expectation of receiving help can act as a placebo
        3. The therapist uses skills to help clients see themselves and situations objectively
            a. The therapist discourages dysfunctional behavior
            b. New behavior is encouraged
    D. A perspective on therapeutic pluralism
        1. Types of therapy interventions target different areas
            a. Affect
            b. Behavior
            c. Cognition
            d. Environment
            E. Physiology
        2. Abnormal behavior maintains itself in a continuous loop.

II. Psychodynamic therapy
    A. Freudian psychoanalysis

1. Free association
2. Analysis of dreams
3. Analysis of resistance
4. Analysis of transference
   B. Psychodynamic therapy since Freud
1. Interpersonal focus is the modern form
2. Interpersonal psychotherapy for depression
   C. Evaluation of psychodynamic therapy
1. It is time-consuming and expensive
2. Immediate life problems may be ignored
3. It appears best suited for economically well-off and cognitively-able persons

III. Behavior Therapy
   A. Extinction
1. Implosive therapy relies on extinction
   a. The person imagines aversive scenes
   b. The therapist attempts to elicit massive anxiety
2. Flooding places a person in a real-life situation of anxiety
   B. Systematic desensitie
1. Wolpe devised the term
2. Relaxation is an incompatible response to anxiety
3. Variants on the procedure include home-based methods
   C. Aversion therapy
1. Punishment is used to modify behavior
2. Autistic children have received aversive therapy
   a. Maladaptive behaviors are interrupted and new behavior substituted
   b. Many critics of this form of therapy have limited its utilization
   D. Modeling
1. Behavior is learned by imitating others
2. Modeling is combined with instruction
   E. Systematic use of reinforcement
1. Response shaping
2. Token economies
3. Behavioral contracting
   F. Assertiveness therapy
1. Therapy to develop coping skills
   a. A person learns open expression of thoughts and feelings
   b. Assertion inhibits anxiety
2. Phobias do not respond to this therapy
   G. Biofeedback treatment
1. A person learns to influence physiological processes
2. Critics view the therapy as having limited generalization to the real world
   H. Evaluation of behavior therapy

1. The treatments are precise
2. Learning strategies are based upon scientifically valid principles
3. The methods are cost efficient

IV. Cognitive-Behavior Therapy
    A. Rational-emotive therapy
        1. Ellis's attempt to change maladaptive thought processes
        2. Irrational beliefs are at the core of maladjustment
        3. Beliefs are reconstructed
    B. Stress-inoculation therapy
        1. A type of self-instruction to alter self-statements
        2. This therapy is a three-stage endeavor
            a. Cognitive preparaton
            b. Skill acquisition
            c. Application and practice
    C. Beck's Cognitive-behavioral therapy for depression
        1. Beck assumes that depression is due to illogical thinking
        2. Clients gather information about themselves in unbiased ways
    D. Evaluation of cognitive-behavior therapy
        1. Depression responds very well to the procedures
        2. The field is continuing to grow

V. Humanistic-Experiential Therapies
    A. Client-centered therapy
        1. The primary objective is to resolve incongruence
        2. Pure client-centered therapy is rarely used today
    B. Existential therapy
        1. The human situation as experienced by the person is of primary importance
        2. The inner world is reconstructed
    C. Gestalt therapy
        1. Fritz-Perls developed this therapy
        2. Self-awareness and self-acceptance are increased
        3. A person becomes aware of the total environment
    D. Evaluation of the humanistic-experiential therapies
        1. Critics point to the lack of a systematized model of human behavior
        2. The approaches have had a major impact on views of human nature

VI. Therapy for Interpersonal Relationships
    A. Couples counseling (marital therapy)
        1. Faculty role expectations play role in discord
        2. Intense emotional involvement can make therapy difficult
        3. Behavior therapy is used as adjunct to couples counseling
    B. Family therapy
        1. A client's problems may be a symptom of family difficulties
        2. Structural family therapy is based upon systems theory

VII. Integration of Therapy Approaches
    A. Dollard and Miller's attempt to integrate learning and psychoanalytic theory
        1. Relationship factors are important in treatment
        2. Learning strategies have been proven to be successful
    B. Because people are multifaceted, integrated approaches are needed
        1. Problems in language used by theorists impedes progress
        2. Conceptual differences preclude full integration

VIII. Evalaution of Success in Psychotherapy
    A. Problems of evaluation
        1. The therapist's impression of changes that have occurred
        2. The client's reports of change
        3. Reports from client's family or friends
        4. Comparisons before and after treatment
        5. Measures of change
    B. Social values and psychotherapy
        1. Therapy is seen as the guardian of the status quo
        2. Therapy needs to pursue the client's good

IX. Unresolved Issues in Psychotherapy
    A. Some therapy may have negative effects
        1. It is unclear how to prevent negatives
        2. The client's life situation cannot be controlled
    B. Sexual misadventures in therapy are increasing
        1. These are destructive events
        2. Therapy should be a safe haven for the client

LEARNING OBJECTIVES

1. List and explain several reasons why people enter psychotherapy, and describe three types of disorders.
2. Describe four general types of therapy, and explain the "continuous loop" perspective.
3. List and describe the four basic techniques of psychoanalysis, summarize the changes that have taken place since Freud, and evaluate the effectiveness of the psychodynamic approach to the treatment of maladaptive behavior.
4. Explain the principle of extinction, and describe several therapeutic techniques that make use of this phenomenon.
5. Explain the learning principles underlying systematic desensitization, and list three steps in its application to maladaptive behavior.
6. Define *aversion therapy*, and give several examples of its use to treat behavioral disorders.
7. Define *modeling*, and explain how it can be used in the treatment of mental disorders.
8. Explain what is meant by systematic use of positive reinforcement, and describe three general techniques based on this plan.
9. Describe *assertiveness therapy* and explain the learning principles that are involved in its

use.
10. List three steps in the biofeedback approach to therapy, and describe several of its applications to maladaptive behaviors.
11. List and explain three advantages that behavior therapy has over other psychotherapies, and indicate why it cannot be a cure-all.
12. Define *cognitive-behavior therapy*, and describe several techniques used by rational-emotive therapists to treat mental disorders.
13. Describe Beck's cognitive-behavior therapy for depression, and explain the theory on which it is based.
14. Describe the three stages of stress-inoculation therapy, and give some examples of the use of this strategy.
15. Compare the outcomes of cognitive-behavior therapy with other psychotherapies, and describe some trends in its use.
16. Describe Carl Rogers' client-centered therapy, and indicate some differences in the way it is practiced today.
17. List several important concepts that underlie existential psychotherapy, and describe its application to maladaptive behavior.
18. Explain the main goals of Gestalt therapy, and describe several techniques used by Perls and others to treat mental disorders.
19. List some criticisms of the humanistic-experiential therapies, and point out some of their positive contributions to the field.
20. Describe several foci of couple counseling, and indicate some of its difficulties and outcomes.
21. Describe two types of family therapy, and give some examples of their use to treat maladaptive behavior.
22. List Kendall's four reasons for the current interest in integrating behavior therapy with other methods, and explain three problems that he sees in achieving this goal.

KEY TERMS

psychotherapy	clinical psychologist
psychiatrist	psychiatric social workers
psychodynamic therapy	free asociation
manifest content	latent content
resistance	transference
counter-transference	behavior therapy
implosive therapy	flooding
systematic desensitization	aversion therapy
modeling	response shaping
token economies	behavioral contracting
assertiveness therapy	biofeedback
cognitive behavioral therapy	rational-emotive therapy (RET)
stress-inoculation therapy	humanistic-experiential therapies
client-centered therapy	person-centered
existential psychotherapy	Gestalt therapy

couples counseling   marital therapy
structural family therapy

FOCUS ON RESEARCH 1

Stein, D. and Lambert, M. (1995). "Graduate training in psychotherapy: Are therapy outcomes enchanced?" Journal of Consulting and Clinical Psychology, 63, 182-196.

This is an informative article that examines the benefits of graduate training in psychotherapy. Although a large body of research has demonstrated that many psychotherapies have demonstrable effects on a wide variety of client problems, researchers have not shown adequately how training programs lead to the positive therapy outcomes. Empirical research has focused on demonstrating the statistical significance in therapy outome studies, and the identification of techniques that promote improvement of symptoms.

On the training issue, research has been done in a retrospective manner. It has identified the current characteristics of therapists and relates them to client improvements. Another focus of research has been on the types of training experiences that are effective in developing specific skills in graduate students. These skills are those that have been previously found to be useful in clinical encounters.

But these researchers suggest that what is lacking in the current literature are longitudinal studies. This type of examination would permit the establishment of any link between skill acquisition in graduate school to the later provision of quality therapy.

The authors then provide a good review of the strategies used by graduate schools and training programs to develop clinical skills. This discussion can provide students with an idea about the nature of training they may receive in graduate school settings. Following this discussion, the authors use the existing studies that have looked at the issue of training and effective therapy in a retrospective manner. They completed a meta-analysis on these studies.

Their results showed that a modest but fairly consistent treatment effect was associated with training level. The effect was strongest for client satisfaction, and post psychological test change. The well trained psychotherapists also experienced fewer therapy dropouts. The authors concluded their report by emphasizing the shortcomings in the area of current research on this topic. They recommend that training programs increase their efforts to provide common factors that have been identified as the best predictors for positive therapeutic outcomes.

Questions for Discussion

1. Discuss the practical problems in influencing various training institutions to include specific training experiences in their curriculum?
2. Discuss the implementation of a longitudinal study to test the effectiveness of psychotherapy training.
3. Should licensing of psychotherapists include the requirement to have experienced a particular type of psychotherapy training?

FOCUS ON RESEARCH 2

Petronko, M., Harris, S., and Kormann, R. (1994). "Community-Based Behavioral Training Approaches for People With Mental Retardation and Mental Illness." Journal of Consulting and Clinical Psychology, 62, 49-54.

The authors provide a review of the treatment of the mentally retarded who have mental illness. The community perpsective has been one of the major forces in the field of mental retardation, yet this model may not be serving the treatment needs of those individuals with mental illness. Earlier research has indicated that for those leaving the developmental centers, their mental health needs were being served by poor or onexistent services. Persons with dual diagnoses were often not given the needed services by community mental health centers. Also the expenditure of funds for such services has been found to vary widely from state to state.

The fact that people with mental retardation can experience emotional problems similar to those in the general population has been well documented. Yet, the existence of self-referrals for psychological services by people with mental retardation is minimal. The need for mental health services to be provided in a number of ways is indicated by the authors.

The first focus is on community-based treatment within the natural family structure. The authors describe the importance of parent-training packages. Overall, successful completion of the program can lead to benefits in behavioral skills and self-help behaviors. Sibling training encourages the beneficial role of a sibling as a teacher and playmate. These methods appear to help not only the child with mental retardation but the family as a whole.

Another area of focus is on the surrogate family. This represents the myriad of community-based home like environments which provide treatment experiences to persons with mental retardation. These treatments are usually regulated by state or federal standards. It is noted that lack of research and lack of planning hamper the effectiveness of many of these treatment opportunities. Assessment is considered to be inadequate in many cases.

The authors report on one comprehensive program that has satisfied what they consider to be the assessment needs of the clients and is based on good planning and research. The Natural Setting Therapeutic Management Project is a psychoeducational program designed to maintain high-risk clients in the natural environment. The project attempts to transform the environment into a therapeutic milieu. The project has teams who visit the natural environment and provides behavioral consultation and training. This project is distinctive from others since it uses a multiple-model perspective. The caregivers receive training to accomplish management skills that are needed to solve many social problems. Continuing assessment during the training process, provides the feedback for evaluating the progress of the participants. This is large scale service delivery system that will require continued funding and support from the professional community.

Questions for Discussion

1. What are some of the unique stresses experienced by both the family and individual with mental retardation?

2. What are the adavantages of community based treatment for persons with mental retardation?

3. How can the professional community handle the problem that few persons with mental retardation request psychological treatment?

FOCUS ON RESEARCH 3

Persons, J. B. (1991). "Psychotherapy Outcome Studies Do Not Accurately Represent Current Models of Psychotherapy." American Psychologist, 46, 99-106.

Students are usually interested in learning about the effectiveness of psychological treatment for various conditions of abnormality. This article is useful to present some of the difficulties that hamper or limit the conclusions stated in outcome studies.

The author contends that the current practice of psychotherapy involves individualized strategies for each patient. The patient's treatment evolves from information garnered through detailed assessment that is placed in the context of a therapist's therapeutic orientation. Thus, each therapist constructs an individualized treatment strategy based upon the characteristics of the patient that are relevant to the theory underlying the threapy preferred by the practitioner. This method of practice is considered to be at odds with the methodology used in most psychotherapy outcome studies.

The controlled outcome studies differ from psychotherapy practice in three major ways. First, the outcome studies lack theory-driven assessment of the patient and rather seek some atheoretical diagnosis which is standardized. Second, many outcome studies utilize subjects who have been assessed and then treated by different professionals. Thus, the close link between a treatment strategy and the assessment process completed by the same person is ignored. Third, the outcome studies are designed to standardize treatment across subjects. Once again the individualized nature of psychotherapeutic practice is lost by this attempt to limit treatment within certain artificial parameters.

The author concedes that some degree of standardization within a treatment modality is required. But therapists practice a theory-driven approach which relies on a care-specific assessment. This permits a flexibility based upon individual needs that is difficult to maintain in controlled outcome studies.

In order to compensate for the proposed shortcomings of current outcome research, the author presents a remedy which he terms the case formulation approach. This procedure closely links assessment and treatment. Investigators could randomly assign patients to treatment condtions, but each therapist carries out an individualized treatment formulated on the results of the assessment. This permits a researcher to study psychotherapy in accord with its theoretical base and bridge the scientist-practitioner gap. This gap suggests that psychotherapy exists in the community in a different form than it is studied by research scientists.

Questions for Discussion

1.   How accurate is the author's premise that psychotherapists design individualized treatments for each patient?
2.   What theoretical orientations ignore or diminish the importance of assessment? Which theories place an emphasis on asessment?
3.   How valuable is the case study method in outcome research?

READINGS

1.   Cote, G., Gauthier, J., and Hugues, J. (1994). "Reduced Therapist Contact in the Cognitive Behavioral Treatment of Panic Disorder." Behavior Therapy, 25, 123-145.

2.   DeBeurs, E., VanDyck, R., and VanKalkom, A. (1994). "Assessing the Clinical Outcome in Agoraphobia Research: A Comparison of Two Approaches." Behavior Therapy, 25, 147-158.

3.   Fals-Stewart, W. and Lucente, S. (1994). "Treating Obsessive-Compulsive Disorder Among Substance Abusers: A Guide." Psychology of Addictive Behaviors, 8, 14-26.

4.   Fals-Stewart, W., and Lucente, S. (1994). "Behavioral Group Therapy with Obsessive-Compulsives: An Overview." International Journal of Group Psychotherapy, 44, 35-51.

5.   Heimberg, R. (1994). "Cognitive Assessment Strategies and the Measurement of Outcome of Treatment for Social Phobia." Behaviour Research and Therapy, 32, 269-280.

6.   Kuruvilla, K., and Rajagopalan, M. (1994). "Group Behavior Therapy for Obsessive-Compulsive Disorder." Journal of Nervous and Mental Disorders, 182, 185-190.

7.   Jenike, M, and Rauch, S. (1994). "Managing the Patient with Treatment Resistant Obsessive-Compulsive Disorder: Current Strategies." Journal of Clinical Psychiatry, 55, 11-17.

8.   March, J., Mulle, K., and Herbel, B. (1994). "Behavioral Psychotherapy for Children and ADolescents with Obsessive-Compulsive Disorder: A New Protocol Treatment Package." Journal of the American Academy of Child and Adolescent Psychiatry , 33, 333-341.

9. McKenszie, S. (1994). "Hypnotherapy for Vomiting Phobia in a 40 year Old Woman." Contemporary Hypnosis, 11, 37-40.

10. Pitman, R., Altman, B., Greenwald, E., and Steketee, G. (1991). "Psychiatric Complications During Flooding Therapy for Posttraumatic Stress Disorder." Journal of Clinical Psychiatry, 52, 17-20.

11. Turner, S., Beidel, D., Cooley, M. and Woody, S. (1994). "A Multicomponent Behavioral Treatment for Social Phobia: Social Effectiveness Therapy." Behaviour Research and Therapy, 32, 381-390.

12. Zerbe, K. (1994). "Uncharted Waters: Psychodynamic Considerations in the Diagnosis and Treatment of Social Phobia." Bulletin of the Menninger Clinic, 58, 3-20.

DISCUSSION AND LECTURE IDEAS

1.   Self-care has become a major issue in health care. A lecture can be developed to supplement the textbook material on therapy to show the importance of self-care strategies. I. Marks (1994) presents a review of studies on this issue with a focus on behavior therapy (Current Directions in Psychological Science, 3, 19-22). The author discusses the problems associated with patients who refuse to comply with self-care strategies. Students can discuss possible methods to enhance compliance.

2.   Are there pre-treatment characteristics that predict treatment outcomes? A lecture on this topic can be developed from an article by Basoglu and his associates (1994), who focused on panic disorder and agoraphobia (Journal of Affective Disorders, 30, 123-132). Students can be asked to suggest characteristics that they beleive would lead to success outcomes for various types of psychotherapy.

3.   In what ways have traditional Freudian concepts influenced our society? Students can be asked to identify the infusion of Freud's ideas into popular attitudes and viewpoints. Are Freudian concepts depicted in movies and television programs? Are treatments influenced by Freudian principles portrayed in the movies and television programming?

4.   Have students discuss what the differences are between a therapist and a good friend. Does a friend serve the same function as a therapist? In what way are they different? What can a person expect from a therapist that would not be expected from a friend? Does a person receive psychotherapy from a friend?

5.   Assertive behavior has been promoted by numerous training programs and groups. Students can discuss the pros and cons of always acting in an assertive fashion. When does assertive behavior become counterproductive? Is assertive behavior often confused with aggression?

6.   Should aversive conditioning be used on patients who are confined? Can a prison

inmate be conditioned to shun undesirable behavior? Can impulses leading to the crimes of rape or incest be removed through aversive conditioning? What dangers exist in the use of this form of treatment?

7.   Should potential graduate students in programs that train them to become psychotherapists be told of the success rate of the programs? What type of therapists are trained by the institution? What type of success do they have with clients? Currently little factual information on therapy outcomes by former students are provided by training institutions. Most information centers on anecdotal evidence of the success for job placement and salary levels attained by graduates. What could potential graduate students ask to know before enrolling at a particular graduate school?

ACTIVITIES AND PROJECTS

1.   Students can be offered a demonstration of deep muscle relaxation. The students can experience the procedure as the instructions are given to the class. The basic induction procedures for deep muscle relaxation are provided in a number of source books. Is muscle relaxation training alone sufficient to reduce fears associated with mental problems? Discuss the process of deep muscle relaxation, or provide a brief demonstration using some class volunteers. Relate the capacity to achieve relaxation with the control of anxiety.

2.   To gain a clear understanding of why individuals seek psychotherapy, students can be assigned the activity of listing the reasons why they would enter therapy. This list can be collected and discussed in the context of the different treatment procedures.

3.   To illustrate the psychotherapeutic process, students can role-play an interview with a person exhibiting some mental disorder. Using the descriptions of mental disorder provided in previous chapters, students can be assigned a particular disorder. They would then role-play that condition while receiving "therapy" from another student.

4.   To help students understand the use of dream analysis in psychoanalysis and other dynamic psychotherapies, they can be asked to keep a "dream diary". Their dreams can be analyzed using Freudian symbolism. (It should be made apparent to the students that this is only an exercise and that the analysis does not reveal hidden results or conflicts.) A good reference source is by John Means (1986, Psychotherapy, 23, 448-452).

5.   Give the class a description of some hypothetical case study. Devise a case exhibiting some life problems and behavior difficulties. Have the students, in groups, devise treatment procedures based on behavior therapy principles for the case problems. Have them include a method to evaluate their therapy outcome.

6.   What methods do students use to deal with problems? Are any of their methods similar to those used in the different forms of psychotherapy? Do students monitor their behavior

and attempt to modify it when it is not appropriate or helpful to them? How aware are students of their maladaptive behavior? Ask students if they can identify someone who they feel could benefit from therapy. Would someone else target them as potential patients?

7.   The procedures used in hypnotherapy could be demonstrated in class. Students often show significant interest in hypnosis. Following a demonstration of the procedures as hypnotic techniques are applied in therapy, discussion can focus on the potential benefits and shortcomings. What type of disorders receive this form of treatment? Are certain patients best suited for this type of treatment?

CHAPTER 18

Contemporary Issues in Abnormal Psychology

CHAPTER OUTLINE

I. Perspectives in Prevention
   A. Primary prevention
      1. Biological measures
         a. Family planning which includes pre- and postnatal care
         b. Genetic defects are detected early in pregnancy
      2. Psychosocial measures
         a. Skills are developed to handle emotions constructively
         b. Self-identity is promoted
         c. Behavioral medicine seeks healthy life-styles
      3. Sociocultural measures
         a. The relationship between the person and society is a reciprocal one
         b. Social conditions can foster healthy development
      4. An illustration of primary prevention strategies
         a. Education programs
         b. Intervention programs for high-risk teens
         c. Parent education and family based-intervention programs
         d. Peer group influence programs
         e. Programs to increase self-esteem
         f. Mass media and modeling programs
   B. Secondary prevention
      1. Crisis intervention
         a. Short-term crisis therapy
         b. The telephone hotline
      2. Consultation and education of intermediaries
         a. Large groups are reached by consultation efforts
         b. Community mental health centers provide educational programs
      3. An illustration of secondary prevention
         a. Post-disaster crisis therapy
         b. Crisis hotline telephone counseling services
         c. Post-disaster debriefing sessions
   C. Tertiary prevention

1. The mental hospital as a therapeutic community
   a. Staff expectations are clearly defined
   b. Patients are involved in decisions
   c. Patients belong to social groups
2. Aftercare programs
   a. They smooth the transition to community life
   b. A halfway period can be involved

II. Controversial Issues and the Mentally Ill
   A. The commitment process
      1. Persons who are a threat to themselves or others are candidates for confinement.
         a. State law dictates the process
         b. Voluntary versus involuntary commitment
      2. Steps in the commitment process
         a. A hearing is called
         b. The court receives a report in sixty days from the facility
   B. Assessment of "dangerousness"
      1. Attempts to predict "dangerousness"
         a. Questions about defining dangerousness
         b. Violence may depend on the situation
      2. Models for assessing potential for dangerousness
         a. Personality tests and personal history provide data
         b. A pessimism exists over the ability to be correct
      3. The duty to warn: implications of the Tarasoff decision
   C. The insanity defense
      1. The McNaghten rule
      2. The irrestible impulse
      3. Durham rule
      4. ALI Standard
      5. Insanity Defense Reform Act
   D. Deinstitutionalizaton
      1. Large state hospitals were seen as warehouses for the disturbed
      2. The hospital population has been reduced since 1970
      3. Care outside of the hospitals has been inadequate
         a. Vagrancy and crime found among discharged patients
         b. Little follow-up data exists for this population

III. Organized Efforts for Mental Health
   A. U.S. efforts for mental health
      1. The federal government and mental health
         a. The National Mental Health Act of 1946
         b. Support has diminished for mental health in the 1980s
      2. Professional organizations and mental health
         a. Standards and ethics promoted by these organizations
         b. They encourage communication between professions

           c.   Social problems are addressed
      3.   The role of voluntary mental health organizations and agencies
           a.   National Association for Mental Health
           b.   National Association for Retarded Citizens
      4.   Mental health resources in private industry
           a.   Employee assistance programs have been developed
           b.   A number of employee problems are addressed by company programs

  B.   International efforts for mental health
      1.   The World Federation for Mental Health
      2.   The World Health Organization

IV. Challenges for the Future
  A.   The need for planning
      1.   There needs to be international cooperation
      2.   Measures must reduce international conflict
  B.   The individual's contribution
      1.   There are opportunities for both the professional and the nonprofessional
      2.   The responsibility must be shared by everyone

V. Unresolved Issues on the Law/Mental Health Interface
  A.   The DSM-IV cautions its diagnoses are not intented as legal definitions
  B.   Insantity defenses remain an unresolved issues
  C.   Malingering can go undetected
  D.   Dissociative Identity Disorder continues to be used as a defense
  E.   Cooperation is needed between the legal and psychiatric communities

LEARNING OBJECTIVES

1. Define *primary prevention* and list several biological, psychosocial, and sociocultural measures that need to be taken.
2. Define *secondary prevention* and list three interventions that can be used.
3. Define *crisis intervention* and describe two types that are in use.
4. Explain how mental health professionals are able to reach a larger group through the process of consultation and the education of intermediaries.
5. List and explain three general therapeutic principles that guide the milieu approach to treatment and compare the relative effectiveness of three treatment approaches.
6. Define *tertiary prevention* and describe several aftercare programs that perform this function.
7. List four conditions that must be met before involuntary commitment to a mental institution can occur and describe the legal process that follows.
8. Describe the incidence of assaultive patients and explain three dilemmas involved in trying to identify or predict dangerousness in psychiatric patients.
9. Describe some methods for assessing a patient's potential for dangerousness and explain the implications of the Tarasoff decision on a therapist's duty to warn persons that a patient is planning to harm.

10. Explain what is meant by the insanity defense in criminal cases and describe four established precedents defining this plea.
11. Define *deinstitutionalization*, briefly describe its history, and list eight principles upon which successful programs have been based.
12. List and describe four major functions of the National Institute of Mental Health (NIMH).
13. List several professional organizations in the mental health field and explain three key functions that they perform.
14. Describe some of the major functions of the National Association for Mental Health (NAMH).
15. Explain why private industry is interested in mental health, and describe Control Data Corporation's Employee Advisory Resource (EAR).
16. Describe the functions of WHO, UNSESCO, and the World Federation for Mental Health.
17. List eight value assumptions with which we must come to grips as we make decisions about the future of mental health.
18. Describe several opportunities that individuals have to contribute to the advancement of mental health, and list five facts that should help them to succeed in those endeavors.
19. Summarize Okin's criticisms of state mental hospitals, and explain why these shortcomings will be difficult to remedy.

KEY TERMS

primary prevention

tertiary prevention

milieu therapy

forensic psychology or psychiatry

Tarasoff decision

secondary prevention

short-term crisis therapy

social-learning programs

deinstitutionalization

the insanity defense

FOCUS ON RESEARCH 1

Palmero, G., and Knudten, R. (1994). "The Insanity Plea in the Case of a Serial Killer." International Journal of Offender Therapy and Comparative Criminology, 38, 3-16.

This article provides a review of how society viewed criminal responsiblity in the past and present. They utilize a recent case of a serial killer who was examined by one the authors for legal sanity as a case example of applying the relevant principles. They describe the early applications of the McNaghten Rule which focused on defect, and the Durham rule which attempted to add the notion of disease or mental infirmity to the legal concept of insanity. This was then replaced by the American Law Institute legal definition which considerd if the defendant lacked substantial appreciation or capacity to conform one's behavior to the requirements of the law. At present it is not just the presence or absence of mental illness that makes an offender legally responsible but rather his state of mind at the time of the offense.

The focus of this article is on the case of Jeffrey Dahmer whose activities were discovered in the summer of 1991, and he was charged witih fifteen counts of first-degree homicide. The first author conducted an expert forensic psychiatric examination following his plea of not guilty by reason of mental illness. The author's forensic evaluation was to determine if Dahmer at the time of the offenses, had the capacity to distinguish right from wrong, refrain from doing wrong, appreciate the nature and quality of his actions, and conform to the requirements of the law.

The assessment consisted of thirteen hours of interviews and testing by the author. A battery of psychological tests including he Wechsler Adult Intelligence-Revised, Minnesota Multiphasic Personality Inventory, and the Rorschac was administered. Dahmer was cooperative during the evaluation and showed no apparent evidence of neurological deficits. He showed reflective capacity, unimpaired thinking, emotional tranquility, and good reasoning skills. The defendant's EEG, CAT scan, and Chromosomal Analysis were reported negative for pathology. He showed a high IQ and lack of psychotic thinking. His MMPI showed a profile consistent with personality disorder.

The author presented the diagnosis of the defendant to be: personality disorder not otherwise specified with alcohol dependence. He concluded that the defendant was legally sane at the time of the offenses.

Questions for Discussion

1. Is it possible for a forensic psychologist to determine the defendant's frame of mind that existed weeks or months previously?

2. What were some of the unusual aspects of the Dahmer case?

3. How cooperative would defendants be with psychological evaluations?

4. Can defendants present themselves in an insane manner for psychologists?

FOCUS ON RESEARCH 2

Bushy, A. (1994). "Implementing Primary Prevention Programs for Adolescents in Rural Environments." Journal of Primary Prevention, 14, 209-229.

The author points to the importance of promoting lifestyle behaviors that increase the likelihood of experiencing a healthful life during the adolescent years. The author makes an important distinction between health promotion programs and primary prevention. The former directs attention towards behaviors that expand the potential for health and well being. Thus, the focus is on approach behaviors. Primary prevention is concerned with avoidance behaviors that may thwart the occurrence of pathogenic insults to health and well being.

Primary prevention programs face additional barriers when they are implemented in rural environments. Persons living in rural areas are suggested to experience a similar rural lifestyle which includes enhanced distances between persons, economics orientation to the land, cyclical work and recreational activities, and face-to-face negotiations. The rural belief systems are categorized as being related to the fatalism of nature, and toward concrete planning or personal orientation. Self-reliance, and self-care with a strong work ethic is identified at the core of the belief system.

Because of the belief systems and enhanced distance between individuals, the author suggests that primary prevention programs targeting adolescents need a community-provider partnership model. This based on cooperatives, coalitions, and alliances with the organizations and individuals in the community. The mental health professional must direct attention toward the development of organizations representing the community at large.

Questions for Discussion

1. What similarities exist between rural and urban areas that would be of concern for primary prevention programs?

2. What types of avoidance behaviors would a primary prevention program for adolescents focus upon?

READINGS

1. Andrews, A. (1994). "Developing Community Systems for the Primary Prevention of Family Violence." Family and Community Health, 16, 11-9.

2. Brown, J. (1991). "The Psychopathology of Serial Sexual Homicide: A Review of Possibilities." American Journal of Forensic Psychology, 12, 13-20.

3. Bushy, A. (1994). "Implementing Primary Prevention Programs for Adolescents in Rural Environments." Journal of Primary Prevention, 14, 209-229.

4. Forbes, N. (1994). "The State's Role in Suicide Prevention Programs for Alaskan Native Youth." American Indian and Alaska Native Mental Halth Research, 4, 235-249.

5. Foster, J, and Cataldo, J. (1994). "Protection from Clinical Depression in Medical Long-Term Care Facilities." International Journal of Geriatric Psychiatry, 9, 115-125.

6. Halpern, A. (1991). "The Insanity Defense in the First Century." International Journal of Offender Therapy and Comparative Criminology, 35, 187-189.

7. Hazelwood, R. and Douglas, J. (1990). "The lust murderer." In, Crominal Investigative Analysis. (pp. 129-133.) Quantico: U. S. Department of Justice.

8. Miller, K, and Billings, D. (1994). "Playing torow: A Primary Mental Health Intervention with Guatemalan Refugee Children." American Journal of Orthopsychiatry, 64, 346-356.

9. Murray, J. , and Keller, P. (1991). "Psychology in Rural America: Current Status and Future Directions." American Psychologist, 46, 220-231.

10. Niccols, A. (1994). "Fetal Alcohol Syndrome: Implications for Psychologists." Clinical Psychology Review, 14, 91-111.

11. Palermo, G., Liska, J., Palermo, M., and Dal Forno, G. (1991). "On the Predictability of Violent Behavior: Considerations and Guidelines." Journal of Forensic Science, 36, 1435-1444.

12. Reynolds, S., and Briner, R. (1994). "Stress Management at Work: With Whom, For Whom and to What Ends?" British Journal of Guidance and Counseling, 22, 75-89.

DISCUSSION AND LECTURE IDEAS

1. The use of primary prevention has often lagged behind outpatient treatment procedures. Some community psychologists suggest that the mental health industry "requires" emotional problems, which means that attempts at prevention would be underminded. Does the class believe that organizations maintain mental disorders for their own benefit?

2. What responsibility does the individual have for the well-being of the community? Should people be concerned with prevention and help other individuals before problems occur? Does the attitude exist that people who suffer emotional problems do so through their own fault? How would this attitude retard efforts in prevention?

3. Can the civil rights of a person with a mental disorder be preserved adequately? Can conditions for involuntary commitment create the problem of locking away normal, yet unconventional or "undesirable," persons? Discuss how the different perspectives on mental disorder (psychoanalytic, behavioral, etc.) could influence the definition of insanity. How could the theoretical perspective influence decisions about commitment?

4. Forensic psychology is a relatively new area of practice. What are the effects of psychologists on the legal situation? Although the DSM-IV was not written for legal proceedings it is widely used in the courtroom. What is the role of psychologists in the courtroom? Are other procedures such as test instruments used inappropriately in the courtroom?

5. Does the government have a basic obligation to care for persons with mental disorders? Should the government provide for care? For treatment? Has the government traditionally limited funds for the care of the mentally disturbed? Should the government regulate the methods used in psychotherapy? Should certain medications and aversive therapy be controlled? What effects might such control have on the practice of psychotherapy?

6. What are the viewpoints of prisoners concerning their punishment? Discuss the possible reactions prisoners have to the imprisonment. Would this be different for a person who was involuntary committed for psychiatric reasons?

7.   Discuss the differences in perception of lay persons and professionals in how dangerousness may be defined. Are there times when a lay person knows who is dangerous even when a professional may not? What are the implications and indicators for dangerousness that students identify?

ACTIVITIES AND PROJECTS

1.   With the availability of Court TV on many cable systems serving university communities, students have increased access to cases that may involve the insanity defense. Before the semester begins, information concerning upcoming cases can be obtained. Students can be assigned the task of reporting on appropriate cases to the class.

2.   Have students develop a program that could prevent many of the problems faced by freshmen when entering a university. Have the students deal with such issues as leaving home, isolation, lack of support systems, drug use, and discouragement. Different groups of students can be assigned different problem areas to focus on.

3.   The university ombudsman can be invited to speak to the class concerning the rights of students in the context of mental disorder and commitment. How does the university handle the situation when a student shows overt signs of dangerousness to himself or herself or to others?

4.   In many communities, local board meetings of mental health centers, rehabilitation centers, and youth service bureaus are open to the public. Students may want to attend these meetings to gain a first-hand understanding of the operation of mental health facilities.

5.   Students can participate in a role-play panel comprised of a psychiatrist, psychologist, social worker, physician, politician, and police officer. What disagreements can be found among what different individuals view as problem behaviors? Would the different professionals suggest solutions to problems that are unique to their professions?

6.   Have the students investigate primary and secondary prevention programs that exist on and off campus. The university counseling center and community mental health center can provide information for this project. The students may interview personnel at their student health center or student services department. What priorities are given for the mental health needs of students?